Reality TV's Real Men of the Recession

Reality TV's Real Men of the Recession

White Masculinity in Crisis and the Rise of Trumpism

Shannon O'Sullivan

LEXINGTON BOOKS
Lanham • Boulder • New York • London

Published by Lexington Books
An imprint of The Rowman & Littlefield Publishing Group, Inc.
4501 Forbes Boulevard, Suite 200, Lanham, Maryland 20706
www.rowman.com
86-90 Paul Street, London EC2A 4NE, United Kingdom

Copyright © 2022 by The Rowman & Littlefield Publishing Group, Inc.

All rights reserved. No part of this book may be reproduced in any form or by any electronic or mechanical means, including information storage and retrieval systems, without written permission from the publisher, except by a reviewer who may quote passages in a review.

British Library Cataloguing in Publication Information Available

Library of Congress Cataloging-in-Publication Data Available

ISBN 978-1-66690-001-9 (cloth)
ISBN 978-1-66690-002-6 (electronic)

*In memory of my mother, Julia O'Sullivan, who
asserted her union rights to the end.*

Contents

Preface	ix
Acknowledgments	xiii
Introduction	1
Chapter 1: Hegemonic Masculinity at Work on Reality TV	33
Chapter 2: White Women with Blue Collars: Rules for Representation	71
Chapter Three: "Real Men" Work in "Real America"	81
Chapter Four: When Wealthy White Men Perform "Real Manhood"	113
Conclusion: The Continuing Relevance of the Blue-Collar Frontier	151
Bibliography	157
Index	171
About the Author	183

Preface

On January 6, 2021, Trumpian devotees stunned the world when they stormed the U.S. Capitol to protest the congressional certification of the Electoral College results solidifying Joe Biden as the 46th president of the United States. To that point, I had closely followed the mainstream reportage of Trump's white, male, and (seemingly) working-class supporters, who media commentators still frequently referred to as *the* working class, despite women and people of color constituting the majority of U.S. workers. I began conducting the foundational research for this project in late 2015, as a billionaire reality television persona surged ahead of his opponents in the Republican primaries. Trump's rhetorical strategy did not reflect his abundant economic and cultural capital, but mirrored a *stereotypical* white male, working-class style of speech. The political punditry, even Trump's critics, largely cast his performative talk as evincing "authenticity," in which overtly sexist, racist, and xenophobic discourse became commensurate with "realness" and "telling it like it is."

Once again, Trump's mastery of television logics garnered him excessive media attention, in which the coverage of his antics and supporters elided much-needed public policy discussions—the push for ratings paired well with an already deeply corrupt political system. To say that media narratives related to voter demographics, especially the working class, lack structural contextualization and nuance would be a profound understatement. As Lauren Shandevel succinctly captures in *In These Times*, "journalists in the US are, by and large, predominantly white, and most come from economically privileged backgrounds—but in spite of this, we still trust them to tell us who the working class are and what they need."[1] This coupled with the increasingly monopolistic corporate ownership of mass media defangs any mainstream political analysis of race, class, and gender, in which social inequities are presented with a highly ahistorical and neoliberal gloss.

I challenge the dominant framing of social categories as authenticated by performance logic alone—a neoliberal tendency designed to remove social

ix

categories, such as race, gender, class, sexual orientation, and ability, from their structural origins. In short, neoliberal rhetoric about diversity and identity promotes the expansion of meritocracy to all, in which social hierarchies remain fundamentally unchallenged. Naomi Klein refers to this in relation to Hillary Clinton's rhetorical strategy in 2016 as "trickle-down-identity-politics."[2] She further elucidates that " . . . this top-down approach to change, if it is not accompanied by bottom-up policies that address systemic issues such as crumbling schools and lack of access to decent housing, is not going to lead to real equality. Not even close."[3]

However, this book does not endeavor to detail at the granular level all that went awry with the media coverage of the 2016 and 2020 elections. Instead, I examine the continued purchase of *performances* of white, rural, working-class masculinity in U.S. culture and the prominent role of reality television in mediating perceptions of masculine authenticity. These hegemonic notions of "real manhood" are inextricably linked to interlocking systems of power, including white supremacy, capitalism, heteropatriarchy, and settler-colonialism. More precisely, this book is about the emergence of a specific subgenre of reality television on History and Discovery networks since the Great Recession, which I am calling the "blue-collar frontier shows." These shows reveal as much about the power of hegemonic *perceptions* of masculine authenticity as they do about the deeper sociopolitical currents that led to Trump's rhetorical strategy and electoral success. These shows provide a rich archive for understanding a seemingly subtle and unsettling iteration of white male identity politics that arose, for a complex constellation of reasons detailed herein, in the last two decades. This book investigates the raced and classed dimensions of dominant perceptions and performances of masculine authenticity in U.S. culture and the significant place of the blue-collar frontier shows in mediating those perceptions.

Thus, I was struck by the regalia of the rioters at the Capitol on January 6, 2021. Overwhelmingly white and male, these rioters looked more like cosplay convention attendees than insurrectionists. The day after the violent melee, Vanessa Friedman of the *New York Times* offered her own assessment of the meaning behind their embodied performances: "When you leave the totems of your usual identity behind you free yourself from the laws that govern that identity and assume those of another character—a *frontiersman* [emphasis added], a hunter, a warrior, even a superhero—that can then be twisted through a dark mirror into the outfits of the insurrection."[4] Friedman's mention of the frontiersman pinpoints a paragon of manliness in U.S. culture, which is showcased on *Deadliest Catch*, *Ax Men*, *Ice Road Truckers*, and *Gold Rush*. Affluent white male politicians since Theodore Roosevelt have recognized the symbolic capital this performance confers. The cosplay of January 6 represents a cartoonish microcosm of a quest to approximate

Preface xi

"real American manhood"—a performance that obfuscates the machinations of capitalism, white supremacy, heteropatriarchy, and settler-colonialism in constructing notions of ideal citizenship.

As incited by a former reality television star, the rioters on January 6 violently enacted their own regressive fantasy of "playing frontiersmen" to "take their country back" in service of the most powerful member of the billionaire class. Once again, the media largely framed this incident as a flashpoint for white, male *working-class* discontent. However, according to political scientist Robert A. Pape writing in *the Washington Post* in April 2021, the data indicate that the overwhelmingly white and male rioters were " . . . by and large, older and more professional than right-wing protesters we have surveyed in the past."[5] To the media, their attire unflinchingly signified working-class status, as opposed to white male professionals angling to present as "authentic" American men.

I was drawn to the study of media depictions of the white working class because of my own background, in which I interloped between the white working, lower-middle, and now, professional-managerial classes. Growing up on the north side of Buffalo, New York, neoliberal economic jolts impacted me and my brother from a young age, as well as our parents' life chances since they entered the workforce amid the widespread deindustrialization of the Northeast and Great Lakes regions in the 1970s. My dad, Gerald O'Sullivan, a committed member of the United Auto Workers, Local 424, left his job at American Axle and Manufacturing in 2006—the assembly plant closed shortly thereafter in 2008. My mom, Julia O'Sullivan, was as an administrative professional and proud member of the Civil Service Employees Association. She suddenly succumbed to cardiac arrest on November 22, 2021, at age sixty-five. In the months leading up to her untimely death, she endured retaliation from her supervisor for asserting her union rights. These distressing workplace challenges arose while she worked on-site throughout the pandemic, despite suffering from asthma. My family's union politics defined the ethos of our family—but was one factor that made us impervious to Trump's appeals. However, the staunch neoliberalism of the dominant wing of the Democratic Party has been deleterious and alienating for workers nationwide. Despite a disproportionate (albeit distorted) focus on the white working class in the context of reporting about electoral demography, my own family's experiences remain elided in media narratives. I suppose white, working-class union members from Buffalo, NY, who backed Bernie Sanders in 2016 and 2020 do not fit the media's cliched culture war dispatches from the Rust Belt.

Like many Americans on January 6, I reached out to friends and family to process and make sense of what was unfolding and what it foretold. Was this the beginning of a troubling and mutinous new chapter, or the end of a chaotic and surreal era? My close friend, Jennifer O'Donnell, a comedian who also worked in reality television development for over a decade, acutely recognized how reality television performance logics infused the Trump presidency. O'Donnell remarked that the day's unruliness fittingly seemed like " . . . the series finale of the Trump show." I took comfort and appreciated her perspective. However, more than one year after the Capitol riot, I see "Trump 2024" signage dotting the Eastern Shore of Maryland, where I now reside. I recall sharing O'Donnell's comment with my friend and fellow communication scholar, Patrick M. Johnson. He agreed but also cautioned that the Capitol riot might only have been " . . . the cliffhanging *season* finale of the Trump show."

This book is premised upon the notion that the reality TV president has forever altered U.S. politics, while cautioning that the public disregards the power of reality television itself at its own peril.

NOTES

1. Lauren Shandevel, "A Bold Experiment in Working-Class Journalism," *In These Times*, August 3, 2021, https://inthesetimes.com/article/working-people-podcast-media-labor-stories.

2. Naomi Klein, *No Is Not Enough: Resisting Trump's Shock Politics and Winning the World We Need* (Chicago, IL: Haymarket Books, 2017), 92.

3. Klein, *No Is Not Enough*, 92–93.

4. Vanessa Friedman, "Why Rioters Wear Costumes," *New York Times*, January 7, 2021, https://www.nytimes.com/2021/01/07/style/capitol-riot-tactics.html.

5. Robert A. Pape, "What an Analysis of 377 Americans Arrested or Charged in the Capitol Insurrection Tells Us," *Washington Post*, April 6, 2021, https://www.washingtonpost.com/opinions/2021/04/06/capitol-insurrection-arrests-cpost-analysis/.

Acknowledgments

Innumerable thanks are due to my husband, Matt Michaud, who stood by my side throughout the trials and triumphs that coincided with working on this project. I am especially grateful to my editor, Jessie Tepper, whose patience, understanding, and support made this book possible. I would like to thank Seema Sohi and Deepti Misri for the critical intellectual spaces they cultivated during my doctoral study at the University of Colorado at Boulder. The genesis of this book can be traced to their classrooms and the invaluable insights they provided. Thanks are also due to Janice Peck and Nabil Echchaibi, who have had an indelible impact on my thinking about media, culture, and class. Special acknowledgment goes to my father for his instrumental role in developing my class consciousness and union pride. Additionally, I wish to thank my brother, as well as countless family members and friends, for their thoughtfulness and humor. Lastly, I want to express my endless gratitude for the city that formed me: Buffalo, NY. Go Bills!

Introduction

The forty-fifth president of the United States, Donald Trump, is a former reality television star. Any resistance to approaching reality television as a subject worthy of scholarly inquiry has arguably faded away with Trump's improbable rise as a political "outsider" to the highest elected office in the nation. As host of *NBC*'s *The Apprentice* (2004–2017), the billionaire real-estate mogul regularly entered U.S. living rooms via the reality television competition format—charting an unlikely course toward the presidency. However, this book is not as much about Donald Trump, as it is about the systems of power and the confluence of social, cultural, and political circumstances that contributed to his election in 2016, as well as subsequent calls for him to run again in 2024. Rather than serve as a political liability, his reality television credentials became an unlikely asset. As Laurie Ouellette cautions in a special issue of *Television & New Media* regarding Trump's improbable ascendence, "Instead of dismissing reality TV as inherently trite, superficial, and trashy, we need to understand the social, economic, and political contexts that have shaped its cultural development and shifting contours. Only then can we really understand the 'first reality TV president.'"[1]

This book explores not only the conditions that gave rise to Trump, but how Trump's supporters were framed in the mainstream media in terms of race, gender, and class. It seems news media reactions to Trump, and especially the political punditry's coverage of his supporters, have proven just as consequential as Trump's policies for understanding how systems of power shape U.S. politics. In short, this book takes as its object of study the relationship between reality television, systems of oppression, and political rhetoric, but with a specific focus on a fecund and enduring subgenre of reality television that quietly signaled the deeper sociopolitical currents that enabled Trump's (seemingly) implausible rise via a racist, xenophobic, sexist, and authoritarian rhetorical strategy.

At the beginning of the economic downturn in 2007–2008, approximately eight years before Trump kicked off his presidential campaign, in a seemingly inconsequential corner of cable television, a new subgenre of reality television emerged on the Discovery and History networks. The so-called blue-collar reality shows[2] have since multiplied into dozens of series in the past decade and a half and remain a staple of U.S. cable lineups. For conceptual clarity, I will subsequently refer to the select series under examination here as the "blue-collar *frontier* shows." This is because I focus on series that dramatize white male survival in wilderness workplaces. The principal casts of these programs are comprised almost entirely of white, heteronormative, working-class men who perform highly hazardous occupations in remote, rural locations. Despite filming these white male subjects almost exclusively on their job sites, the seeming salience of social class and capitalism are subsumed within overarching narrative frameworks that emphasize these workers' perceived status in the dominant visual order as "real men" and "real Americans."

Why did these formulaic reality programs documenting white, working-class men on perilous job sites maintain such popular appeal in the past two decades? I argue that the emergence and enduring popularity of these seemingly banal programs signaled a deeper and more pernicious socio-political backlash that was brewing among white, rural, working and middle-class men—the same demographic of men that both populates the blue-collar frontier world and came out strongly in support of Donald Trump in 2016 and 2020.[3] The upsurge of these series coincided not only with the onset of the Great Recession, but also in relation to the modest advancements made by women, people of color, members of LGBTQ communities, and those living at those intersections of social experience, toward greater social equity in recent years. I assert that this renewed emphasis on white male stories of survival on the frontier speaks to the increased circulation of perniciously false and unfounded threats to white male "survival" as a social group, especially since the 2016 presidential election. More accurately, there have been concerted challenges to white male *dominance* in the twenty-first century—a point which I will engage with extensively in terms of how it relates to neoliberal capitalism and reality television itself as a neoliberal project.

I contend that the blue-collar frontier shows appeared in conjunction with what masculinity studies scholar, Michael Kimmel, refers to as "the contemporary 'crisis' of masculinity."[4] As Kimmel explains, this "crisis" of masculinity is specifically afflicting white, (mostly) rural, males from the working and middle classes. He notes that white male anxiety, fear, and anger over their perceived loss of social status is driven, in part, by the increased economic precarity endemic to neoliberal socioeconomic policies—including deregulating trade, privatizing public resources, defunding social programs, and dismantling union power—coupled with the dominant tendency to link masculinity with economic independence. This perceived masculinity crisis

Introduction 3

is also tied to a misperception and/or a willful ignorance among white, working, and middle-class men regarding the comparative socioeconomic disadvantages women and people of color in the United States endure in relation to white males statistically overall. Naomi Klein astutely captures the economic shocks white, working and middle-class men have sustained since the Great Recession, while noting that this economic upheaval was by no means restricted to their social group. In fact, Black Americans were statistically hit hardest by the housing crisis and the Great Recession.[5] In *No Is Not Enough: Resisting Trump's Shock Politics and Winning the World We Need*, Klein contextualizes the impacts of the Great Recession on comparatively advantaged working and middle-class white males: " . . . accelerating since the 2008 financial crisis, pretty much everyone apart from the one percent has been losing job security as well as whatever feeble safety net used to exist . . . This state of affairs hurts Trump's working-class white male voters just as it does so many others . . . because many of Trump's blue-collar voters had a notably better deal until fairly recently . . . these losses appear to come as more of a shock."[6] I unpack this point at length in the first chapter, but Klein provides the needed foregrounding for why depictions of white males performing conventionally masculine and dangerous jobs resonated so strongly with History and Discovery's majority white male viewership in the late 2000s and 2010s.

Rather than question the unjust and limiting basis of this dominant conceptualization of masculinity, Kimmel finds that many rural, white, working and middle-class men reinvest in traditional metrics of masculine authenticity. It is as though the blue-collar frontier shows assuage the fears of this subset of men through reassuring them that they are still the "real men" at the top of the social hierarchy. In his 2013 text, *Angry White Men: American Masculinity at the End of an Era*, Kimmel documents white men, who would later become identified as Trump's base, expressing deep insecurities about their masculinity, as well as profound resentments toward women and people of color. Unfortunately, Kimmel does not forecast the rise of a demagogic political figure like Trump, who would tap into those anxieties and hatreds, which are deeply rooted in existing white supremacist, heteropatriarchal, and capitalist systems, as part of his meteoric rise to power. In Kimmel's epilogue, he is overly sanguine about the subjects of his investigation and their place in the future of U.S. politics: "It's America 2.0. America the Multicultural. Angry white men are on the losing side of history . . . In fact, they've already lost . . . For the truth is that Angry White Men may make a lot of noise, but they are a fast-disappearing minority."[7] Kimmel's flawed assessment of the hegemony of liberal multiculturalism mirrors much of the mainstream political analysis leading up to the 2016 election, which was remarkably devoid of intersectional frameworks, much less concrete policy discussions. The dominant wing of the Democratic Party labored under the neoliberal illusion

4 *Introduction*

that the country's shifting demographics would be enough to secure electoral victories—it was a mirage that white males collectively lost enough social power to be rendered politically inconsequential, especially given gerrymandering and the Electoral College.

Given Kimmel's prediction in 2013, it is astonishing that in less than four years, Donald Trump would ride on a wave of white male hostility all the way to the White House. Additionally, it would have been nearly impossible to predict the events of January 6, 2021, in which a sizable group of his devotees stormed the Capitol because of a collective unwillingness to accept that Trump lost the election. Clearly, many journalists, pollsters, and scholars missed the mark when it came to understanding the place of white, working and middle-class men within the U.S. sociopolitical landscape leading up to the 2016 election. I contend that the profound changes in programming lineups on U.S. cable networks, specifically History and Discovery from the mid-2000s through the 2010s, represented a reactionary veneration of white, rural, working-class men amid the Great Recession and social movements challenging the hegemony of white supremacy, heteropatriarchy, and capitalism. Additionally, the tenor of these shows does not explicitly evince white male aggrievement as much as they offer a more subtle reverence of white, rural, working-class men as "real men" and even more so as "real Americans." Despite the blue-collar frontier shows appearing ideologically neutral on the surface, I argue that these shows symbolically spoke to the concerns and desires of those who would later become Trump's base of white supporters. In short, as Kimmel and much of the mainstream political punditry dismissed "angry white men" as increasingly irrelevant before Trump's election, History and Discovery were showcasing the deep symbolic power and political purchase of performances of white, rural, working-class manhood.

In this analysis, I specifically examine four of the most popular and longest running series within this subgenre of reality television: Discovery's *Deadliest Catch* (2005-present) follows commercial crab fishermen on Alaska's treacherous Bering Sea; History's *Ax Men* (2008–2016) features commercial loggers in the forests of Oregon, Washington, Alaska, and other locations in the Western United States, as well as swamp and river loggers in Louisiana and Florida; History's *Ice Road Truckers* (2007–2017) documents commercial truck drivers traversing the winter seasonal ice roads in mostly Northwestern Canada and Alaska; and Discovery's *Gold Rush* (2010–present) depicts gold miners in Alaska and the Yukon. These are some of the most statistically dangerous occupations in North America, and the specter of bodily injury permeates the blue-collar frontier shows.

Before moving forward, it is essential to further clarify the parameters of this subgenre of reality television. In referring to the blue-collar frontier shows, I am not including so-called "rednexploitation series"[8] such as TLC's

Here Comes Honey Boo Boo or MTV's *Buckwild*. Unlike the blue-collar frontier shows, these series have mixed gender casts, but also present white, rural, working-class people in more derisive and ridiculing fashions. They also do not center on the workplace, particularly wilderness workplaces. These series tend to document the lifestyles of so-called "rednecks," who eschew middle-class social conventions and the Protestant work-ethic. In contrast, the blue-collar frontier series portray their white, rural, working-class male subjects as hardworking, admirable, and praiseworthy for proving their elite manhood in their execution of highly dangerous occupations.

Thom Beers, who executive produces some of the longest running and highest-rated blue-collar frontier shows, including *Deadliest Catch*, *Ice Road Truckers*, and *Ax Men*, is widely considered the driving force behind the inception and propagation of this subgenre of reality television. Beers also narrates *Ice Road Truckers* and *Ax Men*. In a December 2012 profile of Beers in the *New York Times Magazine*, Charles Homans illuminates his pivotal role in creating a new subset of reality television programming on U.S. cable:

> It is now virtually impossible to surf the cable spectrum without landing on a series built on the Beers template: shows about bush pilots, swamp loggers, wild-pig hunters, gold miners, snake wranglers, repo men, tugboat operators, animal-control officers . . . 'He cornered the market,' says Abby Greensfelder, a former Discovery executive who runs the reality-TV production company Half Yard Productions. 'Now a lot of people have imitated that, but he was the pioneer. He really defined a genre.'[9]

Therefore, this examination explicitly focuses on the Beers template of documenting "real men at work on the frontier" on reality television, as it pertains to deeper sociopolitical currents. A core claim of this book is that the blue-collar frontier shows exemplify a dominant conceptualization of hegemonic masculinity and rugged individualism in the contemporary U.S. neoliberal context. The men of the blue-collar frontier world are not coded within the dominant logics of commercial television as white men or workers, but as "real men" or "rugged individuals." This project also calls attention to which bodies typically constitute neutral individuality in the U.S. context: White men are not typically treated as raced and gendered subjects in the dominant discourse, but often as "neutral" or "normal" in relation to these social categories.

Ryan Broderick of Buzzfeed curiously includes A&E's popular *Duck Dynasty* (2012–2017) in his analysis of "rednexploitation" series in "The Dark Side of America's Redneck Reality TV Obsession."[10] The series centers on the wealthy Robertson family of West Monroe, Louisiana. Despite their economic largesse, the male members of the clan loudly proclaim their "redneck" credentials via their commitment to hunting, fishing, perpetually wearing camouflage, and sporting long, unkempt beards with lengthy, unruly hair to match. Headed by their patriarch Phil, who originally made his millions through establishing Duck Commander—his family-run business, which manufactures duck calls for hunters—the program documents their lifestyle[11]. Unlike the true "rednexploitation" series or the blue-collar frontier shows, *Duck Dynasty* focuses on a wealthy family. Additionally, like their counterparts on *Ax Men, Deadliest Catch, Ice Road Truckers*, and so on, the Robertsons are not framed as worthy of derision, but as quintessentially exemplifying "real manhood" and "family values."

As I have previously contended, *Duck Dynasty* is instructive for understanding the symbolic capital a white, rural, working-class masculine *performance* confers to a man who can approximate it, in which whiteness is a critical prerequisite.[12] The show provides insight into the motivations behind wealthy white males, such as the Robertsons and Donald Trump, embracing white, working-class rhetorical performances, so that they can be perceived as "real men." Juxtaposing the Robertson men with the Capitol rioters, who were largely middle and upper-middle class white men, further illustrates the symbolic currency and ideological underpinnings of performances of white, rural, working-class manhood. Therefore, I include *Duck Dynasty* in this analysis, but maintain an analytical separation between its depiction of wealthy "rednecks" and the blue-collar frontier presentation of "real men" on their job sites. The Robertson men serve as a case study for understanding the hegemony of white, rural, working-class masculinity, as their embodied performances and recreational activities signal a desire to be associated with the "real men" of *Deadliest Catch, Ice Road Truckers, Ax Men*, and *Gold Rush*. Another noteworthy division between the format of *Duck Dynasty* and the rest of the programs included in this examination: It mostly focuses on the Robertsons as a family unit in their home environment and remains more in line with the twenty-two-minute sitcom structure, whereas the other series are more emblematic of forty-four-minute workplace dramas.

It is also significant that *Duck Dynasty* seems more politically charged in terms of the well-documented conservative ideological bent of its audience.[13] The Robertsons publicly supporting Donald Trump, including Willie Robertson endorsing him at the Republican National Convention in July 2016, makes the series look more *overtly* political than the blue-collar frontier shows examined herein. I maintain that the blue-collar frontier shows appearing apolitical belies their ideological heft. In summation, in using the term "blue-collar frontier shows," I am not referring to "rednexploitation" series or *Duck Dynasty*—the latter of which I address separately in the fourth chapter to elucidate the symbolic capital of performances of white, rural, working-class manhood among affluent white men.

Christopher Lockett observes in his analysis of this subgenre of reality television, which includes *Deadliest Catch* and *Ice Road Truckers*, how this trend seems commensurate with a cultural fixation on accessing "real manhood." In his aptly titled piece, "Masculinity and Authenticity: Reality TV's Real Men," Lockett contends "that this idealization of working-class masculinity takes place by way of reality television speaks to its preoccupation with an *authentic masculinity* [emphasis added], one best accessed unalloyed and unmediated."[14] Because reality television is unscripted and includes "real people" as its stars, instead of actors, it maintains an allure of authenticity, despite presenting a product that is highly constructed and mediated. In short, part of the mythology of reality television is that it purportedly presents things "as they are."

Like reality television itself, Donald Trump has been cast as a more "authentic" politician who "tells it like it is." As Halim Shebaya explains in the *Huffington Post,* it is simply the superficial appearance of a certain kind of white masculine authenticity that matters to politically conservative segments of the U.S. electorate: " . . . one way to understand Trump's success is the fact that he is perceived to state things as they really are, without the filter of establishment jargon and what some denounce as 'political correctness' . . . To be sure, Trump is 'telling it like it is' for those who believe what he says. For those who disagree with his views, the 'like it is' is a racist, fascist, Islamophobic, narrow-minded, and essentially false perception of reality."[15]

John Baldoni, in a 2016 *Forbes* editorial titled, "Is Donald Trump a Role Model for Authenticity?" argues that "Politics aside, those who speak in public can admire Trump for his ability to connect with an audience but should be very wary of following what passes for his style of authenticity."[16] The perception of Trump's "realness" underscores how white male supremacy remains deeply entwined with hegemonic conceptualizations of authenticity. As I address at length throughout this text, "real men" typically implies white men in U.S. discourse. Taking this a step further, "real Americans" are often conceived of as white, rural, working-class men. As Lockett observes, the blue-collar reality series are situated " . . . as somehow the norm: 'real America.'"[17] By logical extension, the reality television president not only typifies perceptions of authenticity in a broad sense, but also key elements of an authentic version of masculinity. Trump speaks and performs in a register that gestures toward what it means to be a "real man" in the dominant discourse. This book seeks to answer the question: What systems of power remain embedded in performances deemed authentically masculine, and what is their wider sociopolitical significance?

Before proceeding with a more detailed explanation of the specific aims of this project, for conceptual clarity, I must delineate my understanding of the interlocking systems of power[18] that I consistently refer to in relation to the production and reception of blue-collar frontier television. The intertwined systems of oppression that I argue underpin these series include white supremacy, heteropatriarchy, capitalism, and settler-colonialism. White supremacy in this context does not refer to the overt, ideologically racist rhetoric of far-right, neo-Nazi terrorist groups, as it is commonly conceptualized in the public discourse. White supremacy also refers to how whiteness has become naturalized as an invisible, default racial identity to which all other racial groups are measured. In *The Racial Contract*, Charles Mills characterizes the current racial hierarchy as " . . . de facto white supremacy, when whites' dominance is, for the most part, no longer constitutionally and judicially enshrined but rather a matter of social, political cultural and economic privilege based on the legacy of the conquest."[19] Hence, the whiteness of the principal casts of the blue-collar frontier shows is unremarkable or "normal" in a white supremacist society.

Heteropatriarchy specifically refers to a gender/sexuality system of cis male, heterosexual dominance, in which women and all genders within LGBTQ communities are viewed as subordinate. Settler-colonialism refers to the specific mode of colonization imposed upon indigenous peoples, including the indigenous peoples of North America. Features of settler-colonialism include displacement, genocide, and a loss of cultural sovereignty at the hands of colonizers who permanently settle and fundamentally transform the society they encounter. Although capitalism does not need further explanation, I think it is important to clarify what I mean when I refer to neoliberal capitalism or more simply, neoliberalism. George Monbiot offers a comprehensive sketch of neoliberalism's core socioeconomic features: "So pervasive has neoliberalism become that we seldom even recognise it as an ideology . . . Attempts to limit competition are treated as inimical to liberty. Tax and regulation should be minimised, public services should be privatised. The organisation of labour and collective bargaining by trade unions are portrayed as market distortions that impede the formation of a natural hierarchy of winners and losers."[20]

As I explain in greater detail regarding how this project takes up intersectionality, I understand these systems of oppression as operating in interlocking and mutually constitutive fashions. I argue that the blue-collar frontier shows are invisibly shaped by these systems of power, which have become so naturalized as "common sense" that they often go undetected.[21] In her seminal text, *Black Feminist Thought*, Patricia Hill Collins recognizes the critical role of mass media in reinforcing intersecting systems of oppression, which further legitimates the importance of examining the blue-collar frontier shows as sites of structural domination. Collins examines the common stereotypes applied to African American women, and poignantly refers to them as "controlling images."[22] As she asserts, "Intersecting oppressions of race, class,

Introduction 9

gender, and sexuality could not continue without powerful ideological justifications for their existence."[23] I argue that these series function as one such justification for the preservation of "imperialist white supremacist capitalist heteropatriarchy."[24] Before proceeding, I must detail my theoretical approach to this critical discourse analysis of blue-collar frontier reality television.

INTERSECTIONAL INTERVENTIONS AND THE WORKING-CLASS ASSEMBLAGE

This study incorporates multiple theoretical perspectives from the interdisciplinary arenas of critical whiteness studies; gender and performance studies; and media and cultural studies. These theoretical frames include assemblage, intersectionality, visuality, critical race theory, indigenous critical theory, gender performativity in relation to hegemonic masculinity, and Pierre Bourdieu's formulation of symbolic capital. Because this project makes several theoretical interventions in relation to the study of media texts and social categories as they correspond to systems of power, it is critical to elucidate the applicability of each framework for disrupting the banality, and illuminating the social complexity, of the blue-collar frontier shows. It is critical to qualify that this study's unique theoretical interventions move the analysis beyond the framework of scholarship related to reality television and class alone in favor of bringing the blue-collar frontier shows within the purview of critical whiteness studies and masculinity studies with an emphasis on the explanatory power of women of color and decolonial feminisms.

These popular media representations of working-class subjects reify a deeply entrenched U.S. cultural legacy of conflating working-class status and white manhood. The category "working class" continues to signify white male, blue-collar workers in the dominant U.S. discourse and media. This project aims, in part, to explicate and correct how the social category of "working class" has come to solely represent white male workers in the dominant discourse. This analysis of the blue-collar frontier shows seeks to destabilize the hegemonic and monolithic conceptualization of the "working class" categorization itself through an interrogation of labor along intersecting lines of race and gender.

In investigating the disproportionate visibility of white men within working-class representations in contemporary U.S. media, it is crucial to historicize the diversity of the U.S. working class, in that women and people of color were always already excluded from the "labor aristocracy" because of the intersecting systems of oppression of sexism and racism.[25] The location of the union-organized factory whose workers were predominantly white and male became the primary determinant of recognition and inclusion in the so-called "working class," whereas women and people of color engaged in migrant and domestic work were not identified in the mainstream discourse as such.[26] This legacy endures at present, as women of all races and people of color of all genders remain discursively excluded from working-class identification in the dominant discourse, despite women and people of color constituting the majority of the U.S. working class.[27]

Because reductive and inaccurate images of the working class continue to circulate in mass media, this analysis seeks to theoretically intervene with a more nuanced and complete conceptualization of the U.S. working class that accounts for its complex racial and gendered dimensions. I apply Gilles Deleuze and Felix Guattari's spatial metaphor of assemblage for understanding how the U.S. working class coheres at certain instances of economic exploitation and diverges at other moments in terms of the particularities of race and gender that overlap within the global capitalist system. These flashes of cohesion and divergence ensue concurrently—the U.S. working class is not a fixed or static entity. The working class is continually in the process of becoming, in which multiplicities of bodies varying by race, gender, age, nationality, religion, sexual orientation, ability, and so on, perform numerous occupations—potentially moving in and out of the workforce. As Deleuze and Guattari state, "There are only multiplicities of multiplicities forming a single *assemblage*, operating in the same *assemblage*: packs in masses and masses in packs."[28] It is important to note that this theorization can logically be extended to contexts outside of the United States and transnationally.

This aptly describes the U.S. working class: multiplicities of diverse bodies perpetually in motion, which can be conceptualized as an assemblage at certain junctures within the capitalist system. This dissertation asserts that the unspecified usage of the category "working class" without qualification in terms of race, gender, nationality, sexuality, and so on, is analogous to the problematic deployment of "women" as a monolithic category. In response to this hegemonic tendency, I theoretically locate the U.S. working class as a complex assemblage in which white, heteronormative males remain hegemonic and overrepresented within it—as demonstrated by the blue-collar frontier shows—further illustrating how white supremacist heteropatriarchy cannot be disassembled from capitalism. It is my hope that this study will provide a useful template for other projects, which seek to engage with social class and reality television without succumbing to excessive reductionism. As a spatial metaphor, assemblage allows for an understanding of working-class status as a location of relative economic disadvantage within the global capitalist system, while simultaneously attending to the coexisting power disparities and complex social differentiations within that location.

Aside from this necessary reformulation of social class, this project further legitimates the study of mass media texts for locating the critical place of

Introduction 11

cultural productions within the reification of social hierarchies. More precisely, I intend to challenge dominant conceptualizations of social categories as they are constructed and represented in popular media, especially in terms of the naturalized and concealed reciprocal relationships between white supremacy, heteropatriarchy, and capitalism. I aim for this project to model the affordances of intersectional analytics for the study of reality television.

I maintain that intersectionality is indispensable for unmasking how systems of power, such as white supremacy, heteropatriarchy, settler-colonialism, and capitalism operate in seemingly invisible and naturalized ways. Moreover, intersectionality more accurately conceives of social categories, including race, gender, social class, sexuality, nationality, religion, disability, etc., as dimensions of social experience that remain interlocking and mutually constitutive. In other words, gender, race, social class, and so on, cannot be parsed out into discrete strands and unitary experiences.

In a 2015 *Washington Post* editorial, Kimberlé Crenshaw spotlights that "Intersectionality was a lived reality before it became a term."[29] Crenshaw coined the term in 1989 to specifically address how U.S. discrimination law fails to account for the lived experiences of Black women workers, who experience a uniquely enmeshed form of both racism and sexism. In her landmark piece, "Demarginalizing the Intersection of Race and Sex," she critically observes how dominant legal frameworks and analytical lenses cannot adequately correct the injustices experienced specifically by Black women, which therefore necessitates an explicitly intersectional intervention: "These problems of exclusion cannot be solved simply by including Black women within an already established analytical structure. Because the intersectional experience is greater than the sum of racism and sexism, any analysis that does not take intersectionality into account cannot sufficiently address the particular manner in which Black women are subordinated."[30] Crenshaw contends that through the lens of Black women's experiences, one can clearly discern the necessity of intersectional theorizing and activism. This logic can be extended to the experiences of all women of color, and even further to all those subjects who endure and negotiate multiple forms of domination.

However, I also suggest that as an analytic, intersectionality can be applied to dominant groups, such as heteronormative white men, for the purpose of unmasking how these groups benefit from multiple forms of social advantage. I think Black feminist epistemologies, such as intersectionality, have compelling explanatory power for revealing the innerworkings of white supremacy, heteropatriarchy, and capitalism. Case in point, the subjects of the blue-collar frontier shows are not systematically conferred advantages because of *only* their whiteness or *just* their cisheterosexual manhood—it is how these two structures of domination work in tandem that engenders a specifically advantaged social location. Intersectionality also accounts for capitalism and class, which reveals that the working-class subjects of the blue-collar frontier shows do experience a comparative disadvantage in relation to their economically privileged white male counterparts. I must caution though that this does not imply that middle-class people of color are advantaged overall in relation to working-class white males. Responsible intersectional models are not structured in reductive, additive manners. Intersectionality provides a critical vocabulary for teasing out the complexity of the relationships between multiple axes of one's social location, which are directly tied to systems of oppression.

A critical note: In applying an intersectional lens to dominant groups, the intention is not to further decenter marginalized groups, such as women of color, who are the intended focus of intersectional thinking and activism. (Although I am acutely aware of the risk here.) The objective herein is to unmask and destabilize the ways in which white supremacy, heteropatriarchy, and capitalism appear natural or normal in entertainment media, including reality television. Unless these systems of oppression are explicitly made visible and grappled with in an intersectional manner, white supremacist capitalist heteropatriarchy can continue unchallenged. To further clarify how I conceive of intersectionality within this analysis of systemically advantaged social locations linked to systems of power, I reference Hillary Potter's formulation of intersectionality. In *Intersectionality and Criminology: Disrupting and Revolutionizing Studies of Crime*, Potter elucidates the necessity of intersectionality for criminological research, since it more accurately accounts for dimensions of race, gender, social class, disability, nationality, and other mutually constitutive structures of domination, in relation to hegemonic constructions of crime and criminality. Potter briefly defines intersectionality as " . . . referring to *the concept or conceptualization that each person has an assortment of coalesced socially constructed identities that are ordered into an inequitable social stratum*" [emphasis in original].[31]

I find Potter's working definition of intersectionality to be the most comprehensive and useful, and it is this conceptualization that informs this analysis. This articulation explicitly speaks to how "each person" becomes interpellated into intersecting social categorizations linked to interlocking structures of domination, which engenders power differentials between given positionalities. Although she is explicitly engaging with criminology, her characterization of intersectionality can extend to this media studies application. She further emphasizes that intersectional approaches must center " . . . *social-power differentials based on the social ordering of social attributes that are multiple, multiplicative, and inseparable for each individual*" [emphasis in original].[32]

Potter's emphasis on power differentials speaks to Bonnie Thornton Dill & Marla H. Kohlman's delineation between "strong" and "weak" iterations of

Introduction 13

intersectionality in "Intersectionality: A Transformative Paradigm in Feminist Theory and Social Justice."

Dill and Kohlman contend that intersectionality effectively links theory and practice, since it centers the *embodied* everyday experience of oppressions and steers away from abstract theorizing. Intersectionality's explanatory power and subversive potential shine through in that it " . . . can validate the lives and histories of persons and subgroups previously ignored or marginalized, and it is used to help empower communities and the people in them."[33] As with any theory or research methodology, intersectionality can be interpreted and applied in divergent ways with varying degrees of success.

Dill and Kohlman distinguish "strong intersectionality" as a mode of inquiry that " . . . seeks to ascertain how phenomena are mutually constituted and interdependent, how we must understand one phenomenon in deference to understanding another."[34] In contrast, they explain that " . . . 'weak intersectionality' explores differences without any true analysis . . . [it] eschews the difficult dialogue(s) of how our differences have come to be . . . "[35] The divide between what the authors label as the strong and weak strands of intersectionality mirrors the paradigms of intersectional social justice and (neo)liberal multiculturalism respectively. The latter celebrates difference without acknowledging social hierarchies and systems of oppression, such as white supremacy and heteropatriarchy, which congeal specific meanings and experiences to certain social locations. In short, liberal multiculturalism is ahistorical and lacks needed social contextualization. Therefore, this examination proceeds with the understanding that questions of identity and social categories should not be approached from a flawed liberal, multicultural framework, which celebrates difference at the expense of recognizing asymmetrical power dynamics. I push Dill and Kohlman's characterization of "weak intersectionality" even further and suggest that such analyses should not even be granted the intersectionality label.

I concur with certain aspects of Puar's noted critique of the common implementation of intersectionality in *Terrorist Assemblages*: *Homonationalism in Queer Times*. Puar utilizes Deleuze and Guattari's conceptualization of assemblage as opposed to intersectionality to reveal how gender, sexuality, and race inform logics of U.S. nationalism and imperialism that produce terrorist others. She evaluates the usefulness of assemblage in relation to intersectionality, which is in conversation with Dill and Kohlman's discussion of "strong" and "weak" strands of intersectionality. As she explains, "As opposed to an intersectional model of identity, which presumes that components—race, class, gender, sexuality, nation, age, religion—are separable analytics and can thus be disassembled, an assemblage is more attuned to interwoven forces that merge and dissipate time, space, and body against linearity, coherency, and permanency."[36]

I only agree with Puar's assessment insofar as intersectional paradigms can *potentially* be reductive and problematic. However, I think it is too hasty to do away with intersectionality entirely because some scholars have reproduced "weak intersectionality" in their analysis. This project highlights the usefulness of both assemblage and intersectionality as theoretical frameworks within media studies research—disrupting the notion that the two theorizations are at odds. I argue that assemblage is particularly useful as a spatial metaphor for more accurately locating the working class as a position of economic disadvantage within the capitalist system without erasing the complex heterogeneity of workers and the asymmetrical power dynamics existing among them. Concomitantly, I maintain that intersectionality remains vital for explicating how systems of oppression operate in mutually constitutive and interlocking fashions that structure social experience.

In terms of my contention that intersectionality must be more comprehensively integrated into media studies projects specifically, Patrick R. Grzanka explicates the critical place of media representations within intersectional conceptualizations of social justice in "Media as Sites/Sights of Justice" in *Intersectionality: A Foundations and Frontiers Reader*. Grzanka asserts that "We come to know and create meanings of race, gender, class, sexuality, and other dimensions of difference through representations, so intersectionality is both a structural *and* representational phenomenon."[37] I assert that televisual productions encompass both structural and representational aspects, as per Alison Hearn's discussion of the neoliberal production of reality television.[38] Grzanka further legitimizes the importance of specifically intersectional critiques for properly analyzing media texts: "For example, a single-axis analysis concerned only with evaluating gender representations might prematurely conclude that a film or television series supports gender-progressive ideas while incidentally eliding racist or classist images in the text . . . "[39]

Consequently, intersectionality enables a more precise and critical accounting of the power dynamics embedded in the blue-collar frontier shows. White supremacy, heteropatriarchy, settler-colonialism, and capitalism are not operating independently of each other either in these series or in broader social relations. This is particularly pernicious given that these interwoven systems of oppression seem largely invisible in this subgenre of reality television. Having established how both assemblage and intersectionality inform this project, I will now detail some of the other relevant theoretical frames that disrupt the seeming banality of these series.

I posit that the blue-collar frontier shows are demonstrative of a white male supremacist visuality. Nicholas Mirzoeff characterizes visuality as constituting the hegemonic visual order or the dominant modes of seeing that appear naturalized or "normal" in a given set of social relations.[40] Case in point, it is a taken-for-granted assumption that the subjects of the blue-collar frontier shows—white heteronormative male workers on the job in rural settings—would be interpreted as signifying America's ideal image of "real men." What if one were to rhetorically ask: "What do 'real men' look like?" I argue that the blue-collar frontier shows provide the answer in the current U.S. neoliberal context. For one segment of the population to be designated as "real" or "authentic" relationally defines other groups as inferior and subordinate. In this instance then, men of color are not intelligible as "real men" in the dominant visual domain. Thus, white supremacist logic is encoded within the blue-collar frontier shows with the notable absence of people of color of all genders. This white male supremacist visuality is succinctly captured in the promotional stills from the series described later in subsequent chapters.

With this conceptualization of visuality in mind, it is crucial to more precisely delineate the systems of power that remain invisibly encoded within these series. Critical whiteness studies, a prominent strand of scholarship within critical race theory, challenges dominant configurations of whiteness, as well as maleness, as naturalized or seemingly unremarkable. A salient aspect of how white male supremacy functions is that it exclusively reserves dominant conceptions of individuality for heteronormative white males. For example, a white woman may be discursively reduced to representing her entire gender; a Black man might be reduced to speaking for his entire race; and a queer-identifying person may be called upon to represent all "nonheteronormative" gender identities and sexual orientations. However, it is highly unlikely that a heteronormative white man would ever be reduced to his gender, race, or sexual orientation in mainstream U.S. discourse. In terms of the dominant discourse surrounding social class in the United States, class consciousness remains underdeveloped. Thus, class signifiers are also sublimated within the blue-collar frontier series in favor of narratives that frame these workers as "rugged individuals" who appear unconstrained by the structural realities of capitalism.

The primacy of the individual remains one of the core legacies of Western modernity, which is intimately connected to white supremacy, colonialism, capitalism, and their respective intersections. Within hegemonic white supremacist epistemologies and discourses, racism continues to be reduced to a matter of individual prejudice, as opposed to the reality of its quotidian social and institutional enshrinement. As Neil Gotanda illustrates in "A Critique of 'Our Constitution is Color-Blind,'" the U.S. legal system's claims of racial neutrality belie its systematic history of bolstering white male supremacy, as exemplified via U.S. Supreme Court decisions including *Dred Scott v. Sanford* (1857), *Plessy v. Ferguson* (1896), and numerous other landmark cases, including the court's more recent gutting of the Voting Rights Act in *Shelby v. Holder* (2013). Declarations of colorblindness are connected to the primacy of the individual, in which individuality remains primarily

16 *Introduction*

reserved for white, heteronormative males in both the dominant discourse and sociopolitical practices.

Gotanda addresses how hegemonic conceptualizations of racism are tied to individualism: "Despite the fact that personal racial prejudices have social origins, racism is considered to be an individual and personal trait."[41] This logic enables white supremacy to permeate all aspects of society, including media institutions and their cultural productions, largely unnoticed (at least by the majority of whites). This legacy infuses the blue-collar frontier shows, which have tapped into a deep-rooted U.S. cultural legacy of protecting and valorizing white men as the quintessential rugged individuals.

Cheryl Harris's groundbreaking piece, "Whiteness as Property," is also highly useful for conceptualizing the legal institutionalization of white supremacy; the ramifications of which can be traced to mainstream cultural productions, such as the blue-collar frontier shows. Harris argues that " . . . American law has recognized a property interest in whiteness that, although unacknowledged, now forms the background against which legal disputes are framed, argued, and adjudicated."[42] She astutely grounds the metaphor of whiteness as property in relation to the history of the reservation of full property rights to whites in the United States since the nation's inception. She traces a genealogical sketch of the social construction of race, in which the conflation of whiteness and property underpinned white supremacy, particularly in relation to the enslavement of Black Americans as property and the dispossession of indigenous peoples from their lands. She characterizes whiteness as a form of property interest in that " . . . the law has accorded 'holders' of whiteness the same privileges and benefits accorded holders of other types of property."[43]

Of relevance to the blue-collar frontier shows, which inherently deemphasize class consciousness, is Harris's acknowledgment, which was first notably formulated by W. E. B. Du Bois in *Black Reconstruction in America* (1935), that *all* whites have access to the power that whiteness confers regardless of class status: "The wages of whiteness [Du Bois's phrase] are available to all whites, regardless of class position—even to those whites who are without power, money, or influence."[44] Harris echoes Du Bois's observation that white workers in the nineteenth century became more invested in their white identity at the expense of class consciousness, which continues to have an enduring legacy. This gestures toward the blue-collar frontier shows and the dominant identification of their featured subjects as "real men" and not as workers, which is astounding given that the shows explicitly depict them on their job sites. The field of critical whiteness studies crucially attends to how both class and racial formations remain fundamentally entangled.

The role of place within the white male supremacist visuality of these series also requires further elaboration considering Cheryl Harris's mapping

Introduction 17

of whiteness as property. A formulaic narrative device found throughout these programs is the notion that these men are somehow "taming the wilderness" via their occupations, since their jobs require them to work outdoors in relatively desolate, rural landscapes. Historian Frederick Jackson Turner's "The Significance of the Frontier in American History" provides an historical account of the ideological relationship between the frontier and the U.S. nation-building project; a sociopolitical endeavor rooted in white male supremacy and settler-colonialism. In 1893, Turner put forth his "frontier thesis." With the U.S. Census of 1890 announcing the "closure" of the frontier, Turner believed this would lead to a crisis for the maintenance of the supposedly unique American character—invoking discourses of U.S. exceptionalism. He broadly conceived of (white male) U.S. identity as being continually reified through "westward expansion," which refers to the ongoing colonization of indigenous peoples and their lands in the United States. He believed U.S. culture was preserved through the rugged individualism and egalitarian sentiment supposedly endemic to frontier life: "American social development has been continually beginning over again on the frontier . . . this expansion westward with its new opportunities . . . The true point of view in the history of this nation is not the Atlantic Coast, it is the Great West."[45]

Turner's visuality of an "empty frontier" that erases the presence of indigenous peoples serves to simultaneously obscure and justify colonization and genocide. Contemporary references to the frontier, including on the series examined here, demonstrate its symbolic power and legacy—rendering invisible its historical and ongoing repercussions. Jodi Byrd's articulation of indigenous critical theory in *The Transit of Empire: Indigenous Critiques of Colonialism* unmasks the oppressive structures that constitute the frontier ethos. Byrd's provocation guides this analysis in terms of its engagement with frontier mythology: it is imperative not to reinforce the notion that Native Americans have somehow been relegated to the past tense, or in the case of the blue-collar frontier shows, that they have somehow been always already gone. The filming locations of these programs are framed as perpetual empty wildernesses awaiting the arrival of the rightful frontiersmen to stake their claims. Without Byrd's intervention of indigenous critical theory, one fails to recognize the full extent of the consequences of the replication of frontier mythology. Simply put: Frontier mythology is inseparable from the violent history of the settler-colonization of America's indigenous peoples.

Turner's visuality of the frontier not only erases indigenous peoples, but also naturalizes the presence of white men. As Turner notes in terms of the frontiersman's class status: "Engaged in a struggle to subdue the forest, working as an individual, and with little specie or capital, his interests were with the debtor class."[46] It is noteworthy that Turner qualifies the mythical frontiersman as "working as an individual." This speaks directly to the blue-collar frontier shows, which frame these working-class, white male sub-jects as rugged individuals on the frontier. Turner offers his assessment of the importance of the settling (colonizing) of the frontier within the wider U.S. nation-building project: "And to study this advance, the men who grew up under these conditions, and the political, economic, and social results of it, is to study the really American part of our history."[47] In other words, "real men" forged "the really American part of our history." The blue-collar frontier shows represent a contemporary manifestation of Turner's imperial, white supremacist, heteropatriarchal logic, which inextricably links the visualities of the frontier, "real men," and hegemonic notions of U.S. identity.

Another renowned critical race theorist, George Lipsitz, builds upon Harris's formulation of "whiteness as property" and speaks to the relation-ship between white supremacy and place within his theorization of the "white spatial imaginary." In *How Racism Takes Place*, Lipsitz explicates the ways in which places are always already racialized: "White identity in the United States is place bound. It exists and persists because segregated neighbor-hoods and segregated schools are nodes in a network of practices that skew opportunities and life chances along racial lines."[48] He characterizes the white spatial imaginary as representing " . . . the properly gendered prosperous suburban home as the privileged moral geography of the nation. Widespread, costly, and often counterproductive practices of surveillance, regulation, and incarceration become justified as forms of *frontier defense* [emphasis added] against demonized people of color.[49]"

Lipsitz's analysis focuses on the racialized spaces of cities and suburbs. The white spatial imaginary of the suburban home casts itself as race-neutral, in which the systemic advantages of white supremacy remain concealed through mythic discourses of individual hard work and upward social mobil-ity. Particularly germane to this project is how Lipsitz draws a line of con-tinuity between the contemporary white spatial imaginary of the suburban home and the eighteenth and nineteenth-century dominant conceptualization of the frontier. He puts forth the notion that the U.S. colonial desire for "pure and homogenous spaces"—deemed integral for the U.S. nation-building project—necessitated the removal and marginalization of "'impure' popula-tions."[50] He explains that because the colonial march westward ultimately fell short of the imagined vision of (white male supremacist) freedom that " . . . the properly ordered and prosperous domestic dwelling eclipsed the frontier as the privileged moral geography of U.S. society, as the nation's key symbol of freedom, harmony, and virtue."[51] I argue that the blue-collar frontier shows represent a revival of the frontier as the preferred white spatial imaginary in contemporary U.S. society because of its connection to hegemonic masculin-ity. In the dominant discourse, the suburban home signifies white femininity and domesticity; a place where "real men" cannot thrive. In that sense, the imagined frontier of these shows constitutes a white, heteropatriarchal spatial imaginary. Building off Lipsitz's conceptualization, I argue then that the mythic frontier constitutes a "white male spatial imaginary," as typified by the blue-collar frontier shows.

In his groundbreaking piece, "Encoding and Decoding in the Television Discourse," Stuart Hall explores the salience of the frontier in U.S. culture, particularly through the lens of "The Western" film and television genre. Hall fleshes out the relationship between the historic "American West" and the mythical one that has become embedded in U.S. culture. He explains that "this process, whereby the rules of language and discourse intervene, at a certain moment, to transform and 'naturalize' a specific set of historical circumstances, is one of the most important test-cases for any semiology which seeks to ground itself in historical realities."[52] This project situates the blue-collar frontier shows as operating within the dominant codes of The Western. Hall characterizes this contemporary genre, with its distortion of U.S history, as perpetuating one of the most important mythologies in U.S. culture: "This is *the* archetypical American story, America of the frontier, of the expanding and unsettled West . . . It is the land of *men*, of independent men . . . for a time, in film and television, this deep-structure provided the taken-for-granted story-of-all-stories, the paradigm-action narrative, the perfect myth."[53] In summation, these reality television programs function as part of an ongoing veneration of the Western, frontier myth, in which the intertwined systems of power of white supremacy, heteropatriarchy, and capitalism, and their resultant symbolic and material violence, remain hidden.

A core claim of this project is that the blue-collar frontier shows represent a form of hegemonic masculinity in the current U.S. neoliberal context. Raewyn Connell originally coined the concept of hegemonic masculinity in *Gender and Power: Society, the Person, and Sexual Politics* (1987). In a more recent article, "Hegemonic Masculinity: Rethinking the Concept" (2005), Connell and James W. Messerschmidt claim that " . . . the concept of hegemonic masculinity is in need of reformulation in four main areas: the nature of gender hierarchy, the geography of masculine configurations, *the process of social embodiment* [emphasis added], and the dynamics of masculinities."[54] In essence, hegemonic masculinity should not be collapsed into a monolithic, fixed set of traits. In *Staging Masculinities: History, Gender, Performance* (2003), Michael Mangan succinctly encapsulates the challenges inherent to neatly conceptualizing hegemonic masculinity: "Hegemonic masculinity is that form or model of masculinity which a culture privileges above others . . . Hegemonic masculinity is by nature paradoxical, since it seems to stand still but in fact is always on the move . . . "[55] This necessitates intersectional, socially contextualized approaches to hegemonic masculinity and gender performances more broadly.

It is essential to underline that despite the underlying plurality and malleability of hegemonic masculinity as a concept, I argue that white, rural, working-class masculinity remains a highly privileged masculinity in U.S. culture. I concur with Hugh Campbell, Michael Mayerfield Bell, and Margaret Finney's assessment in *Country Boys: Masculinity and Rural Life* (2006) that white, rural, working-class masculinity implies authenticity, and therefore, legitimacy. I assert that this specific constellation of traits reflects a dominant conceptualization of "real manhood" in the current U.S. neoliberal context, which is evidenced through the proliferation and popularity of the blue-collar frontier shows. As I discuss at length in relation to the Roberston men of *Duck Dynasty*, the perceived legitimacy frontier masculinity confers explains why affluent white males strive to emulate it. Although Donald Trump has not adopted a frontiersman-style presentation, his performative talk and rhetorical strategy evinces a *stereotypical* white, male working-class manner of speech. White, working-class masculine performativity remains profoundly linked with dominant notions of real manhood.

I understand these depictions of hegemonic masculinity as gender performances per Judith Butler's landmark theorizations in *Gender Trouble* (1990). Butler's analytical framework of gender performance unmasks how all subjects become interpellated into a binary gender system, which mandates that all individuals continuously strive to perform in accordance with socially constructed and largely unattainable embodied standards of what it means to be "real men" and "real women." As Butler explains in *Gender Trouble*, " . . . the action of gender requires a performance that is *repeated*. This repetition is at once a reenactment and re-experiencing of a set of meanings already socially established . . . "[56] Consistent with Butler's theorizing, all the men of the blue-collar frontier shows are striving to perform hegemonic masculinity. However, it is noteworthy that the male Robertsons of *Duck Dynasty* underwent an explicit transformation regarding their masculine performances. Through a series of widely publicized photographs, it emerged that the Robertsons had fully embraced so-called "yuppie" or white, upper middle-class appearances before their careers on A&E.[57] This contrasts with their current performance of a self-proclaimed "redneck" masculinity. Building off Butler's framework, Helen Wood and Beverly Skeggs explain in *Reality Television and Class* that " . . . perform*atives* are unconscious repeated gendered and classed enactments, while performances are full-blown conscious actions. What we often see on reality television is the performative made explicit."[58]

The male Robertsons' on-camera performances of redneck masculinity appear highly calculated based upon their prior appearances. To echo Pierre Bourdieu's theorizing, I surmise that despite possessing significant amounts of economic (wealth) and cultural capital (college degrees), the Robertsons

Introduction 21

were still missing the symbolic capital of masculine legitimacy.[59] Thus, their embrace of a hegemonically masculine performance. The Robertsons are not the only notable wealthy, white men to emulate rural, working-class masculine performances. Prominent political figures, such as former President George W. Bush, publicly performing an embodied image of rural masculinity reveals the extent of its perceived legitimacy: " . . . rural occupational and general 'country boy' representations are often appropriated by individuals for self-serving political and commercial purposes. Like the banners of God and flag, rural 'salt-of-the-earth' occupations confer widespread legitimacy."[60] Historicizing this style of political performance even further, one can trace its origins back to Theodore Roosevelt in the late nineteenth century. As Gail Bederman notes in *Manliness & Civilization*, Roosevelt deliberately embraced a highly masculine identity that echoes the Robertsons's contemporary performance of hegemonic masculinity to attain political legitimacy: " . . . he constructed a powerful male identity for himself in the terms of the Western adventure story . . . Now, shooting buffalo and bullying obstreperous cowboys, he could style himself the real thing."[61] When affluent white men take up these rural, working-class masculine performances to be perceived as authentic, it exemplifies the tension endemic to social categories, in which they are commonly understood as both social locations and stylized performances—the latter of which receives greater emphasis in the current neoliberal context.

To further illustrate the relevance of gendered/raced/classed performativity to the analysis of reality television more broadly, Vicki Mayer explains in *Reality Television and Class* how her experience in the industry illuminates the importance of understanding social categories in relation to how they are performed: "My experience with the reality casting process revealed its emphasis on embodied performances. Casters search not only for people within certain demographics, but also for those who act appropriately to the demographic."[62] Usually, one must perform *stereotypically* within the dominant logic of reality television. Despite the notable exception of *Duck Dynasty*, this is consistent with the masculine performances on the other blue-collar frontier shows, in which the white males featured do generally occupy a working-class socioeconomic location. The subjects of *Deadliest Catch*, *Ice Road Truckers*, *Ax Men*, and *Gold Rush* are also *performing* a form of hegemonic masculinity, but by juxtaposing economically privileged white males performing rural, working-class masculinity, it uncovers the desired symbolic capital of this presentation.

I maintain that Pierre Bourdieu's formulation of capital illuminates why this performance has become a strategic maneuver for certain affluent, white male politicians. Bourdieu conceives of social life and the struggle for power through the lens of three fundamental and interrelated concepts: habitus—an individual's predispositions toward certain actions or behaviors, capital—sources of power in its economic, cultural, social, and symbolic forms, and field—a spatial metaphor for the relative distribution of power in a specific context. He characterizes the various forms of capital an individual can acquire as the following: "economic capital (money and property), cultural capital (cultural goods and services including educational credentials), social capital (acquaintances and networks), and symbolic capital (legitimation)."[63] It is the last form of capital, symbolic, that speaks to the power of hegemonically masculine performances, in that they confer masculine legitimacy. Bourdieu's theorization of capital explains why affluent white males, such as the Robertsons and Donald Trump, who already possess large degrees of economic, cultural, and social capital, take up white, working-class masculine rhetorical performances—they are seeking the symbolic capital of masculine legitimacy. The symbolic capital of Donald Trump's *stereotypical* white, working-class masculine rhetorical strategy helped launch him to the presidency.

Having established the rationale for utilizing these specific theoretical frames in this analysis, I will provide a brief overview of the audiences of the programs under examination. Although this book gives primacy to televisual texts within their wider fields of meaning, it is useful to provide a snapshot of the viewers of these programs.

AUDIENCE SNAPSHOT AND THE TRUMP CONNECTION

One of the primary limitations in analyzing demographic data gathered from within the commercial television industry is that is not aggregated intersectionally. Dimensions of age, income, and gender are often given primacy without accounting for how these categories intersect. Race, gender, and region are also less frequently noted in published industry reports. However, based upon the available data and other observations from mainstream television critics, one can get a sense for which segments of the population are primarily watching the blue-collar frontier shows, and why these programs appeal to these groups.

In mapping the general demographic patterns found within the audiences of the series in the sample, it is critical to emphasize that each of these shows tends to attract the same type of viewers. Thus, demographic observations about the audience of *Deadliest Catch* have been generally consistent with findings about the audience of *Ax Men*. With this degree of demographic overlap, it is then safe to refer to the "blue-collar frontier television audience"

Introduction 23

as a group unto itself. As I discuss shortly, television critics often refer to the viewership of this subgenre of reality television as a singular entity.

As an audience metric, age is given a lot of primacy in commercial television. Interestingly, the median age of the viewers of the series under examination leans relatively older—mostly toward the upper end and beyond of the industry's coveted eighteen to forty-nine age demographic. Commercial television's long-held practice of courting this age group has also been subject to increased scrutiny in the past two decades.[64] According to Andy Denhart, the median age of the audiences for the series under examination, of which *Ice Road Truckers* is not included, are as follows: *Deadliest Catch* is forty-seven; *Ax Men* is fifty-one; and *Gold Rush* is fifty-three.[65]

More precise metrics account for both age and gender. With the latter dimension, it becomes clear that the audience is largely comprised of men. In Mitch Metcalf's breakdown of Sunday television ratings and their demographic distribution from March 2015, he notes that "*Ax Men* on History skews toward men 35+."[66] *Entertainment Weekly* reported on *Deadliest Catch*'s record ratings in 2010 and noted the sizable portion of male viewers of a certain age: "For the last two months, *Deadliest Catch* has been the No. 1 program in all of cable on Tuesday nights among persons (an average 3.7 million viewers) and men 25–54 (1.4 million viewers)."[67] October 2014 *Deadline* report discussing *Gold Rush*'s remarkably high ratings for its fifth season premiere notes that Discovery dominated in male viewership across age brackets: "Discovery finished the primetime night in first place among guys 25–54—and guys 18–49, and 18–34."[68] In 2011, the *Los Angeles Times* acknowledged *Ice Road Truckers'* role in making History one of the top-ranked networks among men with its prodigious lineup of blue-collar reality shows: "The network, home also to 'American Restoration,' 'Ice Road Truckers' and 'Swamp People,' is the top-ranked nonfiction network in key viewer demographics and the second-ranked network for men behind ESPN."[69]

An industry report about Discovery Channel's audience from 2012 is highly informative for understanding the viewer profile of the blue-collar frontier programs overall. Scarborough, a local market research subsidiary of Nielsen, not only compiled useful demographic information about the Discovery audience, but also gathered revealing information about the typical recreational and leisure activities of the network's viewers. Their demographic profile offers a substantial level of detail, but notably excludes any information about the racial composition of the network's audience at the time.[70] I speculate that the omission of the racial identities of Discovery's viewers in this demographic composite suggests that most of its viewers are likely white. Whiteness often evades the label of "race" in a white supremacist society, in which it tends to be cast as the "normal" or "default" race.

Therefore, if race goes unremarked upon in a demographic sketch such as this, then one might reasonably argue that the racial subjects under examination are likely white. Additionally, the recreational and leisure activities of its audience are stereotypically associated with white males. Scarborough finds that Discovery's viewers are statistically more likely to have gone hunting, fishing, golfing, camping, and powerboating in the past twelve months. The report specifically credits *Deadliest Catch* for drawing in this subset of viewers: "Deadliest Catch may very well be the show that draws viewers in as Discovery Channel viewers are much more likely than all U.S. adults to have gone fishing or to have gone powerboating in the past year."[71]

It is also noteworthy that Discovery seems to draw viewers from across the class spectrum with a significant portion having blue-collar employment, as well as a sizeable number reporting relatively high income. The network attracting white male viewers from both the working and middle classes remains consistent with Kimmel's psychological profile of U.S. white working and middle-class men in *Angry White Men*. Kimmel notes that despite their differences in income, "The white working class and the white middle class have rarely been so close *emotionally* as they are today . . . "[72] This partially explains Trump drawing white male votes from across the class spectrum as well.[73]

The relationship between Donald Trump and the blue-collar frontier television audience requires further elucidation. In a groundbreaking study regarding television viewership and voting patterns in the 2016 U.S. presidential election, Josh Katz reports in the *New York Times* that "If you had to guess how strongly a place supported Donald J. Trump in the election, would you rather know how popular 'Duck Dynasty' is there, or how George W. Bush did there in 2000? It turns out the relationship with the TV show is stronger."[74] Katz pinpoints that the divide between television preferences mirrors the wider urban/rural divide in the United States, which corresponds with racial divisions. Katz lists *Deadliest Catch* as one of the "shows most common in rural areas"[75], in which whites maintain an overwhelming racial majority.[76] The show registers as having the least similarity to several shows with high popularity in the so-called "Black belt." Katz describes this region as " . . . a swath that extends from the Mississippi River along the Eastern Seaboard up to Washington, but also including city centers and other places with large nonwhite populations."[77] Regarding the rural character of the *Deadliest Catch* audience, Katz more precisely homes in on its regional distribution: "It's most popular in areas that are rural, cold and close to the sea, particularly Alaska and Maine."[78] It seems that perhaps fishermen like to watch other fishermen.

In compiling the available data about the demographic character of the blue-collar frontier shows, in which each report often only focuses on or two social categories, it suggests that the audience tends to be rural white men who are middle-aged and older. This strongly aligns with the demographic characteristics of Donald Trump's supporters. Paralleling the class distribution of Trump voters, the audience appears comprised of both middle and working-class white males. However, as mainstream television critics have observed, the audience tilts more toward the affluent end of the class spectrum overall. In "Grab a Brew While They Face Death," about the now defunct *Coal* on *Spike*, which documented West Virginia coal miners, Dana Jennings of the *New York Times* observed the trend of professional, white-collar men ritualistically reaffirming their masculinity through watching other men perform physically arduous, manual labor on television back in 2011.[79]

Tanja Aho similarly notes how these shows appeal to middle-class men in "Reality TV and Its Audiences Reconsidered: Class and Poverty in *Undercover Boss* (CBS)": "Masculinity-centered reality TV shows such as *Ice Road Truckers, Deadliest Catch,* and *Ax Men* draw on a rhetoric of realism while focusing on the white, male, heroic worker to provide a romanticized ideal of labor. Such an ideal appeals to many middle-class men who feel emasculated by their office jobs."[80] In *Angry White Men*, Kimmel also addresses the place of media escapism for both working and middle-class white men, who he documents as feeling persecuted because of economic shocks, as well as racial and gender-based movements for equity: "If you feel yourself to always be taking it on the chin, media fantasy is the place where you get to pump your first in defiance. If you feel emasculated in real life, you can feel like a man in 'reel life.'"[81]

Thus, the blue-collar frontier shows attract mostly white, rural, middle-class men—a demographic group that largely came out in support of Donald Trump in the 2016 and 2020 elections. It is vital to note that I do not explore, nor do I want to emphasize, the intentionality of show creators in relation to interpreting audience reactions. Ultimately, these programs enter a wider system of meaning upon their distribution within a given sociocultural context—generating specific reactions and signaling deeper trends irrespective of the expressed intentions of show creators. I argue that blue-collar frontier television is in conversation with a wider white, male backlash against feminism, antiracism, and LGBTQ rights, as well as changes in the nature and distribution of work engendered by neoliberal economic policies.

Having established the primary demographic characteristics of the blue-collar frontier television audience (white, rural, middle, and working-class men of middle age), and the principal reasons why this subgenre of reality television appeals to them, it is important to note that I do not think that one's social location is solely deterministic of what one seeks out or enjoys for entertainment. However, there are observable patterns between social location and media consumption, which can offer clues to highly consequential political currents, the likes of which are detailed herein.

The first chapter outlines how white, rural, working-class masculinity, as depicted on the blue-collar frontier shows, signifies hegemonic masculinity in the contemporary U.S. neoliberal context. I detail and historicize the conceptual parameters of this hegemonic masculine performance and illuminate how heteropatriarchy, white supremacy, and capitalism mutually constitute the preferred way to "be a man" in the U.S. dominant domain. I contextualize the emergence of the blue-collar frontier shows in relation to the Great Recession, as well the sizeable white male backlash against the social movements representing the interests of women, people of color, LGBTQ individuals, and those living at those intersections in the past two decades. The casts of these series are comprised almost entirely of white men except for a small number of white women. When men of color do occasionally appear, they are largely relegated to the periphery. Notably, women of color are completely absent. I argue that the popularity of these series, which venerate white, rural, working-class men as authentically masculine, gestured toward a deeper sociopolitical current of white male aggrievement, which cannot be separated from the rise of Donald Trump.

I also attend to the fraught relationship between the blue-collar frontier shows and social class, as they ironically deemphasize the existence of a class system and class consciousness. Moreover, the shows' principal stars, such as the captains on *Deadliest Catch*, more accurately belong to the managerial or ownership classes. The class hierarchies that exist within the blue-collar frontier realm itself require illumination. As I demonstrate, the perception of economic independence and rugged individualism is commensurate with hegemonic masculine status.

In the second chapter, I address the framing of the few white women who are provisionally permitted entry into the male homosocial space of the blue-collar frontier. I spotlight how Lisa Kelly of *Ice Road Truckers*' embodiment of hegemonic femininity allows her to tenuously inhabit this hypermasculine space as long as her appearance satisfies the cisheterosexual male gaze. The show's framing of Lisa strongly aligns with neoliberal feminist logics, which emphasize the triumph of individual (white) women in a manner suggesting the superficiality of sexism and other systemic barriers. In summation, Lisa's exceptionalism in a male homosocial space is tolerated because it generates dramatic tension for the series and does not destabilize the heteropatriarchal order.

Chapter 3 critically illuminates the role of place, specifically the mythic frontier, within the blue-collar frontier shows and in U.S. cultural history by extension. Building off George Lipsitz's conceptualization of the "white spatial imaginary," I contend that the mythic frontier constitutes a "white male

Introduction 27

spatial imaginary." I argue that the blue-collar frontier shows reinvigorate frontier mythology, which is deeply rooted in U.S. exceptionalism and the ideological justification for the settler-colonization of indigenous peoples. I historicize these contemporary depictions of frontier life and labor in relation to U.S. historian Frederick Jackson Turner's landmark thesis, "The Significance of the Frontier in American history." This chapter foregrounds indigenous critical theory for explicating how the dominant conceptualization of the frontier as an empty wilderness both erases indigenous peoples and naturalizes the presence of white men on these terrains. Indigenous critical theory disrupts the seeming banality of frontier narratives, especially those exemplified by the Western film and television genre, which have become some of the most highly venerated and widely circulated stories in U.S. culture. I situate the blue-collar frontier shows within the lineage of the Western and explore why frontier narratives are making a resurgence, albeit in a slightly different iteration, at this juncture.

Chapter 4 exclusively tackles *Duck Dynasty* and the Robertson men's white, rural, working-class or "redneck" masculine performances, despite possessing substantial amounts of economic and cultural capital. I address the history of the term "redneck," and how it has become increasingly dislodged from its class-based origins in favor of its association with masculine authenticity. I argue that the Robertsons, along with affluent white male politicians both past and present, such as Donald Trump, George W. Bush, Ronald Reagan, and Theodore Roosevelt, strategically perform aspects of white, rural, working-class masculinity to attain the symbolic capital of masculine legitimacy that this performance confers.

I discuss Donald Trump's emulation of a stereotypical white, working-class, masculine rhetorical performance at length, and how it has contributed to him garnering support not only from the white working class, but also the white middle class.[82] In exploring some of the class-based demographic misconceptions about Trump's white base, I also touch upon how classism operates within whiteness. Namely, I note how accusations of racism do not collectively stick to middle-class whites as a group. In the mainstream media, racism is often characterized as the exclusive purview of poor and working-class whites. Of course, there is racism among economically disadvantaged whites, but I observe that middle- and upper-class whites are not collectively branded as racist in the same way because of their class privilege. In contextualizing Trump and the Robertson men's gender performances, I unmask the white supremacist, heteropatriarchal, capitalist, and imperial logics that reinforce the performative power of "real manhood."

Lastly, I conclude with a summative assessment of the study's findings and offer my thoughts on the ongoing legacy of blue-collar frontier reality television. Although some of the shows have stopped production, the thematic presence of the blue-collar frontier continues to shape U.S. cable television, even in the streaming era. Moreover, I discuss the continued purchase of white, rural, working-class masculine performances in U.S. culture and politics.

NOTES

1. Laurie Ouellette, "The Trump Show," *Television & New Media* 17, no. 7 (2016): 649, https://doi.org/10.1177/1527476416652695.

2. Kurt Schlosser, "King of Blue-Collar Reality TV Driven by 'Living on the Edge,'" *Today*, March 13, 2013, https://www.today.com/popculture/king-blue-collar -reality-tv-driven-living-edge-1C8842451.

3. Jill Filipovic, "The Revenge of the White Man," *TIME*, November 10, 2016, http://time.com/4566304/donald-trump-revenge-of-the-white-man/; Andrew Prokop, "A New Report Complicates Simplistic Narratives about Race and the 2020 Election," *Vox*, May 10, 2021, https://www.vox.com/2021/5/10/22425178 /catalist- report-2020-election-biden-trump-demographics.

4. Michael Kimmel, *Manhood in America: A Cultural History*, 3rd ed. (New York and Oxford: Oxford University Press, 2012), 187.

5. Michelle Alexander, *The New Jim Crow: Mass Incarceration in the Age of Colorblindness* (New York: New Press, 2020), xli.

6. Naomi Klein, *No Is Not Enough: Resisting Trump's Shock Politics and Winning the World We Need* (Chicago, IL: Haymarket Books, 2017), 88–89.

7. Michael Kimmel, *Angry White Men: American Masculinity at the End of an Era.* (New York: Nation Books, 2013), 279.

8. Tanja Aho, "Reality TV and Its Audiences Reconsidered: Class and Poverty in *Undercover Boss* (CBS) in *Class Divisions in Serial Television*, eds. Sieglinde Lemke & Wibke Schniedermann (London: Palgrave Macmillan, 2016), 89–118.

9. Charles Homans, "A Soap Opera on the High Seas," *New York Times*, December 13, 2012, http://www.nytimes.com/2012/12/16/magazine/how-thom-beers-built-a -reality-tv-empire.html?pagewanted=all&_r=0.

10. Ryan Broderick, "The Dark Side of America's Redneck Reality TV Obsession," *Buzzfeed*, October 27, 2014, https://www.buzzfeed.com/ryanhatesthis/how-hillbilly -reality-tv-got-way-too-real?utm_term=.ao7BEy63W#.efPxN0Bq4.

11. Shannon E.M. O'Sullivan, "Playing 'Redneck': White Masculinity and Working-Class Performance on Duck Dynasty," *Journal of Popular Culture* 49, no. 2 (2016): 367–84, https://doi.org/10.1111/jpcu.12403.

12. Shannon E.M. O'Sullivan, "Playing 'Redneck,'" 367–84.

13. Josh Katz, 'Duck Dynasty' vs. 'Modern Family': 50 Maps of the U.S. Cultural

Divide," *New York Times*, December 27, 2016, https://www.nytimes.com/interactive /2016/12/26/upshot/duck-dynasty-vs-modern-family-television-maps.html?_r=1.

14. Christopher Lockett, "Masculinity and Authenticity: Reality TV's Real Men," *Flow*, October 15, 2010, http://flowtv.org/2010/10/masculinity-and-authenticity/.

15. Halim Shebaya, "Trump 'Tells It Like It Is,'" *HuffPost*, May 5, 2016, https:// www.huffpost.com/entry/trump-tells-it-like-it-is_b_9836974.

16. John Baldoni, "Is Donald Trump a Role Model for Authenticity?," *Forbes*, January 2, 2016, https://www.forbes.com/sites/johnbaldoni/2016/01/02/is-donald -trump-a-role-model-for-authenticity/#1f3e753433bc.

17. Lockett, "Masculinity and Authenticity," http://flowtv.org/2010/10/masculinity -and-authenticity/.

18. Combahee River Collective, *The Combahee River Collective Statement: Black Feminist Organizing in the Seventies and Eighties* (New York, NY: Kitchen Table: Women of Color Press, 1986).

19. Charles Mills, *The Racial Contract* (Ithaca and London: Cornell University Press, 1997), 73.

20. George Monbiot, "Neoliberalism—The Ideology at the Root of All Our Problems, *The Guardian*, April 15, 2016, https://www.theguardian.com/books/2016/apr /15/neoliberalism-ideology-problem-george-monbiot.

21. Arun K. Patnaik, "Gramsci's Concept of Common Sense: Towards a Theory of Subaltern Consciousness in Hegemony Processes," *Economic and Political Weekly* 23, no. 5 (1988): 10.

22. Patricia Hill Collins, *Black Feminist Thought* (New York: Routledge Classics, 2009), 76.

23. Collins, *Black Feminist Thought*, 77.

24. George Yancy and bell hooks, "bell hooks: Buddhis, the Beats and Loving Blackness," *New York Times*, December 10, 2015, https://opinionator.blogs.nytimes .com/author/bell-hooks/.

25. Kathleen Arnold, *America's New Working Class: Race, Gender, and Ethnicity in a Biopolitical Age*, (University Park, Pennsylvania: The Pennsylvania State University Press, 2008), 6–7.

26. Evelyn Nakano Glenn, *Unequal Freedom: How Race and Gender Shaped American Citizenship and Labor*, (Cambridge, Massachusetts: Harvard University Press, 2002).

27. Milia Fisher, "Women of Color and the Gender Wage Gap," *Center for American Progress*, April 14, 2015, https://www.americanprogress.org/issues/women/reports /2015/04/14/110962/women-of-color-and-the-gender-wage-gap/

28. Gilles Deleuze and Felix Guattari, *A Thousand Plateaus: Capitalism and Schizophrenia* (Minneapolis, MN: The University of Minnesota Press, 1987), 34.

29. Kimberlé Crenshaw, "Why Intersectionality Can't Wait," *Washington Post*, September 24, 2015, https://www.washingtonpost.com/news/in-theory/wp/2015/09 /24/why-intersectionality-cant-wait/.

30. Kimberlé Crenshaw, "Demarginalizing the Intersection of Race and Sex: A Black Feminist
Critique of Antidiscrimination Doctrine, Feminist Theory, and Antiracist Politics," in *Critical Race Feminism: A Reader*, ed. A.K. Wing (New York: New York University Press, 2003), 24.

31. Hillary Potter, *Intersectionality and Criminology: Disrupting and Revolutionizing Studies of Crime* (London and New York: Routledge, 2015), 2.

32. Hillary Potter, *Intersectionality and Criminology*, 70.

33. Bonnie Thornton Dill and Marla H. Kohlman, "Intersectionality: A Transformative Paradigm in Feminist Theory and Social Justice" in *Handbook of Feminist Research: Theory and Praxis*, ed. Sharlene Nagy Hesse-Biber (Thousand Oaks, CA: Sage Publications, 2012), 14.

34. Dill and Kohlman, "Intersectionality," 29.

35. Ibid, 29–30.

36. Jasbir Puar, *Terrorist Assemblages: Homonationalism in Queer Times* (Durham, NC: Duke
University Press, 2007), location 4417, Kindle.

37. Patrick Grzanka, "Media as Sites/Sights of Justice," in *Intersectionality: A Foundations and Frontiers Reader*, ed. Patrick Grzanka (Boulder, CO: Westview Press, 2014), 132.

38. Alison Hearn, "Producing 'Reality': Branded Content, Branded Selves, Precarious Futures" in *A Companion to Reality Television*, ed. L. Ouellette (Malden, MA and Oxford: John Wiley & Sons, Inc., 2014), 437–455.

39. Grzanka, "Media as Sites/Sights of Justice," 134.

40. Nicholas Mirzoeff, *An Introduction to Visual Culture* (New York: Routledge, 2009), 89–93.

41. Neil Gotanda, "A Critique of 'Our Constitution Is Color-Blind,'" in *Critical Race Theory: The Key Writings That Formed the Movement* Crenshaw, eds. N. Gotanda, G. Peller, & T. Kendall (New York: The New Press, 1995), 265.

42. Cheryl Harris, "Whiteness as Property," in *Critical Race Theory: The Key Writings That Formed the Movement* Crenshaw, eds. N. Gotanda, G. Peller, & T. Kendall (New York: The New Press, 1995), 277.

43. Cheryl Harris, "Whiteness as Property," 281.

44. Ibid., 286.

45. Frederick Jackson Turner, *The Significance of the Frontier in American History* (London and New York: Penguin Books, 2008), 2.

46. Turner, *The Significance of the Frontier in American History*, 44.

47. Ibid., 4–5.

48. George Lipsitz, *How Racism Takes Place* (Philadelphia: Temple University Press, 2011), 6.

49. Lipsitz, *How Racism Takes Place*, 13.

50. Ibid., 29.

51. Ibid., 30.

Introduction 31

52. Stuart Hall, "Encoding and Decoding in the Television Discourse" in *Channeling Blackness: Studies on Television and Race in America*, ed. D.M. Hunt, (New York and Oxford: Oxford University Press, 2005), 50.

53. Stuart Hall, "Encoding and Decoding in the Television Discourse," 50.

54. Raewyn Connell and J. W Messerschmidt, "Hegemonic Masculinity: Rethinking the Concept," *Gender and Society* 19, no. 6 (2005): 847.

55. Michael Mangan, *Staging Masculinities: History, Gender, Performance,* (*New* York:

Palgrave Macmillan, 2003), 13.

56. Judith Butler, *Gender Trouble: Feminism and the Subversion of Identity* (New York: Routledge, 2006), 191, Kindle.

57. Daniel Luzer, "Duck Decoy," *Washington Monthly*, January 9, 2014, https://washingtonmonthly.com/2014/01/09/duck-decoy/.

58. Beverly Skeggs and Helen Wood, "Introduction: Real Class" in *Reality Television and Class*, eds. Beverly Skeggs and Helen Wood (London: Palgrave Macmillan, 2011), 17.

59. Shannon E.M. O'Sullivan, "Playing 'Redneck,'" 367–84.

60. Hugh Campbell, Michael Mayerfield Bell, and Margaret Finney, *Country Boys: Masculinity and Rural Life* (University Park, Pennsylvania: The Pennsylvania State University Press 2006), 269.

61. Gail Bederman, *Manliness & Civilization: A Cultural History of Gender and Race in the*

United States, 1880–1917 (Chicago and London: The University of Chicago Press, 1995), 174–75.

62. Vicki Mayer, "Reality Television's 'Classrooms': Knowing, Showing and Telling about Social Class in Reality Casting and the College Classroom" in *Reality Television and Class*, eds. Beverly Skeggs and Helen Wood (London: Palgrave Macmillan, 2011), 189.

63. David Swartz, *Culture & Power: The Sociology of Pierre Bourdieu* (Chicago: The University

of Chicago Press, 1997), 74.

64. Brian Dakss, "Is 18–49 Passé as Top Demographic,?" *CBS News*, November 4, 2005,

http://www.cbsnews.com/news/is-18-49-passe-as-top-demographic/.

65. Andy Dehnart, "The Top 201 Reality TV shows and Their Viewers' Ages," *Reality Blurred*, October 5, 2015, https://www.realityblurred.com/realitytv/2015/10/reality-tv-show-viewer-ages/.

66. Mitch Metcalf, "Updated: Showbuzzdaily's Top 150 Wednesday Cable Originals &

Network Finals," *Show Buzz Daily*, July 6, 2016, http://www.showbuzzdaily.com/articles/showbuzzdailys-top-150-wednesday-cable-originals-network-finals-7-6-2016.html

67. Lynette Rice, 'Deadliest Catch' Captures Biggest Audience Ever," *Entertainment Weekly*, June 23, 2010, http://ew.com/article/2010/06/23/deadliest-catch-captures-biggest-audience-ever/.

68. Deadline Team, "Deadline Team 'Gold Rush' 5th Season Debut Hits Ratings Motherlode for Discovery," *Deadline*, October 20, 2014, https://deadline.com/2014/10/gold-rush-ratings-record-5th-season-debut-discovery-channel-856046/.

69. T.L. Stanley, "'Pawn Stars' Helps History Finish in Top Five among Cable Networks," *Los Angeles Times*, December 21, 2011, http://latimesblogs.latimes.com/showtracker/2011/12/history-pawn-stars-top-five-cable-networks.html.

70. Scarborough, "Fishing for Discovery Channel Audience Demographics?," *Nielsen Local*, October 10, 2012, http://dialog.scarborough.com/index.php/fishing-for-discovery-channel-audience-demographics/.

71. Scarborough, "Fishing for Discovery Channel Audience Demographics?," http://dialog.scarborough.com/index.php/fishing-for-discovery-channel-audience-demographics/.

72. Michael Kimmel, *Angry White Men*, 204.

73. Alec Tyson and Shiva Maniam, "Behind Trump's Victory: Divisions by Race, Gender, Education," *Pew Research Center*, November 9, 2016, http://www.pewresearch.org/fact-tank/2016/11/09/behind-trumps-victory-divisions-by-race-gender-education/; Nate Silver, "The Mythology of Trump's 'Working Class' Support," *FiveThirtyEight*, May 3, 2016, https://fivethirtyeight.com/features/the-mythology-of-trumps-working-class-support/.

74. Josh Katz, 'Duck Dynasty' vs. 'Modern Family': 50 Maps of the U.S. Cultural Divide," *New York Times*, December 27, 2016, https://www.nytimes.com/interactive/2016/12/26/upshot/duck-dynasty-vs-modern-family-television-maps.html?_r=1.

75. Katz, 'Duck Dynasty' vs. 'Modern Family,' https://www.nytimes.com/interactive/2016/12/26/upshot/duck-dynasty-vs-modern-family-television-maps.html?_r=1.

76. Housing Assistance Council, "Race and Ethnicity in Rural America," *Rural Research Brief*, April 2012, http://www.ruralhome.org/storage/research_notes/rrn-race-and-ethnicity-web.pdf.

77. Katz, 'Duck Dynasty' vs. 'Modern Family,' https://www.nytimes.com/interactive/2016/12/26/upshot/duck-dynasty-vs-modern-family-television-maps.html?_r=1.

78. Ibid.

79. Dana Jennings, "Grab a Brew While They Face Death," *New York Times*, March 24, 2011, http://www.nytimes.com/2011/03/27/arts/television/coal-on-spike-aims-to-attract-male-viewers.html?_r=2.

80. Tanja Aho, "Reality TV and Its Audiences Reconsidered: Class and Poverty in *Undercover Boss* (CBS)," 91.

81. Michael Kimmel, *Angry White Men*, 218.

82. Jeffry Bartash, "Donald Trump Is Heir to Ronald Reagan in This Way," *MarketWatch*, August 4, 2016, http://www.marketwatch.com/story/shhh-dont-tell-donald-trump-is-not-the-first-republican-to-champion-white-working-class-2016-08-03; Derek Thompson, "Who Are Donald Trump's Supporters, Really?," *The Atlantic*, March 1, 2016, https://www.theatlantic.com/politics/archive/2016/03/who-are-donald-trumps-supporters-really/471714/.

Chapter 1

Hegemonic Masculinity at Work on Reality TV

Suggesting that the blue-collar frontier series narrowly valorize white masculinity at the ideological expense of workers may seem like an incongruous or unfounded claim at first glance. After all, viewers witness workers heroically perform some of the most statistically hazardous occupations in North America. Through watching these programs, one invariably learns about the toils of crab fishing on *Deadliest Catch*; the logistics of logging across various terrains on *Ax Men*; the perils of goldmining on *Gold Rush*; and the risks of hauling massive cargo via semi-trailers across the seasonal ice roads on *Ice Road Truckers*. However, as Christopher Lockett confirms in his critical analysis of this subgenre of reality television, "Ultimately, whether the object is oil or crabs, the drama played out is that of testing one's masculinity against nature . . . "[1] Television critic Robert Lloyd concurs that despite these shows spotlighting working-class subjects, social class itself remains immaterial to the plot: "Blue collars and rednecks aside, these series are not really about class. A little financial struggle is good for the narrative . . . but by and large these are not people operating on the margins."[2] This begets the question: If the blue-collar frontier universe is not intended to be about class and workers, then what are is it about?

In this chapter, I attend to how these programs sublimate the class-stratified reality of capitalism, even though they document workers almost exclusively on manual labor sites in hazardous, outdoor terrains. Despite their focus, not only do these series discourage class consciousness, they also congruently bolster *stereotypical*ly *presenting* white, rural, working-class men as totemic of hegemonic masculinity, rugged individualism, and American authenticity in the contemporary neoliberal context. The emergence of these series coincides not only with the Great Recession, but also in relation to the modest inroads made by women, people of color, and members of LGBTQ communities in recent years toward greater social equity. Thus, I contend that these series appeared in conjunction with what masculinity studies scholar, Michael Kimmel, refers to as "the contemporary 'crisis' of masculinity."[3]

As Kimmel explains, this "crisis" of masculinity is specifically afflicting white, (mostly) rural, males from the working and middle classes. Kimmel pinpoints that this crisis is driven by the increased economic precarity endemic to neoliberal socioeconomic policies—including weakening unions, deregulating trade policies, privatizing public resources, and dismantling remaining social safety nets—coupled with the dominant tendency to link masculinity with economic independence. He calls this ideal conceptualization of masculinity in the United States the "Self-Made Man."[4] To be clear, men of all races, ethnicities, classes, and sexual orientations are measured in relation to the "Self-Made Man" and hegemonic masculinity writ large. I situate Kimmel's mythical "Self-Made Man" as constituting one critical aspect of hegemonic masculinity in the current U.S. context. In sketching out the parameters of hegemonic masculinity, I emphasize the systems of power that underpin it in mutually constitutive ways, including white supremacy, heteropatriarchy, settler-colonialism, and capitalism. A central aim of this chapter is to make these systems of power visible, as they operate in seemingly imperceptible ways, not only in these television programs, but in U.S. sociopolitical institutions and in the dominant culture more broadly.

As Kimmel notes, rather than questioning the socioeconomic order and challenging the constraints of hegemonic masculinity, a sizeable portion of white, rural, working-class men have doubled down on their sense of identity as "real men." In *Angry White Men: Masculinity at the End of an Era*, he describes the increasingly angry, rural, white, male backlash that has been simmering since the 2008 economic collapse: "They don't make common cause with others who have been so marginalized by the class war . . . they are seduced into blaming other people who are in the same situation they are in—other groups who are equally hurting because of the rapacious greed of the bankers and their pals in politics."[5] Consciously or unconsciously, and with profoundly deleterious effect, this segment of men expresses feeling more *deserving* of economic security under the presumption that they are the rightful heirs to the American Dream *as white men*—although this is typically articulated via coded language signaling their perceived status as "real Americans." This sense of worthiness is premised upon the framing of women and people of color as *undeserving* of economic security, as though access to healthcare, housing, and quality nutrition were a zero-sum game. Certainly, white, rural, working-class men have a right to be distressed regarding a decreased and precarious standard of living, which might include losing access to healthcare and retirement. However, it is where that anger is commonly misdirected and channeled, as well as amplified by political elites, that is highly pernicious, erroneous, and counterproductive (to say the least).

Additionally, the mainstream political reporting about this demographic often frames their disaffection as simply amounting to a matter of personal animus toward marginalized groups, as opposed to elucidating the wider power dynamics and structural problems underpinning in it. This is commensurate with neoliberal framings of racism as largely enactments of interpersonal prejudices, as opposed to racist systems, such the prison-industrial complex, producing racist outcomes regardless of the intent or attitudes of the principal actors within them. As Angela Y. Davis powerfully encapsulates in *The Meaning of Freedom and Other Difficult Dialogues*, " . . . if we see these individual eruptions of racism as connected to the persistence and further entrenchment of institutional and structural racism that hides behind the curtain of neoliberalism, their meanings cannot be understood as individual aberrations."[6] Davis's intervention here is highly useful for understanding how mainstream media largely missed the mark in their analyses of Trump's popularity—political pundits and commentators highlighted his overtly racist utterances and Tweets with scant attention to the racist systems and policies that well preceded him. The focus on Trump as a racist individual obscured the country's racist foundations and lasting legacies. If one were to uncritically accept mainstream media narratives about Trump from 2016 through 2020, it might seem that removing Trump from power would suffice as a panacea to the nation's white supremacy. Thus, when analyzing the political expression of white working-class men as a group, it is vital to avoid reproducing neoliberal framings of racism and sexism, wherein the racial and gender diversity of the working class itself remains erased.

Naomi Klein astutely captures how one can analytically situate white, working-class men as both causalities of capitalism, like working class people of all colors, nationalities, and genders, as well as toxic purveyors of racism and sexism in her analysis of white male working-class support for Trump in *No Is Not Enough: Resisting Trump's Shock Politics and Winning the World We Need*. Regarding the white male working class's experience of economic shocks and perceived losses in relation to women and people of color, she pinpoints that "that's part of progress toward equality, the result of hard-fought battles, but it does mean that white men are losing economic security (which everyone has a right to) *and* their sense of a superior status (which they never had a right to) at the same time."[7] This analysis of white male working-class representation challenges the concurrent lionization and normalization of this demographic vis a vis the blue-collar frontier series, while acknowledging the messiness of the U.S. working class as a precarious assemblage containing pronounced power differentials along axes of race, gender, sexual orientation, religion, and other social categories produced by interlocking systems of power.

I maintain that History and Discovery populating their programming with stereotypically presenting white, working-class men is far from incidental or inconsequential. Despite the ostensibly benevolent intentions of showrunners, these shows exemplify how commercial television taps into the legacy of "imperialist white supremacist capitalist heteropatriarchy"[8] at a time characterized by considerable challenges to the hegemony of these interlaced systems of oppression. In essence, these series reinforce white, rural, working-class masculinity as hegemonic masculinity in the contemporary context in direct response to perceived threats to the dominance of that group. One could view it as a highly romanticized call to restore social order in a time of marked social disorganization. As Kimmel notes, U.S. working and middle-class white men are behaving " . . . as if the solution to their problem were simply 'more' masculinity."[9] It is as though both the History and Discovery networks have responded in kind through injecting "more masculinity" into their scheduling. Of course, it is a specific and stereotypical mode of masculinity—white, rural, working-class. They have carved out a space for viewers to watch "real men" at a time when there is a perception that "real men" are losing their grip on the American Dream of economic independence and upward mobility. In the U.S. context, the designation of "real men" can also be directly equated with dominant conceptions of "real Americans" or ideal citizens. As Lockett observes, these series are cast " . . . as somehow the norm: 'real America.'"[10]

In "Reality Television and the Doing of Hyperauthentic Masculinities," Susan M. Alexander and Katie Woods detail the sharp increase in job-related reality television showcasing white male labor spheres as heroic and utopian: " . . . job-focused and survivalist programs with an all-male or mostly male cast have greatly increased in frequency since 2000, a 141% and 118% increase, respectively."[11] Alexander and Woods also critically pinpoint the Great Recession as a significant factor driving the proliferation of these programs: "Men's anxiety about surviving the recession may have created the interest for these types of reality television programs."[12] Despite African American families being hit hardest by the Great Recession,[13] the commercial logic of cable television centered the anxieties and fantasies of the majority white male viewership of History and Discovery. While these shows began to multiply at the beginning of the recession, Barack Obama's election as the first Black president also gave rise to a post-racial discourse pointing to his presidency as definitive proof that white supremacy could forever be relegated to the past tense. Michelle Alexander describes the zeitgeist of the early years of Obama's presidency in the 10th anniversary edition of *The New Jim Crow: Mass Incarceration in the Age of Colorblindness*: "It was a time when our country was awash in post-racialism . . . few people wanted to hear that, despite appearances, since the end of slavery our nation has remained trapped in a cycle of reform, backlash, and reformation of systems of racialized control."[14] Alexander then charts the pronounced discursive shift from postracialism to racialism within the 2010s. She explicates that with the ascendance of Donald Trump via white nationalist rhetoric that " . . . we are now living in . . . a time when many white Americans feel free to speak openly of their nostalgia for an age when their cultural, political, and economic dominance could be taken for granted—no apologies required."[15] Situating these series in relation to the shifting racial politics of the decades in which they emerged reveals how the near universal whiteness (and maleness) of the casts somehow remained both unremarkable and integral to their commercial appeal. In short, when whiteness is not typically coded as a racial identity, as well as maleness with respect to gender, the glamorization of conventionally white male laborers reads simply as television capturing "real America."

Taking this a step further, I argue that the veneration of white masculinity on the blue-collar frontier shows gestured subtly toward a deeper and more pernicious white male aggrievement that enabled Donald Trump's election via an overtly racist, sexist, and xenophobic platform that largely shocked the mainstream political establishment. As Alexander and Woods elucidate, "Before the Trump campaign, however, several reality television programs aimed at men had already offered a vision of hegemonic masculinity set in a White male utopia . . . reality television programs may have set the stage for fervent support shown by some White men for the Trump presidency."[16] As I discuss at length in the fourth chapter, Trump directly appealed to white, rural, working-class voters through his co-option of a stereotypical white, working-class, masculine rhetorical performance. Because these programs found substantial success via a formula that valorizes white, rural, working-class masculinity, they suggest a wider sociopolitical phenomenon in response to the Great Recession and anti-racist, feminist, and pro-LGBTQ social movements. As I note in the introduction, the popularity of the blue-collar frontier shows and the political rise of Donald Trump, who is a former reality television star himself, suggest the legitimacy, and I would argue, the urgency, of approaching reality television as a robust site for scholarly inquiry.

Like Trump, the blue-collar frontier world offers a faux populism, in which white masculine prowess is glorified through the performance of hazardous occupations at the expense of both class consciousness and all those who demographically fall outside the parameters of "real manhood." It is important to emphasize that I am not suggesting that show creators, such as Thom Beers, whose purported intentions for producing these series are discussed in the introduction, consciously or intentionally reproduce imperialist white supremacist capitalist heteropatriarchy. These systems of oppression are naturalized to the extent that they remain largely inconspicuous in the dominant discourse and popular media. Regardless, the point is not to stress the intentionality of show creators, but to challenge dominant narratives circulating in U.S. culture that, on the surface, appear benign. In keeping with the tradition of Cultural Studies, I assert that these shows have consequences outside of attracting advertising dollars and entertaining their audiences—they constitute a site of deeper ideological struggle. How did show producers know that this formula of watching "real men" working in wilderness settings would appeal to U.S. cable audiences? I address the place of frontier mythology and its connection to hegemonic masculinity in U.S. culture at length in the third chapter, but here I will specifically examine the symbolic power of glamorizing tests of *white* manhood within the logic of reality television.

First, I will discuss how these series frame social class overall, and then delve into the fraught class hierarchies that exist within the show's ensemble casts. Second, I sketch out the parameters of hegemonic masculinity, not only in terms of its intersecting demographic characteristics that mirror structures of domination, but also in relation to the occupations and ritualized tests of manhood featured therein. The jobs themselves are rendered as masculine competitions, in which the crews on each show are often pitted against each other in a fictional race for who can catch the most fish; haul the most logs; mine the most gold; or drive the most loads across the ice. The "prize" is symbolic: the right to claim masculine authenticity and dominance.

A considerable amount of gender policing also occurs in the series, which will be dissected at length. Men who do not perform appropriately are often mocked and feminized. Kimmel succinctly encapsulates the deeper meaning behind this tendency within homosocial male spaces: " . . . American men define their masculinity, not as much in relation to women, but in relation to each other. Masculinity is largely a homosocial enactment."[17] This explains the gender homogeneity of the blue-collar frontier world, as well as the resistance and discomfort that arises when women enter these traditionally hyper-masculine arenas. I detail the reactions of male cast members to the introduction of female cast members in the second chapter.

I also address the considerable erasure of people of color across all four series under investigation. When people of color do occasionally appear, they are rarely identified by name, and the audience does not typically hear them utter more than a sentence or two. The relegation of people of color to the periphery speaks to how white supremacy operates within the visuality of hegemonic masculinity. As I note in the introduction, the absence of people of color and the nearly universal whiteness of the principal cast members are rarely noted in entertainment media coverage, as well as in some academic critiques. This speaks to the systemic normalization of whiteness, which typically is not identified as a unique racial identity in the dominant discourse. However, it is worth noting that U.S. media channels have been increasingly remarking upon whiteness in recent years, which is largely attributable to growing antiracist activism. Discussions about white privilege in the media became much more prevalent after Minneapolis police officer Derek Chauvin murdered George Floyd—igniting nationwide protests in the summer of 2020. Despite these inroads, whiteness remains ensconced as the normative racial standard to which all other racial groups are compared. Thus, the all-white casts of these series do not standout as unusual.

ARE "REAL MEN" PART OF AN ECONOMIC CLASS?

Before delving into the boundaries and political consequences of hegemonic forms of masculinity, it is vital to discuss what these series reveal about dominant conceptualizations of class and capitalism in the United States. The maxim that commercial television obfuscates class consciousness and circulates the myth that the United States is a classless meritocracy partially accounts for the relegation of the structural origins of economic realities to the periphery of these programs. As Michael Zweig summarizes in *The Working Class Majority: America's Best Kept Secret*, "The major television networks are owned by Fortune 500 conglomerates whose executives have an interest in downplaying workers' sense of themselves as workers."[18] Therefore, even when the socioeconomic locations of the subjects of the blue-collar frontier shows seem pertinent to the narrative, these instances are typically reduced to individual problems and character flaws. Helen Wood and Beverly Skeggs' *Reality Television and Class* contextualizes the relationship between unscripted television and hegemonic framings of social class. Although this anthology does not include the blue-collar frontier shows examined in this project, it emphasizes the role reality television plays in reifying the naturalization of class inequities in both U.S. and U.K. contexts: " . . . we think it is important to discuss television's intervention in class formations, particularly at a time when political rhetoric is diverting the blame for structural inequality onto personal, individualised failure.[19]" The political rhetoric Wood and Skeggs refer to here relates to the 2008 recession, in which the dominant discourse about equal opportunity and hard work did not abate, despite the clear structural collapse of the global economy.

The post-2008 economic downturn represents a critical moment of rupture in relation to the public acceptance and sustainability of neoliberal socioeconomic policies and paradigms, such as the push for deregulating financial institutions and liberalizing trade agreements. Rather than highlight the shared vulnerability of workers, these series instead ideologically reinscribe the veneration of rugged individualism and meritocracy in U.S. culture in support of the neoliberal status quo, in which the ideal rugged individual is assumed both white and male. The focus on cisheteronormative, working-class, white men in these shows then is not incidental but intentional and essential. White males are framed as the *rightful* heirs to the American Dream, in which they struggle *as* rugged individuals, not as members of a specific class or social location, toward upward economic mobility. Not only did the Great Recession exemplify a crisis for neoliberalism, but it also gestured toward a *perceived* masculinity crisis for white, rural, working and lower middle-class men in the United States. It is the latter "crisis" that the blue-collar frontier shows speak to, as they champion white, rural, working-class masculinity as emblematic of American ideals. In his 2019 book, *No Longer Newsworthy: How the Mainstream Media Abandoned the Working Class*, Christopher R. Martin unpacks the mainstream media's motivation in disrupting worker identification and class consciousness across races and genders: " . . . the news media typically consider the 'working class' not in its entirety, but just in the stereotypical white male form, which nicely serves the purposes of divisive politicians who seek to exploit this image and divide working-class people on every other dimension: race, gender, sexual orientation, disability, and citizenship."[20] Thus, these reality television series mirror the same distortion of the working class found in the news media. Martin properly historicizes this tendency, which is far from a new phenomenon: "Americans have seen the white, male worker deployed as the symbolic representation of the US working class with almost regular repetition in modern politics and news media reports of the past fifty years . . . "[21] This misleading image of the working class also coincides with an enduring perception of what it means to be a "real man" in America, in which economic independence remains a paramount characteristic of hegemonic masculinity.

Kimmel refers to his conceptualization of American hegemonic masculinity as the "Self-Made Man."[22] He traces a critical genealogy of the Self-Made Man throughout U.S history and observes its deep and increasingly volatile connection to class status beginning in the early nineteenth century: "American men began to link their sense of themselves *as men* [emphasis added] to their position in the volatile marketplace, to their economic success—a far less stable yet far more exciting and potentially rewarding peg upon which to hang one's identity."[23] Success in the capitalist system then became a test of manhood unto itself—a legacy that persists today. If a man loses his job, then his masculine identity comes under duress. In contrast, if a woman loses her job, this does not lead to a gendered crisis of womanhood per se. It is vital to note that there are also economic and workplace dimensions to conventional ideals of womanhood. This is especially evident with women from the professional-managerial class who wrestle with social pressures and expectations to "have it all" in terms of both maintaining a high-powered career and properly performing household labor.[24] However, compared to men, metrics of ideal femininity remain strongly linked to the domestic sphere and care work, especially as it relates to fertility and childrearing.[25] In *White Working Class: Overcoming Class Cluelessness in America*, Joan C. Williams details the differing perceptions between white working-class women and professional-managerial elite women when it comes to staying at home to care for children and managing the household. Williams explains that "for working-class white women, becoming a homemaker signals a rise in status, not only for herself but for her entire family. But for PME [professional-managerial elite] women, becoming a stay-at-home mother entails a fall in status, from investment banker to 'just a homemaker.'"[26] Again, this preference and value system remains highly informed by a working mother's social class—is she performing a service job conferring lower status or "leaning in" (to borrow from Sheryl Sandberg) as a mid-level executive? Circling back, although it is vital to account for the complexity and nuances of the relationship between ideal femininity and work, it is undeniable that mastery over one's work serves as a fulcrum for masculine authenticity.

The Self-Made Man conceptualization is inextricably linked to white supremacy, as Kimmel traces its origins to when African American men were still enslaved in the United States. Black masculinity remains wrongfully associated with criminality and economic dependence upon the state in the dominant U.S. public consciousness.[27] As Kimmel further elucidates, " . . . since the nineteenth century, racism has often been cast in gender terms . . . 'They' are not 'real men' either because they are 'too masculine' (savage, rapacious animals) or 'not masculine enough' (irresponsible, absent fathers, dependent on the government)."[28] The complexity and nuance of how all men of color, not only Black men, are measured in relation to white, hegemonic masculinity, cannot be adequately addressed within the scope of this project. The most important takeaway is that the whiteness of the Self-Made Man operates invisibly and functions to oppress all men of color who are barred at the outset from approximating this ideal.

The Self-Made Man is a mythological construct with profound material consequences—deeply interconnected with frontier mythology and rugged individualism, which I explicate in the next chapter. The Self-Made Man's whiteness and maleness confer relative structural advantages, including economic ones, that often go unrecognized by white men themselves. The narrative of the Self-Made Man functions to not only bolster white male supremacy, but to justify the hierarchical class system that capitalism engenders. It suggests that economic success is always possible through the exercise of self-discipline, hard work, self-reliance, and other traits that have been widely coded as masculine in the dominant discourse and public sphere. However, because most white men do not achieve self-made status by the design of the capitalist system, it then generates significant feelings of anxiety and anger when these social expectations do not materialize. Kimmel posits

42   *Chapter 1*

that "the Self-Made Man of American mythology was born anxious and inse-
cure, uncoupled from the more stable anchors of landownership or workplace
autonomy. *Now manhood had to be proved* [emphasis added]."[29] Williams
echoes this postulation in *White Working Class*: " . . . men in general, and
working-class men in particular, tend to ramp up displays of manliness when
their masculinity is threatened."[30]

The blue-collar frontier series document white, rural, working-class men
repeatedly proving their manhood through their occupations. In this context,
work is exclusively a proving ground for masculinity and becomes dislodged
from the structural realities of working-class experience and global capitalism more broadly. Case in point, if men are unable to support themselves
and their families economically, then it is perceived as a failure to live up to
gendered expectations within the logic of heteropatriarchy. As I mention later
in relation to the boundaries of hegemonic masculinity, manual labor jobs,
especially those that pose the threat of bodily injury, are viewed as more
masculine than white-collar or service sector employment. Physical labor,
violence, and "taming the wilderness" typify what it means to be a "real man"
in the U.S. context.

This speaks to why middle and upper-class white men, such as the
Robertsons of *Duck Dynasty*, try to approximate this masculine ideal through
means other than their employment, such as hunting and fishing for recreational purposes. Kimmel refers to author Tom Wolfe's observation about
middle- and upper-class men's insecurities regarding their masculinity:
"Preppies were feminized, Wolfe argues, by a class culture that shielded
them from the harsher realities of masculine life."[31] Manhood has become
so deeply entwined with class status that the former subsumes the latter as
the primary axis of identification—particularly with white males. Thus, the
blue-collar frontier stars are not coded as workers, but as "real men."

Of critical importance to this analysis is that the white males of the
blue-collar frontier are not only framed as untethered to a specific economic
class, but as raceless and genderless. As Donna Haraway asserts in her seminal essay, "The Persistence of Vision," whiteness and maleness remain invisible as race and gender categories respectively: " . . . the gaze that mythically
inscribes all the marked bodies, that makes the unmarked category claim the
power to see and not be seen, to represent while escaping representation. This
gaze signifies the unmarked positions of Man and White . . . "[32] Although
these shows are clearly about displays of (white) masculine prowess, gender
tends to be referenced in the public domain only in relation to women and
gender nonconforming groups. In the same vein, race is often conceptualized
as only having relevance to people of color.

The dominant tendency to identify white males as neutral individuals also
speaks to how class identifications become subsumed by other coexisting

markers. In *Class-Passing: Social Mobility in Film and Popular Culture*, Gwendolyn Audrey Foster observes that " . . . men and manhood are ineluctably connected to class performativity . . . For men, adulthood is inherently associated with a Darwinian business model of class rise. Think of the markers of masculine rites of passage into manhood and note how they are linked to class."[33] Thus, the conventionally masculine expectations of breadwinning are not presented as a barrier for lower and working-class men—they are simply cast as an achievable norm for all men. I emphasize that this acutely demonstrates the explanatory power of intersectionality for making legible how race, gender, and class interact in manners that relatively advantage and disadvantage varying social locations.

Whereas whiteness and maleness remain largely normalized and unremarkable in the dominant discourse and visual domain, social class tends to be framed in the public sphere, including on reality television, in a more ambiguous manner. Laura Grindstaff poignantly summarizes reality television's rendering of social class more broadly: "The performance logic of reality television—in which class-coded performances are dissociated from the socio-economic bases of class inequality in the service of 'class-less' self-expression—is commensurate with and predicted by certain features of late modernity . . . "[34] Working-class people are typically identified and largely configured in reality television—and I argue in mass media more broadly—in relation to their personal appearances and lifestyles. Neoliberal multiculturalism removes social categories from their structural origins and instead pushes for conceptualizations of identity that are delinked from power relations.

In other words, commensurate with neoliberal, multicultural frameworks, working-class people become intelligible within the logic of reality television not in terms of their structural location within capitalism, but via their stylized performances. In keeping with the hegemonic notion that upward economic mobility remains achievable for all contingent upon hard work and prudent choices, the working-class individuals of reality television are typically depicted as solely responsible for their socioeconomic status. It is vital to recognize that the western, liberal value of the primacy of the individual muddles understandings of how systems of oppression, including capitalism, structure individual experiences in common.

Furthermore, particularly in mainstream U.S. discourse, there remains a limited and distorted acknowledgment and discussion of economic class as a social category entirely. Wood and Skeggs note that "the term 'ordinary' is one of the many euphemisms used to stand in for 'working class,' because in many different nations it is no longer fashionable to speak about class identifications."[35] Although U.S. news media discussions of the white working class increased remarkably after Trump's election, conversations about the working class in all its diversity and complexity remain elided—so much so that when media outlets refer to *the* working class, they often mean the *white* working class. Additionally, most news stories narrowly focused on the attitudes and values of white, working-class Trump voters. Martin pinpoints in *No Longer Newsworthy* that not only does the news media misrepresent the U.S. working class demographically, but they also . . . "usually look at the working class only through the lens of a political news story, not through the lens of a labor or workplace news story."[36] Meanwhile, eligible nonvoters of all classes received comparatively scant attention, despite numbering at 80 million in the 2020 presidential election.[37]

As it relates to class, impoverished Americans in particular have some of the lowest voting rates because of a multitude of factors, including logistical impediments and disillusionment with a system that fails to address their needs.[38] Williams also details in *White Working Class* how class hierarchies and class conflict continue to be muted in U.S. discourse, as many Americans across a wide swath of the socioeconomic spectrum identify as belonging to a large, amorphous middle class: "A central way we make class disappear is to describe virtually everyone as 'middle class.' A recent *Bloomburg* story quoted an amusement park worker earning $22,000 a year and a lawyer with an annual income of $200,000, both calling themselves middle class."[39] The acknowledgment of an entrenched class system, which of course is also structured by intersecting racial and gender hierarchies (as I note in the introduction with my formulation of "the working-class assemblage") could potentially lead to a collective challenge of the status quo. Corporate-owned networks remain both materially and ideologically invested in the suppression of class consciousness and in bolstering capitalism. These longstanding class mischaracterizations and misidentifications are no accident.

In representing white working-class subjects on reality television, U.S. cable networks have largely portrayed them in two asymmetrical manners: They are either ridiculed or derided, as is the case with the so-called "rednexploitation" series addressed in the introduction, such as *Here Comes Honey Boo Boo* and *Buckwild*, or they are venerated for their aspirational masculinity, as I elucidate here. Thus, the systemic injustices engendered by the capitalist system remain omitted, and individual agency and personal effort seem to magically determine socioeconomic status both in the realm of reality television and in the wider public discourse. The performance logic of reality television in relation to social class is then inseparable from its production logic within neoliberalism.[40]

This project proceeds with the awareness that reality television is itself a neoliberal project, in which the conditions of its production cannot be exorcised from a critical engagement with its content. The blue-collar reality shows have flourished, not only because their formulaic narratives resonate within mainstream U.S. culture, but because they are comparatively cheap to produce in relation to more conventionally scripted programming. Consequently, neoliberal logics underpin their material production, as well as their ideological content.

ARE THE BLUE-COLLAR REALITY STARS
REALLY PART OF THE WORKING CLASS?

This leads to the analysis of the fraught class dynamics that exist within the casts themselves. The men given the most prominent storylines are the captains of the boats featured on *Deadliest Catch*; the owners of the logging companies on *Ax Men*; drivers that own and operate their own trucks on *Ice Road Truckers*; and the heads of the mining operations on *Gold Rush*. In the opening credits for most of the seasons under examination, particularly for *Deadliest Catch*, *Ax Men*, and *Gold Rush,* the captains/owners are typically pictured standing front and center of their crews—signaling that they are the stars. Within the neoliberal logic of reality television, it is unsurprising that the captains and members of the ownership-managerial class are more venerated than low-level workers. These men are given primacy within the narratives as masculine leaders who exemplify the entrepreneurial American spirit. The men, and on rare occasions women, who labor for them are usually secondary, supporting figures. Within the visual terrain of these series, the captains and owners share the stereotypical *appearance* of white, rural, working-class men. From the standpoint of their masculine performance, it may seem that these men all share the same class position.

Upon closer examination, the owners and captains have significant material advantages over their employees, as well as a greater sense of security and power. As per Michael Zweig's understanding of class, socioeconomic status is not solely determined by income, or even contingent upon whether a worker is paid a yearly salary or by the hour. Ultimately, class is about the control and authority one has over their own work and in society by extension. Zweig defines the working class in a highly inclusive manner in relation to the nature of their work, but identifies their lack of power and autonomy in their occupations as their binding characteristic:

"They are skilled and unskilled, in manufacturing and in services, men and women of all races, nationalities, regions . . . they have relatively little control over the pace or content of their work, and aren't anybody's boss."[41] Martin concurs with Zweig's parameters and notes that " . . . I will opt for Zweig's definition of working class because the state of having 'comparatively little power or authority' as workers and citizens is a condition that captures the

46   *Chapter 1*

lived experience of a vast majority of people."[42] As I argue in the introduction, because the working-class label is so expansive, it can be framed as analogous to the discursive deployment of the term "women." Both groups remain highly diverse and heterogenous unto themselves, wherein they must be understood as always already intersecting with each other as well as with other social categories. As I assert, the spatial metaphor of assemblage can aid in properly conceptualizing both the working class's commonalities and hierarchical differentiations within its ranks at once.

Moving forward, it is essential to note that the blue-collar frontier series mask the class distinctions within the casts themselves and glamorize the captains and owners as risk-takers and entrepreneurs who graciously bestow employment upon their crews. In contemporary discourse, particularly since the recession, news rhetoric often suggests that workers should feel fortunate to have a job at all.[43] Workers are not treated as essential to a company's success *because* they sell their labor in an asymmetrical power dynamic to employers, and businesses are rarely scrutinized for labor exploitation, including a widely documented "epidemic of wage theft."[44] Since the 2020 pandemic, many workers have resisted such exploitive conditions, which has been met with cries from employers that "no one wants to work anymore."[45] Interestingly, these employers fail to recognize that the "labor market" is now logically demanding more just compensation and benefits.

Executives and business owners have also been praised as "job creators," as Republican presidential candidate Mitt Romney famously called them during his 2012 campaign.[46] Mike Rowe, the narrator of *Deadliest Catch*, reproduces this conceptualization with the captains of the commercial fishing vessels in Season One: Episode 10: "The Final Run": "In a job where every second counts, the strategy and planning of the captain makes the difference between rags and riches for the deckhands."[47] I am not suggesting that the captains' decisions are inconsequential for their crews or that they do not take risks and endure relative economic precarity within late capitalism. I am spotlighting how the captains and owners throughout the four series are given more favorable and developed storylines in relation to their employees who have significantly less power and economic security as proper members of the working class.

Case in point, Peter Liske, captain of the *Lady Alaska*, seems blasé about the economic precarity of his crewmembers in the same episode. Peter bemoans the crew's performance during that crab season: "We should have done better. We're a big boat . . . But I am thankful. The guys made some money, and they're just gonna have to go get a job somewhere else."[48] He makes these comments at the end of a season in which a partner shipping vessel, the *Big Valley*, sank and lost five crewmembers. Deckhands risk their lives to only make a modest living, and like a lot of workers in the neoliberal era, they must work multiple jobs to support themselves and their families. In addition, the captains navigate the ships from where it's warmer, drier, and far safer than on deck, where their subordinates contend with heavy equipment, hazardous weather, and rough waves. The captains are narratively framed as bold risk-takers, but the deckhands withstand the worst hazards of commercial fishing on the Bering Sea.

The captains often call for their crews to work long hours without breaks and little sleep. For example, Sig Hansen, captain of the *Northwestern*, forces his crew, including his brother Edgar, to work more than 24 hours straight in Season Four: Episode Four: "Unsafe and Unsound." Rowe narrates that "although the crew is ready for a break, Sig wants to fish."[49] As his exhausted crew continues to haul in crab on deck, Sig leans back with his feet up, and says to the camera: "I'd rather work until my eyes pop out of my head than sleep . . . Quite honestly, the longer you work, the better I feel."[50] It is far easier for Sig to remain awake and continue working from where it is comparatively warm and comfortable. In Season Five: Episode Three: "Stay Focused or Die," Sig again forces the crew to work more than 24 hours without stopping. Jake Anderson, a deckhand in his 20s, mentions that working long hours on little sleep is common on the *Northwestern*: "You up for 20 hours a day—mandatory, ya know? Right now, we're up for over 24 . . . we've been up for 28."[51] In relation to the grueling schedule, Sig, looking exhausted himself, dismissively comments from the wheelhouse: "Who the hell says 9:00 to 5:00 is normal anyway?"[52] For context, outside of the fishing industry as well, Americans notoriously work longer hours and for comparatively stagnant pay and paltry benefits compared to their counterparts in other countries.[53]

The show makes light of a particularly disturbing incident involving Sig and his crew in Season Five: Episode 15: "Day of Reckoning." In the episode, a dangerous Arctic hurricane is descending upon the fleet. Sig turns back the ship's clock below deck, so his crew loses track of how long they have been working in subzero temperatures. At one point, the crew has been laboring for more than 48 hours nonstop, and Sig appears unconcerned about their health and safety. He pretends to give the crew the "option" of either staying up all night or working during the height of the incoming storm. He says flippantly to the camera: "I'm like the king of manipulation with them."[54] Of course, this functions to build dramatic tension, but over the course of the show's 18 seasons as of 2022, Sig is framed as being more worthy of lionization than loathing. Violating his workers' rights is portrayed as a tough but necessary mechanism for triumphing in the world of commercial crab fishing—the ends of profits justify the means of workplace exploitation.

Sig's abusive management style generates significant tension on the *Northwestern* in Season Six: Episode 10: "The Darkened Seas." Deckhand

Jake Anderson expresses grievances about the workplace culture on the boat: "You always deserve some time to relax when you're done fishing, but apparently not on this boat, it's just one job after the next."[55] The camera cuts to the deckhands doing repairs on deck, as Sig sleeps below. Matt Bradley, another deckhand, complains to the camera: "I'm a little tired. Job takes a toll on you. It's not like you ever get a day off. I haven't had a day off in 20 days already."[56] The camera jumps to Sig dismissing the crew's legitimate protests: "I find it insulting that you've got a gripe when you're sleeping every night. Hell, it ain't that often that they sleep at all."[57] This feeds into the dominant narrative that workers should always be grateful and deferential to their employers, irrespective of the conditions. The show highlights deckhand grievances, since they convincingly aid in building dramatic tension, but ultimately, Sig is depicted as more of a firm disciplinarian and hero than a villain for pushing his crew to their limits.

Within the performance logic of hegemonic masculinity, these hazardous occupations are framed as tests of manhood. Therefore, if a man complains about his job, then he risks emasculation: If you cannot endure the pain and suffering, then you are not a "real man." This specter of emasculation enables abuse like Sig's to continue unabated. Sig's dismissal of his employees' objections culminates with him defiantly stating to the camera: "Eat me, ya know? That's not my problem."[58] Sig is one of the most prominently featured captains throughout the show's eighteen seasons—one of its true "stars." It is surprising then that more analyses have not spotlighted the class hierarchies present within the cast of *Deadliest Catch*, especially considering Sig's treatment of his employees.

On the cover of the DVD for the fourth season of *Deadliest Catch*, Sig and all the other captains are triumphantly perched atop piles of crab.[59] The fact that only the captains of the vessels make the cover, and not any of the low-level deckhands, establishes who the intended stars are of the series. Additionally, the captains on the cover typify a lot of the burly presentation and manner of dress associated with white, rural working-class masculinity, including wearing jeans, ball caps, and keeping facial hair. This image is highly representative of the visual order of hegemonic masculinity depicted across the blue-collar frontier shows, in which the owners, captains, and managers remain at the top of the masculine hierarchy.

Hugh Rowland is one of the stars of *Ice Road Truckers*, and in addition to driving his own truck, also owns several of the trucks driven by fellow cast members. As is the case for all the series included here, the more economic capital a cast member possesses, the more likely they are to be given primary and mostly flattering storylines. Hugh, like Sig, has a domineering personality and is harsh with his drivers. In Season One: Episode Nine: "The Big Melt," Rick Yemm, one of Hugh's drivers who is prominently featured throughout the series, suffers from frostbite because the floor heater in his truck is malfunctioning. Because Hugh owns the truck, it is his responsibility to ensure that it is operating appropriately. Hugh dismisses Rick's concerns, and Rick decides to quit working for him accordingly. After the two argue on the phone, Hugh emasculates Rick to the camera for expressing grievances about his working conditions: "He hung up on me, that's how mad at me he is (laughs), it's like a little fucking girl, eh?"[60] After their altercation, Rick vents at a local bar: "I'll starve before I go back and work for him again. This is not how you treat your right-hand man and your best friend . . . this is just unacceptable. I'm freezing up there. I tell him that and he laughs at me like it's a joke."[61]

After learning officially that Rick quit, Hugh mocks and emasculates him further: "He was a carpet cleaner before I got a hold of him. I made a man out of me [*sic*]."[62] Hugh shirks his responsibility of maintaining the quality and safety of his trucks for his drivers by accusing Rick of not being tough enough to endure subzero temperatures without a proper heater. Because Hugh also "wins" that season's fictional race for who can haul the most loads across the ice, the show casts him in a positive light overall since he was "tough enough" to finish out the season on top. The tendency to delegitimize genuine health and safety concerns in the workplace as trivial complaints from men who fail to live up to ideals of masculine toughness is one of the most pernicious currents running through these series. Industry and workplace deregulation remains one of the hallmarks of neoliberalism—framing these hazardous occupations as masculinized competitions of survival of the fittest further justifies the practice.

Health and safety regulations are particularly germane to the workers of the blue-collar frontier world because they perform some of the most statistically dangerous jobs in the United States.[63] Janet Webb, chief forester and president of Big Creek Lumber in central California, explains that the high fatality rate is partially attributable to the remote, rural locations in which these jobs are performed: "Whether it's logging, fishing or agriculture jobs, when you're working in wilderness type settings you're not right there next to [a] facility that can bail you out."[64] On *Ax Men*, the viewer is regularly reminded of the dangers of commercial logging, in which narrator and executive producer, Thom Beers, explains the perils of the job with the occasional assistance of computer animations. These animations graphically simulate loggers being impaled by branches, losing limbs, and enduring other violent injuries.

With the dangers of the occupation firmly established, viewers witness living proof of those hazards with Jay Browning, the owner of J. M. Browning Logging, who lost his hand in an accident with a saw many years prior. Jay, who now uses a prosthetic hand, explains with a sense of pride in Season One: Episode Two: "Risk and Reward" how he refused workers' compensation insurance after the incident: "When I got out of the hospital, they sent me workmen comp checks. I even sent 'em back. I just never felt that I should cash those checks because it was my stupid move that created the whole problem, so kinda had to fight with them. They didn't wanna take the checks back, but they finally did."[65]

His comments suggest that safety is the sole responsibility of the worker, and therefore, workers' compensation programs are unnecessary. This rationalizes the neoliberal practice of eroding any semblance of a social safety net and worker protections. Of course, Jay is not a low-level worker, but the owner of a successful commercial logging company. The fact that Jay has enough economic security to refuse workmen's compensation is precluded from the narrative. His remarks also likely suggest that he does not believe the loggers who work for him should receive workers' compensation in the event of an accident. As one of the principal cast members who receives a highly developed storyline, Jay exemplifies how class-based power differentials remain sublimated throughout the series. He is depicted as a self-made success story, in which his status as the owner and manager of a company coupled with his embodied performance of white, rural, working-class masculinity, signals his masculine authenticity. The show's emphasis on masculinity subsumes the class stratification between he and his employees. Within the visuality of *Ax Men*, all the men featured are "real men," but Jay and the other owners are positioned at the apex of the hierarchical masculine order, concealing the presence of a distinct and inequitable class hierarchy. This is consistent with the U.S. mythos of rugged individualism and the classless society.

Gold Rush is premised upon the Great Recession more than any other series included in the sample. The pilot episode documents Jack and Todd Hoffman, a father and son team, who are forced to sell their family's airfield business because of the economic downturn. The Hoffmans decide to mine for gold in Alaska, not with the hope of maintaining a middle-class standard of living, but with the lofty aspiration of striking it rich. As show narrator, Paul Christie, intones with dramatic emphasis, "With the price of gold at an all-time high, Jack and Todd are about to risk everything they own on the biggest gamble of their lives."[66] Despite their economic woes, the Hoffmans still have a substantial amount of economic capital—hundreds of thousands of dollars to purchase high-powered machinery and supplies—which enables them to even attempt an Alaskan mining expedition in the first place.

With this degree of economic capital, it would be highly inaccurate to claim that the Hoffmans share the same socioeconomic status as the workers mining at their behest. In fact, the miners they are employing are purportedly foregoing wages until they find gold and begin raking in profits. In Season One: Episode One: "No Guys, No Glory," Jack says unflinchingly about his crew: "These guys are paying their own way until we strike gold."[67] The show glamorizes the Hoffmans' economic risk-taking as demonstrative of masculine prowess and not necessarily reflective of socioeconomic advantages.

In summation, the common embodied performance of white, rural, working-class masculinity in the blue-collar frontier shows contributes to the perception of a lack of class distinctions among their casts. This is highly demonstrative of neoliberal conceptions of social class, which frame class identity in relation to individual, stylized performances as opposed to a shared structural location produced by the capitalist system. Because of their economic advantages and power over their subordinates, the owners and captains more closely align with Kimmel's core conceptualization of U.S. hegemonic masculinity, the "Self-Made Man." Of course, these men are far from self-made and heavily rely upon their racial, gender, and economic privileges, as well as the labor of their employees, in enabling their success. Building off Kimmel's formulation of the "Self-Made Man," I will now discuss one of the central claims of this book: The blue-collar frontier shows exemplify hegemonic masculinity in the contemporary United States.

BLUE-COLLAR REALITY TV: A RESPONSE TO U.S. HEGEMONIC MASCULINITY IN CRISIS

Nicholas Mirzoeff delineates visuality as the hegemonic visual order or the dominant mode of seeing that appears naturalized or "normal" within a particular set of social relations.[68] Case in point, it is assumed that the subjects of the blue-collar frontier shows—white, heteronormative men working in rural settings—signify an idealized image of "real men" in the United States. If one were to rhetorically ask what "real men" look like, the blue-collar frontier shows provide the answer in the contemporary U.S. neoliberal context. Whether an individual observer contests this notion does not change the fact that these subjects are widely recognized as "real men" in the dominant visual rhetoric. It is worth reiterating that I am approaching these programs from Hall's conceptualization of the *"dominant-hegemonic position,"* in which I engage with a reading of these series that "decodes the message in terms of the reference code in which it has been encoded."[69]

Before proceeding, it is integral to delineate the conceptual parameters of hegemonic masculinity. Raewynn Connell originally coined the concept of hegemonic masculinity in 1987 in *Gender and Power: Society, the Person, and Sexual Politics*. Connell asserts that patriarchy "requires the construction of a hypermasculine ideal of toughness and dominance.[70]" I argue that the primary objective of *Deadliest Catch*, *Ax Men*, *Ice Road Truckers*, and *Gold Rush* is to construct a visuality of (white) masculine toughness. These occupations function as repeated and ritualized tests of manhood within the narrative logic of these series, which further contributes to the subdual of the casts' structural locations as workers, or as discussed previously, as manager-owners. In short, these white male subjects are not overtly coded based on their economic status but based upon their gender expression as "real men." Robert Hanke's formulation of hegemonic masculinity is also highly instructive for this analysis: "Hegemonic masculinity thus refers to the social ascendancy of a particular version or model of masculinity that operates on the terrain of common sense and conventional morality that defines 'what it means to be a man,' thus securing the dominance of some men (and the subordination of women) within the sex/gender system."[71]

As Christopher Lockett notes in his aptly titled piece, "Masculinity and Authenticity: Reality TV's Real Men," hegemonic masculinity is often identified as "real" or "authentic" masculinity. In his discussion of this subgenre of reality shows, which includes *Deadliest Catch* and *Ice Road Truckers*, he observes "that this idealization of working-class masculinity takes place by way of reality television speaks to its preoccupation with an *authentic masculinity* [emphasis added], one best accessed unalloyed and unmediated."[72] For there to be "real men," it then suggests that there are "fake" or "inauthentic" men. Lockett connects that there seems to be no better way to showcase "real men" than on reality television, which despite remaining highly mediated and constructed, projects a compelling gloss of authenticity.

The demographic of men that inhabit the blue-collar frontier milieu—white, rural, (mostly) working-class, cis-heterosexual men—are the group of men that Kimmel documents as most outwardly experiencing a perceived "masculinity crisis" because of their increased economic precarity since the Great Recession. As Kimmel elucidates, this perceived crisis of masculinity has " . . . pressed men to confront their continued reliance on the marketplace as the way to demonstrate and prove their manhood."[73] The blue-collar frontier shows respond to this perceived crisis through valorizing and reinvigorating the notion that masculinity must be proved through workplace performance. I argue that it is the specific occupations featured therein—highly hazardous, manual labor jobs in remote locations—as performed by white males, wearing the clothes and speaking in the gruff manner typically associated with working-class manhood, that collectively signify hegemonic masculinity in the contemporary U.S. neoliberal context.

I concur with Hugh Campbell, Michael Mayerfield Bell, and Margaret Finney's assessment in *Country Boys: Masculinity and Rural Life* that white, rural, working-class masculinity implies authenticity, and therefore, legitimacy, since it signifies the most preferred form of masculinity in the U.S. gender hierarchy. This is evidenced through wealthy, white male politicians, such as Ronald Reagan and George W. Bush, embodying the dress, mannerisms, and speech of working-class white males, to attain the symbolic capital such a gender performance confers. Campbell, Bell, and Finney provide a vivid description of this performance through the lens of former President George W. Bush, which closely characterizes the masculine performances endemic to the series included in the sample:

> But there will be no blush on President George Bush's face as he faces the cameras at the next photo opportunity at his Crawford, Texas ranch. Wearing his boots and Stetson, posing with his horses, leaning on the rail of his cattle yards, clearing brush, and striding out across his land, Bush uses the imagery of rural life to portray not just a persona of authority and control but a *masculine* persona of authority and control . . . Real men don't drink latte. They drink beer, smoke Marlboros, and ride their SUVs through mud and up mountains . . . *Real men are rural men* [emphasis added]: this cultural idea wields not only enormous political power but enormous economic power.[74]

It is noteworthy that Bush's movements and physical labor are included as part of the description of his performance of "real manhood." As John Berger poignantly captures in his groundbreaking text, *Ways of Seeing*, in the dominant visual culture, " . . . *men act* and *women appear*."[75] For men to live up to hegemonic masculine ideals, they must always be active and exercise physical control in a public, outdoor environment.

The narrators of these programs frequently describe these men as "battling" the elements and "wrestling" with heavy machinery. Unlike women, these men's actions are emphasized, not their appearances. This does not suggest that their looks are immaterial to their perceived masculine authenticity, however, their appearances alone rarely if ever elicit narrational commentary. These workers are not only described as powerful and in control but as confronting death at every conceivable turn. Rowe does this frequently in his narration of *Deadliest Catch*. He offers a typical example in Season Six: Episode 10: "The Darkened Seas," when he stresses the dangers faced by the crew of the *Time Bandit*: "With the deck barraged by ice chunks, every step the crew takes could be their last."[76] Rowe regularly reminds the viewer throughout the series that commercial fishing is the most dangerous job in the world. His narration signals that these men exemplify hegemonic masculinity because of their willingness to risk serious injury. In the beginning of Season Three: Episode Seven: "New Beginnings," Rowe provides his near standardized description of crab fishing on Alaska's Bering Sea: "Die-hard crews are back to face down bigger waves . . . more boat crippling ice . . . and deadly steel . . . the vicious Bering Sea will unleash surprises on the 400 brave souls tempting fate for fortune . . . "[77] His narration is intercut with action-packed footage of crews fishing on decks with crashing waves, in which frequent, quick edits create a sense of urgency and suspense.

54 *Chapter 1*

Thom Beers, who produces and narrates both *Ice Road Truckers* and *Ax Men*, frequently invokes a sense of peril and suspense through his narrational approach. Beers provides his usual introductory narration for *Ice Road Truckers* at the beginning of Season One: Episode Four: "The Big Chill": "At the top of the world, there's an outpost like no other. And a job only a few would dare . . . The rewards are great . . . the risks even greater . . . These are the men who make their living on thin ice."[78] Like *Deadliest Catch*, the introductory remarks are interspersed with fast-paced edits, jumping from one driver to the next. Earlier seasons also include an animation of a tractor trailer falling completely through the ice—an event that, although possible, fortunately, does not occur during filming of the show's 11 seasons.

As mentioned previously, the shows are framed as masculine competitions. Nowhere is this theme given more weight than in *Ax Men*. Beers offers one of his most overt invocations of hegemonic masculinity in his narrational preview of Season Two: Episode 10: "Clash of the Titans": "Crews endure subzero temperatures . . . rising water . . . and a brawl on the landing. With just one week left, *it's give up or man up* [emphasis added]."[79] The message is clear: These real men prove their manhood through performing some of the world's most statistically dangerous jobs. Moreover, the specter of bodily injury coincides with the connection between hegemonic masculinity and violence. As Kimmel points out, "Today, the capacity for violence is a marker of authentic masculinity . . . a test of manhood."[80] In that same episode, Beers even employs warlike imagery in describing the show's fictional contest between the Rygaard and J. M. Browning logging companies: "Deep within the mountains of Oregon and Washington, an epic battle rages between two titans of logging."[81] The term "battle" recurs throughout the episodes in the sample. Beers similarly invokes violent imagery in his introductory remarks in Season Four: Episode One: "Alaska,": "From coast to coast, it's an all-out assault."[82]

In *Gold Rush*, Season Two: Episode 17: "Frozen Out," narrator Paul Christie also suggests that gold mining is an aggressive enterprise: "Up in the frozen north, three crews continue their battle against the elements to strike it rich."[83] This brief description touches upon two of the primary features Kimmel identifies as commensurate with U.S. hegemonic masculinity: violence and self-made, upward economic mobility. The association with hegemonic masculinity and violence can be observed in a promotional, still photo for *Gold Rush* from 2011.[84] In this photo, one can observe some of the conventional visual codes of masculinity: All the men pictured are standing up straight with stern expressions. Visual codes that are specific to white, rural, working-class masculinity include the men sporting hard hats and work boots; wearing blue jeans, flannel shirts, and safety vests; and grasping shovels and other mining equipment in an assertive, domineering manner. This image is highly similar in its construction to many of the promotional stills used to advertise the blue-collar frontier shows. Noticeably, Jack Hoffman, who is pictured directly to the right of his son Todd, is holding what appears to be a hunting rifle and aiming it slightly to his left. The placement of the firearm in the image further cements the association between hegemonic masculinity and violence.

It is critical to stress that violence is only palatable within hegemonic masculine performances because of the whiteness of the men therein. The role of white supremacy within hegemonic masculinity cannot be overstated, especially given that whiteness often operates invisibly as a racial identity that confers systemic advantages. Kimmel touches upon white supremacist, heteropatriarchal framings of masculinities of men of color: "The 'other'— whether racial, sexual, religious, or any other identity—was either 'too masculine' or not 'masculine enough,' . . . They're either wild, out-of-control animals, violent and rapacious (too masculine, uncivilized), or they are weak, dependent, irresponsible (not masculine enough)."[85] Therefore, the violence that underpins the blue-collar frontier shows only receives an honorable and romanticized gloss because of the near-exclusive presence of white men.

Case in point, Edgar Hansen, deckhand and brother to captain Sig Hansen of the *Northwestern*, menacingly lights his throwing hook aflame before hurling it into the Bering Sea to retrieve pots full of crabs in Season One: Episode 10: "The Final Run." Edgar announces to the camera: "I'm gonna light my throwing hook on fire. Why? For the hell of it."[86] He also briefly sets himself on fire before doing so and is applauded by his brother Sig over the loudspeaker from below deck. One could surmise that such behavior would not be interpreted the same way if enacted by a man of color. In Season Three: Episode Seven: "New Beginnings," Edgar comments on how he plans to treat the greenhorn deckhands, while simultaneously making a repeated punching gesture with his hand: "I gotta pack in as much abuse as I can over the next few weeks."[87] These overt displays of hegemonic masculine behavior are presented playfully and favorably, which cannot be separated from Sig's whiteness.

In the same episode, it is also revealed that one of the greenhorns on the same boat, Matt Bradley, a young white male in his twenties, has a criminal record. Matt explains his sentencing to the camera: "I got home in time for my court date, and the judge was pretty lenient. I didn't get the eight-month sentence, like I would've got if I missed that court date. I ended up getting a couple weeks."[88] The nature of the charges against Matt are not revealed in the show, and in the same episode, the cameras cut to his fellow crewmates making light of his brief incarceration. Because there are marked sentencing disparities along racial lines in the U.S. criminal justice system, particularly in relation to black male defendants receiving far more severe prison sentences than white male defendants for similar crimes,[89] it is telling that Matt received a comparatively lenient sentence. Furthermore, because criminality is so heavily and unjustly tied to black masculinity in the United States,[90] Matt's criminal past does not stigmatize him on account of his race or reflect upon young white men as a group in the same fashion. One cannot separate Matt's whiteness from how his criminal record is framed on *Deadliest Catch*—as a relatively minor mistake that does not define him (which of course, it should not). In illuminating this, I am not suggesting that he should have been dealt a more severe punishment. In terms of racial justice and equity, the goal is to eliminate racial disparities and upend the ongoing legacy of the systematic criminalization of people of color. In short, violence and unlawful behavior are far more palatable to mainstream audiences within the confines of whiteness.

Despite whiteness and compulsory heterosexuality (no cast members on the blue-collar frontier shows are explicitly identified as LBGTQ) remaining consistent features of hegemonic masculinity throughout U.S. history, hegemonic masculinity itself should not be collapsed into a monolithic, fixed set of traits. In *Staging Masculinities: History, Gender, Performance*, Michael Mangan succinctly encapsulates how hegemonic masculinity is dynamic and often evolves in relation to wider systemic changes: "Hegemonic masculinity is by nature paradoxical, since it seems to stand still but in fact is always on the move . . . Connell's history indicates the way in which these changes relate to wider social and economic movements."[91] That being the case, I think it is worth underlining the conditions that gave rise to white, rural, working-class masculinity increasingly constituting hegemonic masculinity since the Great Recession.

I maintain that the emergence of the blue-collar frontier shows is a direct response to the Great Recession engendering a perceived threat to white masculine dominance, which consequently, reasserts white, rural, working-class masculinity as hegemonic masculinity. It is worth restating that the 2008 downturn disproportionately harmed people of color, especially African Americans.[92] Since women of all races and people of color of all genders were hit hard by the recession, then why did the Great Recession lead to a gendered crisis among white men? Kimmel addresses the substantial impact of the 2008 recession on white males in the United States, which he refers to as the "he-cession" in his prescient 2013 text, *Angry White Men: American Masculinity at the End of an Era*.[93] Although Kimmel does not forecast the rise of a former reality TV star presidential candidate appealing to the nation's deeply rooted sexism, racism, and xenophobia, as was the case with Donald Trump, he does identify an emergent and palpable anger among working and middle-class white men during this time of socioeconomic uncertainty.

The decline of traditionally masculine spheres of labor since the Great Recession, such as U.S. manufacturing, contributes to the *perception* among white men that there is an assault on *exclusively white men*. This contrasts with the more complicated reality of the neoliberal attack on working people across races and genders, with more vulnerable groups, such as African Americans, suffering disproportionately because of the compounding nature of systemic racism. Kimmel contextualizes the effects of dramatic declines in traditionally male-dominated employment sectors, coupled with the increased presence of women in the workforce in recent years: "During the first five years of the twenty-first century alone, 2.5 million manufacturing jobs were lost. The unemployment rate for men is nearly two percentage points higher, at 8.8 percent, than the rate for women . . . If women's entry into the labor force stirred up men's ability to anchor their identity as family provider, women's emergence as primary breadwinner is a seismic shift, shaking men's identity to its foundation."[94]

The sizeable change in the gendered distribution of labor contributes to the misnomer that women are somehow systemically advantaged over men and that sexism is a myth. Traditionally feminized occupations, such as jobs in the service sector, have become the primary source of job growth since the Great Recession.[95] It is important to contextualize that the growth in traditionally feminized occupations has not led to women surpassing men in earnings overall. Not only do conventionally female-dominated fields remain more precarious and pay lower wages, but as women enter traditionally male-dominated sectors, the payrates tend to drop as well. Claire Caine Miller explains in the *New York Times* article, "As Women Take Over a Male-Dominated Field, the Pay Drops," that "It may come down to this troubling reality, new research suggests: Work done by women simply isn't valued as highly."[96]

Additionally, according to a report from the Women's Bureau in the U.S. Department of Labor, women of color endured some of the highest rates of unemployment compared to white women during and after the Recession: "For each year from 2007–2012, Black women had the highest unemployment rate (peaking at 14.1 percent in 2011 and dropping to 12.8 percent in 2012) . . . Latinas had the next highest, peaking at 12.3 percent in 2010 and dropping to 10.9 percent in 2012."[97] Women of color are also overrepresented in low-wage service sector positions and experience a much more pronounced gender wage gap with white men as compared to the pay deficit between white women and white men.[98]

The data indicate that this sense of economic precarity is a relatively new phenomenon for working and middle-class white men *as a group*. Naomi Klein contextualizes this newfound sense of precarity for working and middle-class white males in *No Is Not Enough*: " . . . because many of Trump's blue-collar voters had a notably better deal until fairly recently—able to access well-paid, unionized manufacturing jobs that supported middle-class lives—these losses appear to come as more of a shock . . . Another way of thinking about it is: when a building starts to collapse, it's the people on the higher floors who have further to fall—that's just physics."[99] Furthermore, this thinking destructively ignores the structural disadvantages women and people of color endure in the United States in relation to white males overall. Klein rightfully observes that "to a terrifying degree, skin color and gender conformity are determining who is physically safe in the hands of the state, who is at risk from vigilante violence, who can express themselves without constant harassment, who can cross a border without terror, and who can worship without fear."[100] Because whiteness and maleness are constructed as the default racial and gender identities in the United States, white males, as per Kimmel's analysis, are more likely to view themselves as individuals and not as members of wider social groups. Moreover, it appears that white males are even less likely to recognize that they systemically *benefit* from their social location at the intersection of white supremacy and patriarchy. Combine this tendency with the potential for a racial and gender-inclusive class consciousness not materializing, in part, because of an attachment to achieving hegemonic masculine ideals (among other complex sociopolitical factors), and you have a recipe for misplaced blame and aggression toward women and people of color in an imperialist white supremacist capitalist heteropatriarchal system.

Interestingly, Kimmel identifies white working-class and middle-class men as having an increasingly shared sense of commonality despite their class differences, which are gradually becoming negligible as neoliberal economic policies continue to shrink the middle class entirely.[101] As Kimmel explains, "The white working class and the white middle class have rarely been so close *emotionally* as they are today; together they have drifted away from unions; from big government; from the Democratic Party, into the further reaches of the right wing."[102] This partially explains Trump drawing white male votes from across the class spectrum. It is noteworthy that Trump's white working-class supporters have come under the most scrutiny in main-stream political reporting, but as discussed previously in this chapter, news rhetoric about the white working class leaves much to be desired in terms of understanding race and class hierarchies in the United States. I contend that the dominant characterization of working-class whites as racist is attributable to how classism operates among whites, since charges of racism do not collectively adhere to middle-class whites as a group. Certainly, there is racism to be found within the ranks of the white working class, but the common perception that working-class whites are the sole purveyors of racism in the United States needs correction. Williams explicates this tendency in *White Working Class*:

There's an element here of privileged whites distancing themselves from racism by displacing the blame for racism onto less-privileged whites . . . Implicit association test results show that MDs, college grads, and MBAs did not score lower for implicit racial bias than did high school grads . . . Among liberals it's a mark of sophistication to acknowledge that everyone's a little bit racist, yet professional-class racism slides conveniently out of sight in discussions about working-class whites.[103]

Regardless, all whites systemically benefit from a white supremacist racial caste system. It is also critical not to conflate systemic racism with personal prejudice or racist attitudes among whites—in a white supremacist system, racial disparities and inequitable outcomes result even if there are no intentionally or overtly racist actors therein.

The increased sense of commonality between working-class and middle-class white men speaks to how the blue-collar frontier shows appeal to both groups. These shows venerate a form of hegemonic masculinity that is presented as potentially attainable to able-bodied, white men of all classes. As Kimmel points out, "If you feel yourself to always be taking it on the chin, media fantasy is the place where you get to pump your first in defiance. If you feel emasculated in real life, you can feel like a man in 'reel life.'"[104] In this sense, the emergence of these programs is in direct conversation with white male fears and anxieties regarding their social status in the United States. These shows document occupations that remain white, male-dominated spheres at a time when white-male dominated employment sectors, such as manufacturing, are in decline. Alexander and Woods explain that these reality series tend to depict jobs that " . . . reinforce stereotypical ideas about what men do—'real men' work on cars, survive in the wilderness, hunt, discover essential resources, make manly objects such as swords and beer, and collect manly objects such as tools, fishing lures, or rare car parts."[105] This is not a coincidence. It is as though the shows rhetorically console their white male viewership by saying: "Don't worry, you're still on top as the real men of the United States." In "Portrayals of Masculinity in the Discovery Channel's *Deadliest Catch*," Burton P. Buchanan poignantly encapsulates the deeper social meaning behind this program for white male viewers: " . . . white male power has endured encroachment as women, gays and minorities have gained social power in recent decades. *Deadliest Catch* serves as a fine example of a reality television program that demonstrates an environment where traditional masculinity is exercised, a place where white males can perform masculine rituals, compete with one another in an adverse environment and reassert their position in the social cultural hierarchies.[106]"

In addition, since both working and middle-class white men recognize white, rural, working-class masculinity as the most "legitimate" form of

60   *Chapter 1*

masculinity in the contemporary U.S. context, class distinctions, even those that exist within the casts of these series, become sublimated within the visuality of "real men." Upon establishing that the blue-collar frontier shows reaffirm white, rural, working-class masculinity as hegemonic masculinity in the contemporary U.S. context in response to the socioeconomic upheaval generated by the Great Recession, I will now detail with greater specificity the role of gender policing within performances of hegemonic masculinity.

THE BLUE-COLLAR REALITY WORLD: POLICING MASCULINITY IN HOMOSOCIAL SPACES

Since the blue-collar frontier shows provide a visual archive of hegemonic masculinity in the United States over the past two decades, it may come as a surprise that gender policing itself remains a central aspect of the narratives. If the men of the blue-collar frontier world signify "real men" at the level of commonsense, then why would the men in these series explicitly engage in gender policing? I delineate gender policing in this context as the occasions in which men overtly call attention to their supposed masculine superiority *at the expense of other men*, or more simply, when men ridicule other men with feminizing insults. I configure this teasing in homosocial spaces as a ritualized practice commensurate with the performance of hegemonic masculinity. The preoccupation with *proving* one's manhood suggests that one's place at the top of the masculine hierarchy is never fully secured, and these programs provide an opportunity to bear witness to "real men" ritualistically doing so in relation to their workplace subordinates or coworkers.

Kimmel points out in *Manhood in America* that men can only appropriately demonstrate their masculinity in exclusively male spaces: "Throughout American history American men have been afraid that others will see us as less than manly, as weak, timid, frightened . . . American men define their masculinity, not as much in relation to women, but in relation to each other."[107] Because these workplaces are almost entirely homosocial spaces—with women only occasionally entering the perimeter with significant resistance from men—the series entail a substantial amount of gender policing. Kimmel further elucidates the significance of single-gender environments for men in proving their masculine worth: "Masculinity defined through homosocial interaction contains many parts, including the camaraderie, fellowship, and intimacy often celebrated in male culture. It also includes homophobia."[108] He elaborates that homophobia is not merely about fearing or discriminating against homosexuals, but that it also " . . . is the fear of other men—that other men will unmask us, emasculate us, reveal to us and the world that we do not measure up, *are not real men* [emphasis added] . . . "[109]

I contend that this mode of ridicule constitutes one of the primary ways in which men enforce gender normative expectations of one another, in which compulsory heterosexuality is considered integral to ideal manhood. It also functions to correct seemingly undesirable behaviors through peer pressure—as there is no worse insult to a man than feminizing him. In Season Eight: Episode Four: "The Hook," *Deadliest Catch* viewers witness one of the more brutal instances of feminized insults being deployed to purportedly modify behavior. Captain Bill Wichrowski of the *Kodiak* grows frustrated as he watches his son, deckhand Zack Larson, unsuccessfully throw the hook to retrieve the pots full of crab from the Bering Sea multiple times in a row. After scolding him on deck for his performance, Bill returns to the wheelhouse and then declares over the loudspeaker so that the entire crew can hear: "Zack, I've got to say—you've probably made your mom proud throwing the hook this season. She always wanted a girl."[110] He then removes Zack from throwing the hook.

Evidently, Bill thinks the best way to help improve his son's performance is to deride him by claiming he is "throwing like a girl." The implication, of course, being that a woman could never perform a job that requires that kind of physical strength and coordination. This type of gender policing further solidifies the linkage between job performance and masculinity: If a man does not perform his job well, or have a job at all, then he is not living up to masculine ideals. In Season 11: Episode Nine: "Hell's Bells," one of the deckhands engages in a similar type of gendered harassment against a fellow crewmember. Veteran deckhand, Danny Chiu, is relentlessly hounding twenty-something deckhand, Phillip Hillstrand, aboard the *Time Bandit*. Danny's behavior on deck is erratic, as he aggressively taunts Phil: "We're crabbing. It's a crab deck. Move your ass little girl . . . Come over here and be a man."[111] Danny's abusive behavior culminates with him slapping Phillip. Although Danny's actions are perceived as wild and unsafe by most of his crewmates, and are presented as such, it is not until he physically strikes a fellow crewmember that anyone intervenes, or the show suggests that a line of social acceptability has been crossed. The gendered verbal harassment that preceded it remains consistent with the kind of gender policing endemic to the homosocial male spaces catalogued across the series in this study.

The viewers witness a seemingly more jovial instance of gender policing in Season Two: Episode 10 of *Ax Men*, "Clash of the Titans." This episode highlights the manufactured competition to haul the most lumber between the J. M. Browning and Rygaard logging companies in Oregon and Washington respectively. The Rygaard crew sends the Browning loggers pink gloves to suggest that they are too feminine to win the competition. In return, the Browning crew sends them pink tutus. As Jay Browning reiterates, "It's important that they're pink."[112] Although lighthearted, the notion that pink is

62   *Chapter 1*

an intrinsically feminine color that would inherently emasculate any "true" man wearing it, is a common form of gender policing. Gender policing in relation to the colors pink and blue begins at birth for most U.S. children based upon their biological sex characteristics. Even if done in a humorous fashion, the cumulative effects of this type of gender patrolling in cisheterosexual, male homosocial spaces enforces and naturalizes hegemonic masculine standards of conduct. In short, "real men" do not wear pink.

In Season Four: Episode One: "Alaska," *Ax Men* continues with the plot device of pitting crews against each other, in which the "winners" can claim bragging rights to having proven themselves as the toughest and truest of men. Within the narrative arch of *Ax Men*, the winners are given the title of "King of the Mountain." In this installment, the viewer is introduced to Papac Logging in Alaska. An unidentified logger from Papac proclaims in the introduction of the episode that Alaska is "where the real men come to log the real wood."[113] (The relationship between place, specifically the mythic frontier and hegemonic masculinity in the U.S. context is addressed in the third chapter.) Logger, Mike "Costsy" Coats, announces later in the episode that " . . . it's just the terrain's way tougher up here. I mean, my daughter could log down there where Rygaard logs [Washington]."[114] Again, women are used as a reference point to demonstrate another man's supposed inferiority. Hegemonic masculinity in the U.S. context requires the performance of these discursive rituals of gender policing for its maintenance—it is never fixed or assumed and requires repeated, performative expression.

Given that the most cutting way to insult a man is to feminize him within the logic of hegemonic masculinity, then the best way to compliment him is to praise his masculinity in homosocial spaces. The primary way of recognizing a fellow man's masculine prowess is through complimenting his toughness or "guts." In Season Four: Episode Four: "Unsafe and Unsound," *Deadliest Catch* viewers witness a young deckhand on the *Wizard*, Jason Moilanen, aka Moi, struggling to keep up with the pace of the workload in a harsh environment. Mike Rowe narrates as Moi continues to complain, "Jason Moi is barely hanging on."[115] Captain Keith Colburn expresses irritation at Moi's complaints. Shortly thereafter, Moi smashes his finger in the door of an 800-pound steel pot used to catch crabs. Keith minimizes the extent of his injury, and then has Moi poke his finger with a hot tweezers. Moi does not emote as blood pours out of his heavily bruised and swollen digit.

Rowe then contextualizes the significance of this event in relation to Moi's standing with the captain: "Moi has yet to impress the skipper with his deck work, but he does prove he may have some guts."[116] The camera then cuts to Keith praising Moi for enduring pain without much complaint or display of emotion: "You're a tough guy. That was impressive. Should have given you a shot of whiskey first."[117] A critical aspect of hegemonic masculinity is enduring pain or the threat of violence without displaying emotions that have become stereotypically coded as feminine, such as fear and sadness. Although Moi is not wholly successful in proving his masculinity through his job performance, he remains in good standing with his male peers and supervisor through his display of masculine toughness in the face of serious injury. The show frames this incident as redemptive for Moi since his masculine authenticity was coming under scrutiny until that point.

Season Five: Episode Three: "Stay Focused or Die" is one of *Deadliest Catch*'s most emotional episodes. The episode recounts the season's greatest tragedy—the sinking of the *Katmai*, in which seven fishermen perished and four survived. Although the vessel and its crew were not directly taking part in the filming of the series, the viewer sees the Coast Guard deployed on a rescue mission and the reactions of principal cast members to the devastating news. The narrative jumps back and forth in time, in which much of the episode consists of studio interviews with three survivors of the tragedy. During a moving interview with survivor Ryan Appling, he holds back tears as he lauds his fellow fishermen who died: "There's not much you can say other than that they were hell of good guys. *They were real men* [emphasis added], real men with character and real men to really be around, have a part of your life, and I enjoyed each and every second of that."[118] Ryan has clearly been through an incredibly traumatic event and the aim here is not to criticize his heartfelt expression of that. If anything, the show deserves credit for depicting a man's sincere expression of grief, as heteropatriarchy encourages the restriction and repression of men's emotional expression, especially as it relates to sadness and pain. However, it is noteworthy that he chooses to honor and pay tribute to his deceased crewmates through calling them "real men." It provides insight into how highly valued that designation is *to men* in the contemporary context and why it matters to them to discursively call attention to their own masculinity, as well as their peers, in both positive and negative fashions accordingly. To be a real man is to have truly attained a highly venerated status. In short, that is the overriding message of all the blue-collar frontier programs: These shows claim to document real men, and they reinforce that this subset of men has a preferred status in the current U.S. social climate. Consequently, this masculine performance confers a significant degree of symbolic capital, which explains why upper-class white males seek to emulate white, rural, working-class masculinity.

Because homosocial spaces are a linchpin to the visuality of hegemonic masculinity, in the next chapter, I will detail how the small number of white women who have been included in the blue-collar frontier milieu are portrayed.

NOTES

1. Christopher Lockett, "Masculinity and Authenticity: Reality TV's Real Men," *Flow*, October 15, 2010, http://flowtv.org/2010/10/masculinity-and-authenticity/.

2. Robert Lloyd, "TV's Rugged, Rural Breed," *Los Angeles Times*, December 1, 2011, https://www.latimes.com/archives/la-xpm-2011-dec-01-la-et-1130-redneck-tv-20111201-story.html.

3. Michael Kimmel, *Manhood in America: A Cultural History*, 3rd ed. (New York and Oxford: Oxford University Press, 2012), 187.

4. Michael Kimmel, *Manhood in America*, 7.

5. Michael Kimmel, *Angry White Men: American Masculinity at the End of an Era* (New York: Nation Books, 2013), 223.

6. Angela Davis, "Recognizing Racism in the Era of Neoliberalism," *Truthout*, May 6, 2013, https://truthout.org/articles/recognizing-racism-in-the-era-of-neoliberalism/.

7. Naomi Klein, *No Is Not Enough: Resisting Trump's Shock Politics and Winning the World We Need* (Chicago, IL: Haymarket Books, 2017), 89.

8. George Yancy and bell hooks, "bell hooks: Buddhis, the Beats and Loving Blackness," *New York Times*, December 10, 2015, https://opinionator.blogs.nytimes.com/author/bell-hooks/.

9. Michael Kimmel, *Manhood in America*, 240.

10. Christopher Lockett, "Masculinity and Authenticity," http://flowtv.org/2010/10/masculinity-and-authenticity/.

11. Susan M. Alexander and Katie Woods, "Reality Television and the Doing of Hyperauthentic Masculinities," *The Journal of Men's Studies* 27, no. 2 (2019): 161, https://doi.org/10.1177/1060826518801529.

12. Alexander and Woods, "Reality Television and the Doing of Hyperauthentic Masculinities," 162.

13. Michelle Alexander, *The New Jim Crow: Mass Incarceration in the Age of Colorblindness* (New York: New Press, 2020), xli.

14. Michelle Alexander, *The New Jim Crow*, x.

15. Ibid., xi.

16. Alexander and Woods, "Reality Television and the Doing of Hyperauthentic Masculinities," 153.

17. Michael Kimmel, *Manhood in America*, 5.

18. Michael Zweig, *The Working-Class Majority: America's Best Kept Secret* (Ithaca: Cornell University Press, 2000), 56.

19. Beverly Skeggs and Helen Wood, "Introduction: Real Class" in *Reality Television and Class*, eds. Beverly Skeggs and Helen Wood (London: Palgrave Macmillan, 2011), 2.

20. Christopher R. Martin, *No Longer Newsworthy: How the Mainstream Media Abandoned the Working Class* (Ithaca and London: Cornell University Press, 2019), 3.

21. Christopher R. Martin, *No Longer Newsworthy*, 2.

22. Kimmel, *Manhood in America*, 7.

23. Ibid., 7.

24. Ann-Marie Slaughter, "Why Women Still Can't Have It All," *The Atlantic*, August 15, 2012, https://www.theatlantic.com/magazine/archive/2012/07/why-women-still-cant-have-it-all/309020/.

25. Ada Calhoun, "The New Midlife Crisis: Why (And How) It's Hitting Gen X Women," *Oprah.com,* https://www.oprah.com/sp/new-midlife-crisis.html.

26. Joan C. Williams, *White Working Class: Overcoming Class Cluelessness in America*, (Boston, MA: Harvard Business Review Press. 2017), 76.

27. Michelle Alexander, *The New Jim Crow: Mass Incarceration in the Age of Colorblindness* (New York: New Press, 2020).

28. Kimmel, *Manhood in America*, 284–85.

29. Ibid., 7.

30. Williams, *White Working Class*, 80.

31. Kimmel, *Manhood in America*, 200.

32. Donna Haraway, "The Persistence of Vision," in *The Visual Culture Reader*, ed. Nicholas Mirzoeff (London and New York: Routledge, 2013), 356.

33. Gwendolyn Audrey Foster, *Class-Passing: Social Mobility in Film and Popular Culture* (Carbondale, IL: Southern Illinois University Press, 2005), 43.

34. Laura Grindstaff, "From *Jerry Springer* to *Jersey Shore*: The Cultural Politics of Class in/on US Reality Programming," In *Reality Television and Class*, eds. B. Skeggs and Helen Wood (London: Palgrave Macmillan, 2011), 203.

35. Beverly Skeggs and Helen Wood, "Introduction: Real Class" in *Reality Television and Class*, eds. Beverly Skeggs and Helen Wood (London: Palgrave Macmillan, 2011), 2–3.

36. Martin, *No Longer Newsworthy*, 3.

37. Erin Karter, 'Nonvoters 2020: Counted Out' Examines Reasons 80 million Americans Opted Out of Presidential Election," *Northwestern Now*, December 15, 2020, https://news.northwestern.edu/stories/2020/12/nonvoters-2020-counted-out-examines-reasons-80-million-americans-opted-out-of-presidential-election/&fj=1.

38. Matt Stevens, "Poorer Americans Have Much Lower Voting Rates in National Elections than The Nonpoor, a Study Finds," *New York Times*, August 11, 2020, https://www.nytimes.com/2020/08/11/us/politics/poorer-americans-have-much-lower-voting-rates-in-national-elections-than-the-nonpoor-a-study-finds.html.

39. Williams, *White Working Class*, 9.

40. Alison Hearn, "Producing 'Reality': Branded Content, Branded Selves, Precarious Futures" in *A Companion to Reality Television*, ed. L. Ouellette (Malden, MA and Oxford: John Wiley & Sons, Inc., 2014), 437–455.

41. Zweig, *The Working-Class Majority*, 3.

42. Martin, *No Longer Newsworthy*, 5.

43. Jacquelyn Smith, "10 Things the Best Leaders Never Say," *Business Insider*, September 15, 2014, http://www.businessinsider.com/successful-leaders-never-say-these-things-2014-9.

44. Brady Meixell and Ross Eisenbrey, "An Epidemic of Wage Theft Is Costing Workers Hundreds of Millions of Dollars a Year. *Economic Policy Institute*, September 11, 2014, https://www.epi.org/publication/epidemic-wage-theft-costing-workers-hundreds/.

66   *Chapter 1*

45. Amanda Holpuch, "No One Wants to Work Anymore': The Truth Behind This Unemployment Benefits Myth," *The Guardian*, May 7, 2021, https://www.theguardian.com/business/2021/may/07/truth-behind-unemployment-benefits-myth

46. Alexander Burns, "Romney: Obama Waging 'War on Job Creators,'" *Politico*, May 23, 2012, http://www.politico.com/blogs/burns-haberman/2012/05/romney-obama-waging-war-on-job-creators-124350

47. *Deadliest Catch*, season 1, episode 10, "The Final Run," written by Ethan Prochnik, narrated by Mike Rowe, aired June 14, 2005, *Original Productions* for *Discovery Channel*.

48. *Deadliest Catch*, season 1, episode 10, "The Final Run."

49. *Deadliest Catch*, season 4, episode 4, "Unsafe and Unsound," narrated by Mike Rowe, aired April 29, 2008, *Original Productions* for *Discovery Channel*.

50. *Deadliest Catch*, season 4, episode 4, "Unsafe and Unsound."

51. *Deadliest Catch*, season 5, episode 3, "Stay Focused or Die," narrated by Mike Rowe, aired April 28, 2009, *Original Productions* for *Discovery Channel*.

52. Deadliest Catch, season 5, episode 3, "Stay Focused or Die."

53. Gregory Bresiger, "Americans Work Harder Than Any Other Country's Citizens: Study," *New York Post*, September 3, 2017, https://nypost.com/2017/09/03/americans-work-harder-than-any-other-countrys-citizens-study/; Ben Winck, "Having a Job Right Now Means Longer Hours and Slow Pay Growth," *Business Insider*, June 14, 2021, https://www.businessinsider.com/labor-shortage-employed-americans-longer-hours-slow-pay-growth-jobs-2021-6.

54. *Deadliest Catch*, season 5, episode 15, "Day of Reckoning," narrated by Mike Rowe, aired July 21, 2009, *Original Productions* for *Discovery Channel*.

55. *Deadliest Catch*, season 6, episode 10, "the Darkened Seas," narrated by Mike Rowe, aired June 15, 2010, *Original Productions* for *Discovery Channel*.

56. *Deadliest Catch*, season 6, episode 10, "The Darkened Seas."

57. Ibid.

58. Ibid.

59. *Deadliest Catch*, Season 4 DVD Cover Image, 2008, https://pisces.bbystatic.com/image2/BestBuy_US/images/products/9224/9224083_so.jpg.

60. *Ice Road Truckers*, season 1, episode 9, "The Big Melt," narrated by Thom Beers, aired August 12, 2007, *Original Productions* for *History Channel*.

61. *Ice Road Truckers*, season 1, episode 9, "The Big Melt."

62. Ibid.

63. David Johnson, "The Most Dangerous Jobs in America," *TIME*, May 13, 2016, https://time.com/4326676/dangerous-jobs-america/.

64. Johnson, "The Most Dangerous Jobs in America," https://time.com/4326676/dangerous-jobs-america/.

65. *Ax Men*, season 1, episode 2, "Risk and Reward," narrated by Thom Beers, aired March 16, 2008, *Original Productions* for *History Channel*.

66. *Gold Rush: Alaska*, season 1, episode 1, "No Guts No Glory," narrated by Paul Christie, aired December 3, 2010, *Raw TV* for *Discovery Channel*.

67. *Gold Rush*, season 1, episode 1, "No Guts No Glory."

68. Nicholas Mirzoeff, *An Introduction to Visual Culture* (New York: Routledge, 2009), 89–93.

69. Stuart Hall, "Encoding/Decoding" in *Media and Cultural Studies KeyWorks*, eds. M.G. Durham and D.M. Kellner (Malden, MA and Oxford, UK: Blackwell Publishing, 2006), 171.

70. Raewyn Connell, *Gender and Power: Society, the Person, and Sexual Politics* (Stanford, California: Stanford University Press, 1987), 80.

71. Robert Hanke, "Hegemonic Masculinity in Transition. in *Men, Masculinity, and the Media*, ed. S. Craig (Newbury Park: Sage Publications, 1992), 190.

72. Lockett, "Masculinity and Authenticity," http://flowtv.org/2010/10/masculinity-and-authenticity/.

73. Kimmel, *Manhood in America*, 216.

74. Hugh Campbell, Michael Mayerfield Bell, and Margaret Finney, *Country Boys: Masculinity and Rural Life* (University Park, Pennsylvania: The Pennsylvania State University Press 2006), 1–2.

75. John Berger, *Ways of Seeing* (London and New York: Penguin Books, 1977), 47.

76. *Deadliest Catch*, season 6, episode 10, "The Darkened Seas," narrated by Mike Rowe, aired June 15, 2010, *Original Productions* for *Discovery Channel*.

77. *Deadliest Catch*, season 3, episode 7, "New Beginnings," narrated by Mike Rowe, aired May 15, 2007, *Original Productions* for *Discovery Channel*.

78. *Ice Road Truckers*, season 1, episode 4, "The Big Chill," narrated by Thom Beers, aired July 8, 2007, *Original Productions* for *History Channel*.

79. *Ax Men*, season 2, episode 10, "Clash of the Titans," narrated by Thom Beers, aired May 11, 2009, *Original Productions* for *History Channel*.

80. Kimmel, *Manhood in America*, 269.

81. *Ax Men*, season 2, episode 10, "Clash of the Titans."

82. *Ax Men*, season 4, episode 1, "Alaska," narrated by Thom Beers, aired December 12, 2010, *Original Productions* for *History Channel*.

83. *Gold Rush*, season 2, episode 17, "Frozen Out," narrated by Paul Christie, aired February 17, 2012, *Raw TV* for *Discovery Channel*.

84. *Gold Rush*, *Raw TV* for *Discovery Channel*, 2011, https://www.adgully.com/img/800/54456_gold-rush-discovery-channel.jpg.

85. Kimmel, *Angry White Men*, 257.

86. *Deadliest Catch*, season 1, episode 10, "The Final Run," narrated by Mike Rowe, aired June 14, 2005, *Original Productions* for *Discovery Channel*.

87. *Deadliest Catch*, season 3, episode 7, "New Beginnings," narrated by Mike Rowe, aired May 15, 2007, *Original Productions* for *Discovery Channel*.

88. *Deadliest Catch*, season 3, episode 7, "New Beginnings."

89. Joe Palazzolo, "Racial Gap in Men's Sentencing," *The Wall Street Journal*, February 14, 2013, https://www.wsj.com/articles/SB10001424127887324432004578304463789858002.

90. Michelle Alexander, *The New Jim Crow: Mass Incarceration in the Age of Colorblindness* (New York: New Press, 2020).

91. Michael Mangan, *Staging Masculinities: History, Gender, Performance* (New York: Palgrave Macmillan, 2003), 13.

68 *Chapter 1*

92. Alexander, *The New Jim Crow*, xli.

93. Kimmel, *Angry White Men*, 209.

94. Kimmel, *Manhood in America*, 288.

95. Justin Fox, "Where the Job Growth Is," *Bloomberg*, February 5, 2015, https://www.bloomberg.com/view/articles/2015-02-06/job-market-gains-aided-by-slowdown-in-government-layoffs.

96. Claire Cain Miller, "As Women Take Over a Male-Dominated Field, the Pay Drops," *New York Times*, March 18, 2016, https://www.nytimes.com/2016/03/20/upshot/as-women-take-over-a-male-dominated-field-the-pay-drops.html?_r=0.

97. "Economic Status of Women of Color: A Snapshot," Women's Bureau in the U.S. Department of Labor, https://www.in.gov/icw/files/WB_WomenColorFactSheet.pdf.

98. Milia Fisher, "Women of Color and the Gender Wage Gap," *Center for American Progress*, April 14, 2015, https://www.americanprogress.org/issues/women/reports/2015/04/14/110962/women-of-color-and-the-gender-wage-gap/

99. Klein, *No Is Not Enough*, 89.

100. Ibid., 90.

101. Richard Fry and Rakesh Kochhar, "The Shrinking Middle Class in U.S. Metropolitan Areas: 6 Key Findings," *Pew Research Center*," May 12, 2016, http://www.pewresearch.org/fact-tank/2016/05/12/us-middle-class-metros-takeaways/.

102. Kimmel, *Angry White Men*, 204.

103. Williams, *White Working Class,* 60–61.

104. Kimmel, *Angry White Men*, 218.

105. Alexander and Woods, "Reality Television and the Doing of Hyperauthentic Masculinities," 162.

106. Burton P. Buchanan, "Portrayals of Masculinity in the Discovery Channel's *Deadliest Catch*," in *Reality Television: Oddities of Culture*, eds. A. F. Slade, A. J. Narro, and B. P. Buchanan (Lanham, Maryland: Lexington Books, 2014), 2.

107. Kimmel, *Manhood in America*, 5.

108. Ibid., 6.

109. Ibid.

110. *Deadliest Catch*, season 8, episode 4, "The Hook," narrated by Mike Rowe, aired May 1, 2012, *Original Productions* for *Discovery Channel*.

111. *Deadliest Catch*, season 11, episode 9, "Hell's Bells," narrated by Mike Rowe, aired June 9, 2015, *Original Productions* for *Discovery Channel*.

112. *Ax Men*, season 2, episode 10, "Clash of the Titans," narrated by Thom Beers, aired May 11, 2009, *Original Productions* for *History Channel*.

113. *Ax Men*, season 4, episode 1, "Alaska," narrated by Thom Beers, aired December 12, 2010, *Original Productions* for *History Channel*.

114. *Ax Men*, season 4, episode 1, "Alaska."

115. *Deadliest Catch*, season 4, episode 4, "Unsafe and Unsound," narrated by Mike Rowe, aired April 29, 2008, *Original Productions* for *Discovery Channel*.

116. *Deadliest Catch*, season 4, episode 4, "Unsafe and Unsound."

117. Ibid.

118. *Deadliest Catch*, season 5, episode 3, "Stay Focused or Die," narrated by Mike Rowe, aired April 28, 2009, *Original Productions* for *Discovery Channel*.

Chapter 2

White Women with Blue Collars: Rules for Representation

In framing the blue-collar frontier series as a case study for understanding the visuality of hegemonic masculinity, it is vital to dissect how these four series under examination portray the exceptionally small number of white women featured on screen. It is telling that women of color are completely absent from the blue-collar frontier shows—white masculinity is so entrenched in the frontier mythology and visuality of these series that the presence of women of color would appear highly incongruous and perhaps even menacing to white male dominance. Only one of the white women featured in this sample, Lisa Kelly of *Ice Road Truckers*, receives top billing as a main cast member. Notably, Mandy Hansen, the daughter of the captain of the *Northwestern*, Sig Hansen, joined the cast of *Deadliest Catch* at the start of the show's tenth season in 2014 and has remained through the end of the seventeenth season in 2021. Her presence is consequential, in which her gender identity in a male-dominated profession, as well as her relationship to her father, spur the narrative along in a predictable and gimmicky fashion. The timing of Mandy's appearance in the series in its tenth season is also a noteworthy attempt at generating needed dramatic tension within the all-male cast. As I will detail momentarily, the introduction of young white women into these hypermasculine environments is a common ploy within this subgenre of reality television. However, because Mandy's inclusion in the series occurs relatively late in the show's production and is heavily centered upon her relationship to an existing male cast member, I have elected to exclude her from this analysis. Instead, I focus on why Lisa Kelly is permitted entry into the blue-collar frontier world of *Ice Road Truckers*, as well as how she is marginalized and stereotyped in accordance with hegemonic framings of white femininity.

Because the premise of these series is predicated upon displays of masculine toughness, palpable tensions arise when women do occasionally enter

72   *Chapter 2*

the scene. As mentioned previously, there are no women of color depicted, even peripherally. This is not solely incidental and suggests a penchant for white femininity, if any femininity, within the visual logic of the blue-collar frontier shows. As per the strict gender policing endemic to performances of hegemonic masculinity that I document in the first chapter, the women of the blue-collar frontier world are only granted entry within the confines of hegemonic femininity, in which whiteness remains an inescapable metric.

First, the only woman conferred star status in any of the series included here is Lisa Kelly of *Ice Road Truckers*. Lisa is included in the opening credits and is given a significant storyline after she is introduced in the third season. Lisa stars in the series for a total of seven seasons. Although Maya Siber is introduced as a main cast member in the fifth season, her stint on the series is limited to a single season with an underdeveloped story arch. Lisa is a conventionally attractive twenty-something with long blonde hair, and I maintain that this is a prerequisite for her inclusion in the series. Notably, Maya is also conventionally attractive, in her twenties, but with long dark hair. As per Berger's adage regarding the portrayal of men and women in the dominant visual domain, " . . . *men act* and *women appear.*"[1] Because physical attractiveness is so foundational to a woman's social experience, treatment, and wider representation, it is unsurprising that the only woman who receives a prominent and robust multi-season storyline embodies conventional standards of beauty, which are profoundly linked to white supremacist logics.

Despite performing the same job, Lisa's physical attractiveness is the linchpin to her marketability as compared to her male counterparts. In fact, most of the men throughout the blue-collar frontier shows do not exemplify conventional standards of attractiveness. I argue that this indicates that cisheterosexual male audiences only accept the inclusion of women cast members if they visually appeal to the male gaze. As per Laura Mulvey's groundbreaking 1975 essay, "Visual Pleasure and Narrative Cinema," Lisa's portrayal coincides with the visual expectations and desires of heterosexual male spectators. This is particularly evident when looking at promotional stills of Lisa. None of the male cast members in any of the blue-collar frontier shows have ever been photographed in a similar fashion. In one such photograph, Lisa is bent over suggestively on her knees, as she appears to be superficially fixing a truck.[2] She is in a vulnerable position consistent with what sociologist Erving Goffman describes as the "ritualization of subordination" in his pioneering work investigating the patterns of women's depictions in advertising, *Gender Advertisements* (1979). In contrast, if any of the men of the blue-collar frontier shows were pictured in the same bent over position on their knees, it would seem bizarre and comical. Lisa's positioning suggests passivity and vulnerability—two traits associated with dominant conceptions of femininity in U.S. culture. Hegemonic masculine performances necessitate

White Women with Blue Collars: Rules for Representation 73

standing up straight, grasping objects with authority, and appearing in control of one's surroundings. In short, dominant codes of masculinity suggest power, whereas dominant codes of femininity suggest weakness within a patriarchal system.

In the same image, Lisa peers back over her shoulder, which signals that she is aware that she is being observed. In *Ways of Seeing*, Berger notes that this is one of the canonical ways women are represented in commercial photography, which has its roots in Western European nude portraiture. Berger explains that in these images, "Women watch themselves being looked at."[3] Lisa displays a similar over-the-shoulder glance in another posed photograph, as she stands in front of a semi-trailer truck in a formal ball gown.[4] In this image, her back and shoulders are exposed by the halter-style dress she is wearing. None of the men featured in these series are ever photographed in attire that deviates from their codified white, rural, working-class masculine performances—they are always depicted in what they wear to work. Although she is pictured in front of semi-trailer truck, the photo does not connect to her exceptional driving and mechanical abilities but solely accentuates her appearance.

In accordance with hegemonically feminine visual codes, Lisa is also highly sexualized. Her sexuality is integrated into her performance on the series in both overt and subtle ways. In Season Three: Episode Six: "Arctic Ice," Lisa must manually fix her truck's frozen brake lines. Before lying down beneath the truck to hammer ice off the wheels, she comments suggestively to the camera: "I like being on the ground anyway."[5] As she finally gets her truck running, the sexual innuendo continues with her provocatively stating, "Bend me over and spank me. Crack that whip."[6] The men on these shows are never sexualized—by themselves or otherwise—in any capacity. Lisa is performing in accordance with hegemonic expectations of femininity for male spectators. Especially with Lisa's comments here, the show depicts her as agentic and empowered in her own objectification—she is not only in on the joke, but the one making it. In "Posting Racism and Sexism: Authenticity, Agency, and Self-Reflexivity in Social Media," Rachel E. Dubrofsky and Megan M. Wood explicate the discrepancies between white women and women of color when it comes to the framing of their participation in appealing to the male gaze: " . . . unlike the white women who are presented as working hard to attract this gaze . . . and therefore empowered in attracting this gaze, women of color are not framed as agentic or empowered."[7] As a white woman, *Ice Road Truckers* consistently portrays Lisa as agentic in her self-objectification for male visual pleasure—it is a palatable mode of "empowerment" within heteropatriarchal capitalism. In short, Lisa can transgress heteropatriarchal expectations through truck driving insofar as she remains visually pleasing to the assumed cisheterosexual male viewer.

74   Chapter 2

I argue that for Lisa to gain any degree of acceptance in male homosocial spaces, she must not deviate from the strict feminine gender codes of physical attractiveness and sexual appeal to men. Otherwise, her presence would be too threatening to masculine hegemony. The show underscores Lisa's sexuality in indirect ways as well. In the same episode, the camera cuts to an image of a wild, artic fox on the ice on two occasions before segueing to Lisa driving. This hints toward associating Lisa with the term "arctic fox." Regardless of her driving abilities, which prove to be formidable throughout her tenure on *Ice Road Truckers*, her physical attractiveness remains her defining characteristic within the narrative logic of the series.

It is important to emphasize that although Lisa is permitted entry into the homosocial male landscape of blue-collar frontier television because of her appearance, she is never on equal footing with her male counterparts. She shoulders an added burden as one of the only women working in her field, in which her job performance remains under intense scrutiny. Unlike the men of the series, any mistake she makes is more likely to be attributed to her gender. Thom Beers describes Lisa's recent admission into the occupation of commercial truck driving in his narration in Season Three: Episode Two: "Rookie Run": "And as a woman working in a man's world, she had to want it more than anyone else . . . Lisa's career choice often shocks the guys."[8] Aside from satisfying the male gaze, including Lisa in the series functions as a plot device to keep the show engaging: She is the sole outsider within the cast, which provides significant dramatic tension. One might argue that her presence inspires female viewers, especially as she navigates sexism while performing as well, if not better, than the male drivers. However, the show's framing of Lisa contending with sexism does not ultimately challenge the status quo—suggesting the superficiality of systemic barriers wherein exceptional individuals can always succeed.

Season Seven: Episode One: "Collision Course" exemplifies how Lisa's gender generates narrative conflict. Hugh Roland, one of the stars of the series, declares that Lisa is unfit to drive on the ice roads because she is a woman. Hugh explains his objections to the camera: "It's not safe for her. Don't matter who she's with or anything, it's just not safe for her. They're the roughest toughest roads in North America, and I don't even think Lisa will make it on these roads, like, because she's a girl."[9] The camera then cuts to Lisa driving, and she defends herself against Hugh's unfounded allegations: "Just because you're a woman doesn't mean you can't do a thing. I may be a woman in a man's world, but I'm not gonna try to change it, I'm not gonna try to feminize it, and I'm not gonna be pretending to be a man."[10] Lisa's rhetorical strategy in defense of her occupation is an intriguing one: She asserts that her gender does not preclude her from performing her job, but she also suggests that truck driving itself is somehow inherently masculine. This is not to nitpick her observation—it is simply noteworthy that most occupations have become naturalized as either masculine or feminine in accordance with the gender binary.

The camera then returns to Hugh, in which he refers to the show's manufactured competition between the drivers for who can haul the most loads across the ice: "I don't think Lisa's even cut out—she shouldn't even be here. She's not really a truck driver. She's no threat to me whatsoever. Not even in the least."[11] Obviously, this tension is fostered for dramatic effect. However, based upon Kimmel's findings in *Angry White Men*, a sizeable portion of rural, white, working-class men do resent women performing occupations that they view to be exclusively "their jobs." Hugh does seem genuinely afraid that Lisa will defeat him in the competition. If she were to do so, Hugh would feel highly emasculated. The fear of emasculation is so deeply entrenched that Hugh (perhaps at the show's urging) wants women barred from the competition. Despite the threat Lisa poses to hegemonic masculine dominance, she is begrudgingly accepted within the logic of the series because her physical appearance satisfies the male gaze; her presence creates narrative tension; and her success as an individual does not threaten the white heteropatriarchal capitalist order.

Arguably, including Lisa in the series could also be designed to attract female viewers, as she could be read as an empowering figure due to her driving acumen and courageous willingness to perform such a dangerous occupation. Regardless, for Lisa, or for any woman to be spotlighted in the blue-collar frontier realm, they must conform to a highly restrictive gender performance—one that does not destabilize or threaten the legitimacy of heteropatriarchy, white supremacy, and capitalism. Thus, through Lisa's story arc, the show *could* be read as feminist—however, I argue this constitutes a form of faux feminism, aligning with neoliberal or "lean-in" feminism, as popularized by Facebook Chief Operating Officer Sheryl Sandberg in 2013. Catherine Rottenberg pinpoints the core features of this hegemonic mode of feminism:

> Yes, neoliberal feminism might acknowledge the gender wage gap and sexual harassment as signs of continued inequality. But the solutions it posits elide the structural and economic under-girding of these phenomena. Incessantly inciting women to accept full responsibility for their own well-being and self-care, neoliberal feminism ultimately directs its address to the middle- and upper-middle classes, effectively erasing the vast majority of women from view. And, since it is informed by a market calculus, it is uninterested in social justice or mass mobilisation. With the rise of neoliberal feminism, which encourages individual women to focus on themselves and their own aspirations, feminism can more easily be popularised, circulated, and sold in the market place.[12]

76   *Chapter 2*

Additionally, neoliberal feminism also remains complicit in white supremacy—representing the interests and concerns of primarily white, middle, and upper-middle class, cisheterosexual women. In essence, Lisa is situated as an exceptional woman who succeeds in a man's world because of individual merit and hard work—suggesting that any woman can advance accordingly in any field. Of course, this logic of inclusion into oppressive systems sustains their validity and even more perniciously conceals the existence of these structures and their profound impacts on women's life chances writ large.

Moreover, Lisa typifies hegemonic femininity, which dovetails well with neoliberal feminist tenets and representations. Hamilton et al. identify the affordances of hegemonic femininity with Patricia Hill Collins' intersectional conceptualization of the matrix of domination: "Performances of hegemonic femininities are motivated, whether intentionally or not, by the pursuit of a *femininity premium*—a set of individual benefits that accrue to those who can approximate these ideals . . . White, affluent, heterosexual women are typically best positioned to collect a femininity premium."[13] Although Lisa presents as working class in the series, it is noteworthy that in the still photographs discussed previously, she passes as middle class—aligning even more closely with feminine ideals. Regardless of her attire while driving, her conventional attractiveness allows her to maintain the "femininity premium" required for entry into a male homosocial space. Additionally, because the job itself is a more solitary endeavor, especially as compared to working on a crab boat or in a mining crew, the male homosocial space of ice road trucking is comparatively siloed. In short, Lisa's presence may not have been as well tolerated if she were working in a more collaborative dangerous job with all men.

I contend that, in contrast to Lisa, a woman driver briefly featured in the first season, Karen McDougal, does not receive top billing or a developed story line because she falls short of attaining the femininity premium. In Season One: Episode Four: "The Big Chill," Thom Beers notes that she is one of the few women drivers on the winter ice roads. As Karen is shown driving her truck, the viewer can see that she is white, middle-aged, and sports long, blonde dreadlocks. Unlike Lisa, Karen does not embody ideal beauty standards. As she is driving, Karen discusses the challenges of being away from her home and children for more than two months during the driving season: "I do have a son at home, and I'm gonna be out here. I'm gonna miss his 16th birthday . . . I'm probably gonna have a crappy day that day."[14] Karen's personal story of sacrifice, especially as one of the only women who works this job, is compelling and full of narrative potential. Many of the male drivers on the show have children as well, but according to the dominant and highly asymmetrical gendered expectations of parenthood, a mother being away from her children is considered far less palatable. The show does not provide more details about Karen's circumstances, so the viewer does not get a sense of the conditions that brought her to this juncture. Karen attests to the notoriety she received shortly after her arrival on the ice roads: "I was out here for, like, two days, and everybody knew my name. They don't see a lot of women out here, and they don't see a lot of dreadlocks."[15] Despite Karen's exceptional story, this is the last the viewer sees of her. I assert that because Karen does not possess the femininity premium required to satisfy the male gaze of the target audience, her presence is too threatening to the masculine hegemony of the blue-collar frontier milieu. Only women who can do the job while looking the part, like Lisa, are endorsed.

In *Ax Men* Season Four: Episode One: "Alaska," the series introduces Leah Proctor, a woman logger, who looks to be in her twenties, to Pihl logging company. Although Leah does not become a prominently featured cast member, she does closely approximate feminine beauty ideals commensurate with the femininity premium. Before owner Mike Pihl introduces her to the crew, Thom Beers narrates that " . . . Mike is trying something few logging crews would dare."[16] As Leah approaches the crew, the men look stunned. Mike instructs them to " . . . just give her a handshake like she's a man, yeah."[17] In a cutaway interview, Leah expresses her concerns about joining an all-male logging crew: "I definitely had a lot of anxiety about coming out today. Hopefully the guys will take me in and not judge me for being a girl."[18] Leah has experience as a wild land firefighter, but despite her credentials, her gender is instantly perceived as a limitation.

One of her fellow loggers, Stacey Robeson, expresses his reservations and doubts about her ability to do the job of setting chokers on logs that need to be pulled uphill: "I've never worked around a girl setting chokers. I don't know. They're gonna send some little 5-foot-nothing girl out here who might weigh 100 pounds. It'll be something to watch anyway."[19] His last statement signals the rationale behind her introduction—producing narrative tension. Introducing hegemonically feminine women into male homosocial spaces is a reliable device for achieving this aim. It is noteworthy that Stacey refers to Leah as a "girl" and not a woman. Referring to women by this more infantilizing designation evidences the patriarchy's pervasive impact on everyday discourse. It becomes apparent immediately that Leah's gender precludes her from equal status within the crew when Mike tells his crew explicitly to "treat her with respect."[20] She ends up performing quite well, but always under the added pressure that if she makes a mistake, it will be attributed directly to her gender. Mike explains his rationale for hiring her toward the end of the episode: "You know, logging is somewhat of a man's world. It's just never anything we considered, hiring a woman . . . Actually, looks like Leah's doing great. She's getting around like a deer, keeping up with Stacey."[21] Mike seems surprised by her job performance and reinforces the notion that logging is intrinsically a man's job. Once could safely surmise that the idea of hiring a woman originated with show producers as a plot device, since Mike indicates it was something he had never thought of previously. Even when women perform these highly masculinized jobs well, they are never fully accepted or framed as truly belonging in that sphere because they are viewed as intruding upon men's rightful territory.

In Season Three: Episode Three: "Secret Weapons," *Gold Rush* introduces a woman miner for the first time who is working for "Dakota" Fred Hurt's mining operation. Christie provides some background in his narrative introduction: "Melody Tallis, a rodeo rider from Arizona, has been gold-mining for the last four years."[22] Melody appears middle-aged and has blonde hair. Youthful appearance is integral to feminine standards of beauty, which explains why Lisa and Maya of *Ice Road Truckers*, who are in their twenties, receive comparatively more attention within that series. The show reveals that Fred, who appears to be in his sixties, hired her, much to the dismay of his son Dustin, who looks middle-aged as well. Dustin complains about his father brining in Melody: "I wasn't expecting a woman. I really wanted a big strong guy to do all the lifting for me or help me with the lifting. But now, what I get is a little woman."[23] Fred dismisses his son's concerns and then tellingly remarks upon Melody's appearance: "Dustin's worrisome about having a woman on the job and not a bad-looking one at that."[24] Fred's comments reveal the extent to which women's physical appearances are always given primacy. Additionally, because Melody does not fully embody ideal standards of beauty—the complete femininity premium—the show does not feature her prominently or give her much of a storyline. Her introduction into a male homosocial space only suffices to spur some short-lived narrative tension, as women are always interpreted as trespassing on men's territory, irrespective of their appearances—a discernable pattern across the series under examination.

CONCLUSION

Regardless of their appearances, there remains an underlying hostility toward women who dare to enter and challenge male dominance in homosocial spaces. The small number of women introduced into the realm of the blue-collar frontier are done so in service of a narrative gimmick, in which only women who emblematically satiate heteropatriarchal male visual pleasure, like Lisa from *Ice Road Truckers*, are tolerated to the extent that they do not threaten masculine dominance. The blue-collar frontier shows touch upon a wider sociopolitical current of male resentment toward women's presence in the workforce, in which they are scapegoated for neoliberal capitalism's shocks to the male-dominated and formerly high-paying (and unionized) manufacturing sphere. As noted in the first chapter, when women enter an occupation in significant numbers and it resultantly becomes "feminized" in the public consciousness, the pay drops for all workers in that sector regardless of gender. Since the Great Recession, one of the primary sectors that experienced growth was the highly precarious and low-paying service industry—although this sector has notably suffered significant employment losses because of the pandemic and the emergence of "The Great Resignation."[25] Regardless, as Claire Caine Miller posits regarding the pattern of wage regression in feminized occupations: "Work done by women simply isn't valued as highly."[26] Thus, the men on these series vocally protesting and resisting the entry of women into their homosocial work environments may also stem from a patriarchal fear that the presence of women will devalue their jobs writ large.

Per Kimmel's findings in *Angry White Men*, one can see how Trump's antifeminist and misogynistic rhetoric resonated with perceptions that women's apparent gains in the workforce were the primary driver of middle and working-class men's economic suffering since the Great Recession. Although the shows under examination take a lighthearted and arguably neoliberal feminist approach to their depiction of the handful of women therein, it reifies the following hegemonic perceptions: occupations are either inherently masculine or feminine; barriers to women's advancement in the workplace are superficial and can be transcended by the "right kind of woman"; and women are only granted conditional entry into male homosocial spaces if they exemplify hegemonic femininity and satisfy the male gaze.

In the next chapter, I explicate the critical role of place within these series, as frontier mythology remains deeply entwined with hegemonic masculinity and capitalism.

NOTES

1. John Berger, *Ways of Seeing* (London and New York: Penguin Books, 1977), 47.

2. *Ice Road Truckers*, Image of Lisa Kelly, *Original Productions* for *History Channel*, https://m.media-amazon.com/images/I/4185i25ebZL._AC_.jpg.

3. John Berger, *Ways of Seeing* (London and New York: Penguin Books, 1977), 47.

4. *Ice Road Truckers*, Image of Lisa Kelly, *Original Productions* for *History Channel*, https://i.pinimg.com/474x/15/ac/f3/15acf320e4523cf32d1514ae0d8398bc--cool -trucks-sexy-trucks.jpg.

5. *Ice Road Truckers*, season 3, episode 6, "Arctic Ice," narrated by Thom Beers, aired July 5, 2009, *Original Productions* for *History Channel*.

6. *Ice Road Truckers*, season 3, episode 6, "Arctic Ice."

7. Rachel E. Dubrofsky and Megan M. Wood, "Posting Racism and Sexism: Authenticity, Agency and Self-Reflexivity in Social Media," *Communication and Critical/Cultural Studies* 11, no. 3 (2014): 283.

8. *Ice Road Truckers*, season 3, episode 2, "Rookie Run," narrated by Thom Beers, aired June 7, 2009, *Original Productions* for *History Channel*.

9. *Ice Road Truckers*, season 7, episode 1, "Collision Course," narrated by Thom Beers, aired June 9, 2013, *Original Productions* for *History Channel*.

10. *Ice Road Truckers*, season 7, episode 1, "Collision Course."

11. Ibid.

12. Catherine Rottenberg, "How Neoliberalism Colonised Feminism—and What You Can Do about It," *The Conversation*, May 23, 2018, https://theconversation.com /how-neoliberalism-colonised-feminism-and-what-you-can-do-about-it-94856.

13. Laura T. Hamilton, Elizabeth A. Armstrong, J. Lotus Seeley, and Elizabeth M Armstrong, "Hegemonic Femininities and Intersectional Domination," *Sociological Theory* 37, no. 4 (2019): 316.

14. *Ice Road Truckers*, season 1, episode 4, "The Big Chill," narrated by Thom Beers, aired July 8, 2007, *Original Productions* for *History Channel*.

15. *Ice Road Truckers*, season 1, episode 4, "The Big Chill."

16. *Ax Men*, season 4, episode 1, "Alaska," narrated by Thom Beers, aired December 12, 2010, *Original Productions* for *History Channel*.

17. *Ax Men*, season 4, episode 1, "Alaska."

18. Ibid.

19. Ibid.

20. Ibid.

21. Ibid.

22. *Gold Rush*, season 3, episode 3, "Secret Weapons," narrated by Paul Christie, aired November 9, 2012, *Raw TV* for *Discovery Channel*.

23. *Gold Rush*, season 3, episode 3, "Secret Weapons."

24. Ibid.

25. Bryan Lufkin, "What We're Getting Wrong about the 'Great Resignation,'" *BBC*, October 28, 2021, https://www.bbc.com/worklife/article/20211028-what-were -getting-wrong-about-the-great-resignation.

26. Claire Cain Miller, "As Women Take Over a Male-Dominated Field, the Pay Drops," *New York Times*, March 18, 2016, https://www.nytimes.com/2016/03/20/ upshot/as-women-take-over-a-male-dominated-field-the-pay-drops.html?_r=0.

Chapter Three

"Real Men" Work in "Real America"

A crucial component of the popular appeal and commercial success of the blue-collar frontier shows is that they reinvigorate frontier mythology in the United States. The series under examination, including *Deadliest Catch*, *Ice Road Truckers*, *Ax Men*, and *Gold Rush*, are filmed primarily in rural, wilderness settings in the northwestern continental United States, Alaska, and northwestern Canada. Only *Duck Dynasty* is filmed exclusively in the southern United States, specifically rural and suburban Louisiana, where the Robertson men are portrayed as asserting their masculine prowess via their outdoor recreational activities, including hunting and fishing. As I detail in chapter four, *Duck Dynasty* functions as an exception within this sample of American reality television because its approximately 22-minute narratives align more with domestic, family sitcoms than the roughly 44-minute episodes of *Deadliest Catch*, *Ice Road Truckers*, *Ax Men*, and *Gold Rush*, which more closely resemble workplace dramas. Additionally, because *Duck Dynasty* gives primacy to heteronormative, nuclear family structures, in which traditional U.S. gender roles are policed within the show's overarching narrative, the viewer sees more women present than in the other series. The presence of women within this stereotypically patriarchal purview necessitates their depiction in the home, whereas the other programs focus exclusively on men in the workplace. In addition, the Robertsons are also far wealthier than their blue-collar frontier counterparts, and I explicate the symbolic capital their white, rural, working-class, masculine performance confers in the contemporary U.S. neoliberal context in the fourth chapter.

Through the lens of the blue-collar frontier shows in their entirety, the role of place, specifically the frontier, remains integral to understanding the parameters of hegemonic masculinity, white supremacy therein, and its connection to two of the most deeply embedded myths in U.S. culture: rugged individualism and U.S. exceptionalism. These mythologies function to both ideologically justify and obscure social inequities, in which the latter specifically validates U.S. settler-colonialism and imperialism both past and present. The role of place in relation to hegemonic masculinity and its intersections with race and social class, as they pertain to rugged individualism, constitutes a critical linkage that needs to be teased out within an intersectional media studies framework. Additionally, I assert that this renewed emphasis on white male narratives of survival on the frontier speaks to the increased circulation of perniciously false and unfounded threats to white male "survival" as a social group since 2016.

For the purposes of conceptual clarity, I must delineate how I am operationalizing myth/mythology and ideology before proceeding with this analysis, as there is significant overlap between the two concepts. First, Stuart Hall defines ideology as a "way of representing the order of things which endowed its limiting perspectives with that natural or divine inevitability which makes them appear universal, natural, and coterminous with 'reality' itself."[1] Thus, the systems of power embedded within the portrayals of "real men" on the blue-collar frontier shows go largely unnoticed and unquestioned because they appear "real" and "natural." This definition is particularly relevant to reality television, which is highly constructed and mediated, but has the appearance of capturing people "as they are."

Because there is no singular definition of ideology, I further complement Hall's understanding with John Storey's characterization of ideology specifically in relation to media forms: " . . . texts (television fiction, pop songs, novels, feature films, etc.) always present a particular image of the world . . . of society as conflictual rather than consensual, structured around inequality, exploitation, and oppression. Texts are said to take sides, consciously or unconsciously, in this conflict."[2] I proceed from the premise that the blue-collar frontier shows are taking sides ideologically with their perpetuation of frontier mythology and the systems of power inscribed therein. I think it is accurate to suggest that the creators of these programs, such as Thom Beers, take sides unconsciously. Regardless, the cumulative effects of the continued circulation of the interlocking racial, gendered, classed, and colonial ideologies embedded in these programs must be made visible.

Mythology is related to ideology, but some critical distinctions need to be outlined. Paul M. Gaston describes myths as "combinations of images and symbols that reflect a people's way of perceiving the truth. Organically related to a fundamental reality of life, *they fuse the real and the imaginary* [emphasis added] into a blend that becomes a reality itself, a force in history."[3] Gaston's definition informs this analysis regarding the interconnected mythologies under scrutiny here: the frontier ethos, rugged individualism, and U.S. exceptionalism. These myths are imagined and constructed, but have generated real, material consequences. Additionally, it is widely disseminated and accepted in the United States that these myths are true, and thus, they underpin dominant notions of America's collective identity. Therefore, unlike ideology, myths are typically highly valued and venerated within a given cultural context.

Richard Slotkin also offers a critical distinction between ideology and myth in *Gunfighter Nation*: *The Myth of the Frontier in Twentieth Century America*, which is highly pertinent herein. Slotkin refers to ideology as "the basic system of concepts, beliefs, and values that defines a society's way of interpreting its place in the cosmos and the meaning of its history."[4] He explains that a "myth expresses ideology in a narrative, rather than discursive or argumentative, structure."[5] Therefore, I view the blue-collar frontier shows as retelling frontier myths within the narrative structure of reality television, which ideologically reinforces heteropatriarchal, white supremacist, and colonial logics in naturalized and seemingly undetectable ways. Slotkin also acknowledges the critical place of mass media within the circulation of dominant mythologies: "The mythology produced by mass or commercial media has a particular role and function in a cultural system that remains complex and heterodox. It is the form of cultural production that addresses most directly the concerns of Americans as citizens of a nation-state."[6] As I discuss at length in the first chapter and will touch upon again shortly, the Great Recession played a significant role in the resurgence of the frontier myth on reality television, as frontier mythology reifies U.S. exceptionalism, rugged individualism, and white male supremacy. The widespread economic precarity engendered by neoliberal capitalism and the Great Recession, as well as the social advancements made by women and people of color in recent years, signaled that there were substantial challenges to the hegemony of these myths and the power structures underpinning them in the United States.

For example, in the pilot episode of *Gold Rush*, Todd Hoffman explains that he and his father are responding to their economic misfortune by heading up to Alaska to mine for gold. Todd invokes frontier mythology to justify his decision: "So, like my forefathers—they balls-ed up, and they went out into the frontier."[7] Were Todd's literal forefathers "pioneers" who went westward as incentivized by the U.S. federal government? Whether he is a direct descendant of those who made that journey or not, it is significant that he conceives of himself as a rightful heir to that highly venerated U.S. mythology. As a white male who owned an airfield in Oregon with his father Jack that was hit hard by the 2008 economic downturn, Hoffman wants to convey that he is reacting to his circumstances as he ought to be. He overtly connects the frontier ethos to masculine prowess, and the whiteness of his forefathers remains implicit and unremarked upon, as whiteness often is the dominant discourse.

84   *Chapter Three*

Todd does not simply state that he and his father are taking an economic gamble by travelling up to Alaska to mine for gold; he essentially declares that he is exercising his birthright (as a white male) by going "out into the frontier." It is also significant that the Hoffmans have a substantial amount of economic capital—hundreds of thousands of dollars to purchase high-powered machinery and supplies—which enables them to even attempt their mining expedition in the first place. Are they enduring precarious economic times? Certainly. However, the Hoffmans and their white, male crew's structural location is comparatively advantaged within the working-class assemblage overall. As I discuss later in the chapter, the socioeconomic status of the mythical frontiersman necessitates further scrutiny.

This leads to an important clarification regarding frontier mythology: What and where exactly is the frontier? As Richard Drinnon notes, "The West was quite literally nowhere—or everywhere, which was to say the same thing."[8] This echoes Gaston's parameters of myths in the sense that "they fuse the real and the imaginary."[9] Within frontier mythology, the frontier is in "the West," which throughout U.S. history, can be charted as a relative geographic destination. The series under examination are filmed in the following locations, which vary occasionally throughout their multiple seasons: *Deadliest Catch* follows commercial fishermen on the Bering Sea off the coast of Alaska; *Ax Men* features commercial loggers in the forests of Oregon, Montana, Alaska, and other locations in the Western United States, as well as swamp and river loggers in Louisiana and Florida; *Ice Road Truckers* documents commercial truck drivers traversing the winter seasonal ice roads in mostly Northwestern Canada and Alaska; *Gold Rush* depicts gold miners in Alaska and the Yukon, but also follows the Hoffman crew down to the jungles of Guyana for one season; and *Duck Dynasty*'s wilderness locations include the woods and swamps of Louisiana. Although these series primarily take place in the Western portions of the United States and Canada, all filming occurs in relatively remote wilderness settings, in which the elements themselves provide the backdrop for the overarching narrative of white men demonstrating their masculine prowess as they "tame the wilderness" through their occupations (or in the case of *Duck Dynasty*, through their recreational activities). It is the element of danger that nature itself poses that signal to audiences that these are not just workers, but "real men."

Therefore, I conceive of the frontier in this analysis as an actual geographic terrain, primarily confined, but not limited to, western North America, characterized by remote, unindustrialized, and sparsely populated natural landscapes, including forests, swamps, and large bodies of water. Simultaneously, I conceptualize the frontier in relation to its mythological function as a "spatial imaginary." More specifically, I describe the frontier as a "white, heteropatriarchal male spatial imaginary." I am building upon critical race scholar George Lipsitz's theorization of "the white spatial imaginary" in *How Racism Takes Place*, which speaks to the relationship between white supremacy and place.

Lipsitz's conceptualization of the "white spatial imaginary" is in conversation with critical race theorist Cheryl Harris's formulation of "whiteness as property," which is also useful for this analysis. Harris argues that " . . . American law has recognized a property interest in whiteness that, although unacknowledged, now forms the background against which legal disputes are framed, argued, and adjudicated."[10] She astutely grounds the metaphor of whiteness as property in relation to the history of the restriction of full property rights to whites in the United States since the nation's inception. She traces a critical genealogy of the social construction of race, in which the conflation of whiteness and property underpinned white supremacy, particularly in relation to the enslavement of Black Americans *as* property and the dispossession of indigenous peoples from their lands. She characterizes whiteness as a form of property interest in that " . . . the law has accorded 'holders' of whiteness the same privileges and benefits accorded holders of other types of property."[11] Harris recognizes how whiteness functions as a linchpin to full citizenship and individuality: " . . . whiteness became the quintessential property for personhood."[12] Frontier mythology propagates the notion that the frontier exists as an empty terrain awaiting the settlement of whites, specifically white males. Thus, the frontier is a place reserved *for* white males.

Lipsitz explicates how places are always already racialized: "White identity in the United States is place bound. It exists and persists because segregated neighborhoods and segregated schools are nodes in a network of practices that skew opportunities and life chances along racial lines."[13] His analysis primarily focuses on the racialized spaces of cities and suburbs. He characterizes the white spatial imaginary as representing " . . . the properly gendered prosperous suburban home as the privileged moral geography of the nation. Widespread, costly, and often counterproductive practices of surveillance, regulation, and incarceration become justified as forms of *frontier defense* [emphasis added] against demonized people of color."[14] The literal and figurative fortification of both the suburban home and the frontier is premised upon the white supremacist notion that only white people are *worthy* of inhabiting those spaces. The white spatial imaginaries of the suburban home and the frontier are cast as race-neutral terrains, in which the systemic advantages of whiteness remain concealed through mythic discourses of individual hard work and upward social mobility.

Particularly germane to this project is how Lipsitz draws a line of continuity between the contemporary white spatial imaginary of the suburban home and the eighteenth and nineteenth-century dominant conceptualization of the frontier. He puts forth the notion that the U.S. colonial desire for "pure

86 *Chapter Three*

and homogenous spaces"—deemed integral for the U.S. nation-building project—necessitated the removal and marginalization of "'impure' populations."[15] He explains that because the colonial march westward ultimately fell short of the imagined vision of (white male supremacist) freedom that " . . . the properly ordered and prosperous domestic dwelling eclipsed the frontier as the privileged moral geography of U.S. society, as the nation's key symbol of freedom, harmony, and virtue."[16] I argue that the blue-collar frontier shows represent a revival of the frontier as the preferred white spatial imaginary in contemporary U.S. society because of its connection to hegemonic masculinity. In the dominant discourse, the suburban home signifies white femininity and domesticity; a place where "real men" are constrained by a culture attempting to neutralize their masculine impulse to tame the wilderness.

Consequently, the frontier itself within frontier mythology functions as both a geographically tangible place *and* a white, heteropatriarchal male spatial imaginary. It is the latter conceptualization that is of utmost relevance to the visuality of the blue-collar frontier shows and understanding the systems of power congealed within their production and reception. As I will explain, U. S. historian Frederick Jackson Turner's "frontier thesis" constitutes the ideological basis of frontier mythology. Turner views the frontier as an indispensable aspect of the social and cultural fabric of the United States, and claims it is the linchpin for U.S. exceptionalism. Moving forward, I refer to the frontier, rugged individualism, and U.S. exceptionalism as fundamentally interrelated myths, and to white supremacy, heteropatriarchy, capitalism, and settler-colonialism as the mutually constitutive ideological systems of oppression that underpin said myths.

In this chapter, I explore and historicize the presence of frontier mythology in the contemporary U.S. cultural context through the lens of the blue-collar frontier shows. What cultural legacy do the remote, wilderness filming locations of these series tap into with U.S. audiences? I trace the origins of the frontier myth to U.S. historian Frederick Jackson Turner's landmark thesis, "The Significance of the Frontier in American History," which Turner delivered at the 1893 meeting of the American Historical Association in Chicago. I contend that the frontier thesis ideologically underpins the contemporary frontier ethos, which is predicated upon the erasure and *ongoing* colonization of North America's indigenous nations. It remains noteworthy that one of the most renowned U.S. historians of the last two centuries cites U.S. colonial expansion westward as fundamental to the preservation of what he refers to as the exceptional "American character."[17] Therefore, this chapter not only aims to make the intertwined systems of power of settler-colonialism, heteropatriarchy, capitalism, and white supremacy visible within the context of current mainstream media representations, but to also do so within the confines of orthodox U.S. historiography.

First, I will discuss Turner's legacy within frontier mythology and "the Western" film and television genre. I contend that the series under examination signify a contemporary iteration of "the Western" narrative. Although the blue-collar frontier shows do not strictly adhere to all the conventions typically associated with the Western, they echo critical aspects of this distinctly American genre. Why are the narratives typically associated with this genre experiencing a cultural resurgence, albeit in a slightly different iteration, in the past two decades? I argue that the Great Recession spurred the production and popularity of these series in conjunction with the white male backlash to the modest social gains made by women, people of color, LGBTQ communities, and those living at those intersections. This constellation of events has generated significant anxiety and anger among working and middle-class white, cisheterosexual men and parallels the successful rise of President Donald Trump, which I discuss in greater detail in the first and fourth chapters. The blue-collar frontier shows revive frontier mythology, which is commensurate with white male supremacy and U.S. exceptionalism, in the same spirit as Trump's 2016 campaign slogan: "Make America Great Again."

Second, I assert that indigenous critical theory is essential for understanding how frontier mythology, Westerns, and the blue-collar frontier shows by extension reify settler-colonial logics and the erasure of North America's indigenous peoples given the dominant conceptualization of the frontier as an empty or uninhabited wilderness. Although some Westerns include conflict with Native Americans as a prominent component of their narratives, the blue-collar frontier shows make no explicit reference to indigenous peoples. It is only through the lens of indigenous critical theory that one can discern how the blue-collar frontier shows reinscribe the ideological justification for the *continuing* colonization of indigenous nations and their lands. Lastly, after laying the theoretical foundations for unmasking the systems of power that ideologically buttress the frontier ethos as exemplified through the blue-collar frontier shows, I will then detail how *Gold Rush*, *Ax Men*, *Ice Road Truckers*, and *Deadliest Catch* specifically evoke frontier mythology within their narratives and visuality. I contend that uncovering the systems of power entrenched within frontier mythology is a critical first step toward destabilizing the oppressive ideologies contained therein and, ultimately, delegitimizing and transforming them.

"THE ARCHETYPICAL AMERICAN STORY"

In his groundbreaking piece, "Encoding and Decoding in the Television Discourse," Stuart Hall explores the salience of the frontier in U.S. culture, particularly through the lens of "The Western" film and television genre.

88   *Chapter Three*

Hall fleshes out the relationship between the historic "American West" and the mythical one that has become embedded in U.S. culture. He explains that "this process, whereby the rules of language and discourse intervene, at a certain moment, to transform and 'naturalize' a specific set of historical circumstances, is one of the most important test-cases for any semiology which seeks to ground itself in historical realities."[18] This project situates the blue-collar frontier shows as operating within some of the dominant codes of The Western. Hall pinpoints this contemporary genre, with its distortion of U.S history, as perpetuating one of the most consequential mythologies in U.S. culture: "This is *the* archetypical American story, America of the frontier, of the expanding and unsettled West . . . It is the land of *men*, of independent men . . . for a time, in film and television, this deep-structure provided the taken-for-granted story-of-all-stories, the paradigm-action narrative, the perfect myth."[19] These reality television programs can be situated within the lineage of the Western, frontier myth, in which the intertwined systems of power of white supremacy, heteropatriarchy, settler-colonialism, and capitalism, and their resultant symbolic and material violence, remain hidden.

Before I outline the genre conventions that the blue-collar frontier shows share with the Western, I want to stress that I am not offering an exhaustive description of tropes endemic to this category of film and television—only the characteristics most germane to the series under examination. Richard Slotkin attests to the extensive influence of frontier mythology on U.S. media and popular culture in his own analysis: " . . . its characteristic conventions have strongly influenced nearly every genre of adventure story in the lexicon of mass-culture production . . . I have chosen, therefore, to limit this study to the genres that may be described as 'Westerns': story-forms whose connection to the characteristic images, characters, and references of frontier mythology is observably direct."[20] This analysis echoes Slotkin's observation, and I argue that like Westerns, the blue-collar frontier shows are highly instructive for directly observing frontier mythology produced in the contemporary, neoliberal context.

In *Riding the Video Range: The Rise and Fall of the Western on Television*, Gary A. Yoggy provides a detailed analysis of the history of the genre on television. Yoggy defines the Western as follows: "Time *and* place are both important criteria. A program should be considered a Western if it takes place west of the Mississippi *after* 1900, or east of the Mississippi prior to 1800."[21] It is critical to note that the blue-collar frontier series take place within the past two decades, but most episodes are filmed west of the Mississippi, with the exception of some episodes of *Ax Men* featuring river loggers in Florida. Either way, the remote, wilderness settings remain a constant. In *The Western: Parables of the American Dream*, Jeffrey Wallmann offers a more expansive definition of Westerns, which aligns more closely with the blue-collar frontier shows: "Because the frontier serves as the symbolic 'cutting edge' of American civilization and progress, there is no specific region or time period, and consequently there are westerns set on the Canadian frontier, the Alaskan frontier . . . westerns are adventures."[22]

It is this understanding of the Western that most aptly frames the emergence and popularity of the blue-collar frontier shows in the past decade: They depict "real men" who within frontier mythology are depicted in their rightful place on the "'cutting edge' of American civilization and progress." Thus, the cultural and symbolic power of the frontier for reasserting U.S. exceptionalism, rugged individualism, and white male supremacy. As Wallmann concisely states, " . . . westerns are fundamentally allegories of the American dream."[23] Therefore, when the American dream of upward economic mobility comes under more widespread duress and scrutiny because of the worst global economic downturn since the Great Depression, a reinvigoration of frontier mythology within the commercial television landscape aids in reaffirming the viability of those entwined myths within the U.S. context.

As John E. O'Connor and Peter C. Rollins note in *Hollywood's West: The American Frontier in Film, Television, and History*, "Contemporary politics clearly affect the construction of Westerns . . . "[24] The blue-collar frontier shows provide a space where "real men" or white, rural, working-class men can be reified as the rightful purveyors of rugged individualism on the frontier at a time when their socioeconomic and cultural status has come under increasing external pressure and scrutiny. In short, these white males are configured as the standard bearers of the American dream itself. As Wallmann notes regarding the mythology of Westerns, "Only the strong were able to survive."[25] The blue-collar frontier series configure their subjects as paragons of survival and manliness at the expense of those who fall outside of the social categories that define the frontiersman.

In *Westerns in a Changing America, 1955–2000*, R. Philip Loy addresses the wider cultural significance of the popular perception of John Wayne, a landmark figure for the performance of white, rural, working-class masculinity in the Western film genre, particularly during the sociocultural upheaval of the 1960s and 70s. I argue that Loy's characterization of Wayne's impact parallels the cultural significance of the frontiersmen of the blue-collar frontier world since the late 2000s: "The notion that John Wayne came to be identified as *the* American at that moment in American history (when many Americans believed that the country they loved was passing away) is seminally important for understanding Wayne's impact on the country during the last twenty years that he lived."[26] It is telling that Loy largely omits the integral role of white male supremacy within the dominant perception of Wayne as "*the* American" at a time when struggles for justice for women, people of color, and LGBTQ individuals were gaining more traction in mainstream U.S.

90   *Chapter Three*

political and popular culture. I contend that the frontiersmen of the blue-collar frontier shows are perceived similarly as "*the* Americans." I argue that the like Westerns, these series reaffirm frontier mythology, which concurrently conceals and justifies white male supremacy as the linchpin to ideal U.S. citizenship and belonging.

Interestingly, Yoggy's discussion of the 1955 Western anthology series, *Frontier*, touches upon some of the common threads within the series in this sample: "Realism was stressed and most plots portrayed settlers coping with the harsh environment . . . Although *Frontier* stressed human emotions and psychological influences, rather than gun duels and chases, it did not lack for action."[27] The primary action of the blue-collar frontier shows centers on white, male characters as they "tame the wilderness" via their occupations, in which the specter of bodily injury remains an indispensable component of the plot. Realism, as with all reality television programming, is emphasized as well, regardless of its genuine verisimilitude. Wallmann reiterates that " . . . westerns are considered to be adventure stories, set on a frontier, about personal character striving to overcome perilous circumstances."[28]

As Thom Beers, who serves as producer for *Deadliest Catch, Ax Men*, and *Ice Road Truckers*, as well as the narrator for the latter two series, remarks about his now cancelled series *Coal,* "It's a great, epic man-against-nature story."[29] This characterization applies to all of Beers' series under examination here. Unlike many conventional Westerns, the blue-collar frontier programs align more stylistically with series like *Frontier*, in which gun battles and conflicts between "cowboys and Indians" do not transpire. As I discuss later, cowboy references do appear within these series—solidifying the association between the Western and contemporary U.S. hegemonic masculinity. As always, the threat of violence, due to the natural elements and the operation of heavy machinery in the case of the blue-collar frontier programs, is a prominent feature within the Western and its underlying frontier mythos. For the frontiersman to be a "true man," he must expose himself to danger and violence in the wilderness.

Slotkin charts the popularity of the Western throughout the nineteenth and twentieth centuries. He notes that despite the genre waning in overall popularity at certain points, its overriding ideological power remains endemic to U.S. culture: "The displacement of the Western from its place on the genre map did not entail the disappearance of those underlying structures of myth and ideology that had given the genre its cultural force."[30] The popularity and proliferation of the blue-collar frontier shows gestures toward the sustainability of frontier mythology as a cultural force in the United States. Although some purists would scoff at the suggestion that this subgenre of reality television programming constitutes an iteration of the Western, I maintain that its core premises and ideological bases fall within the narrative parameters of the genre.

The essence of frontier mythology within the Western remains intact in *Ax Men, Gold Rush, Ice Road Truckers*, and *Deadliest Catch*. With the understanding that blue-collar frontier series can be traced back to the Western film and television genre, I must turn to the foundational ideology that underpins the Western, frontier myth and its counterparts of rugged individualism and U.S. exceptionalism: Turner's "frontier thesis."

TURNER AND TEDDY'S TALES OF "REAL MEN" TAMING THE WILDERNESS

Turner's frontier thesis is encapsulated within this excerpt from his 1893 address: "American social development has been continually beginning over again on the frontier. This perennial rebirth, the fluidity of American life, this expansion westward with its new opportunities, its continuous touch with the simplicity of *primitive society* [emphasis added], furnish the forces dominating American character. The true point of view in the history of this nation is not the Atlantic Coast, it is the Great West."[31] With the U.S. Census of 1890 announcing the "closure" of the frontier, Turner warns that this will foster a crisis for the maintenance of the supposedly unique American character—invoking discourses of U.S. exceptionalism. He broadly conceives of (white male) U.S. identity as being continually reified through "westward expansion." This term diminishes the brutal reality of the settler-colonization and genocide of indigenous peoples throughout U.S. history. He believes U.S. culture is preserved through the rugged individualism and egalitarian ethos supposedly endemic to frontier life. His visuality of an "empty frontier" that erases the presence of the indigenous peoples of the United States imposes symbolic violence upon them, which contributes to and justifies the *actual* violence of settler-colonialism. Contemporary references to the frontier, including on the blue-collar frontier shows, demonstrate the symbolic power and legacy of frontier mythology, in which its historical and ongoing repercussions are rendered invisible.

Turner's conceptualization of the frontier, which has become the dominant one in U.S. culture, not only erases indigenous peoples, but also naturalizes the presence of white males therein. Although Turner does not specify that the frontiersman is white, whiteness often operates as the "default" race and typically remains unmentioned. It is evident that Turner is referring specifically to white men when he refers to individuals, as is typically the case in the dominant U.S. discourse—individuality tends to be discursively reserved for white men. As he notes in relation to the frontiersmen's class status: "Engaged in a struggle to subdue the forest, working as an individual, and with little specie or capital, his interests were with the debtor class."[32] It is noteworthy that Turner characterizes the mythical frontiersman as "working as an individual." This speaks directly to the blue-collar frontier shows, which frame their working-class, white male subjects as rugged individuals conquering the wilderness. Furthermore, the blue-collar frontier shows remain largely consistent with Turner's understanding that the frontiersman's "interests were with the debtor class." However, both Turner and these series present frontiersmen as generally unrestrained by their socioeconomic location.

Turner's brief acknowledgment of the existence of a class system belies his overriding assertion that rugged individualism and upward mobility thrive via an endlessly expanding frontier: "The self-made man was the Western man's ideal, was the kind of man that all men might become. Out of his wilderness experience, out of the freedom of his opportunities, he fashioned a formula for social regeneration—the freedom of the individual to seek his own."[33] He configures the frontier as an empty wilderness awaiting white frontiersmen to advance their individual social standing, which he theorizes also advances the United States as a nation-state. Per Turner, " . . . the frontier is productive of individualism . . . The frontier individualism has from the beginning promoted democracy."[34] He conceives of the frontiersmen as the linchpin to U.S. democracy, despite his thesis being predicated upon the erasure of indigenous peoples and the subordination of all those who fall outside of the intersecting social categories that comprise the social location of the frontiersman. He demarcates white males as the universalizing individual persons to whom the frontier belongs. The role of place in relation to hegemonic masculinity cannot be overstated, as well as Turner's notion that U.S. exceptionalism itself depends upon frontiersmen.

Turner offers his assessment regarding the significance of the settling (colonizing) of the frontier within the wider U.S. nation-building project: "And to study this advance, the men who grew up under these conditions, and the political, economic, and social results of it, is to study the really American part of our history."[35] In other words, "real men" forged "the really American part of our history." The blue-collar frontier shows represent a contemporary manifestation of Turner's imperial, white supremacist, heteropatriarchal logic, which inextricably links the visualities of the frontier, "real men," and hegemonic notions of U.S. national identity. Again, the Western, frontier myth has become so commonplace and normalized within U.S. culture that upon engaging in dominant readings of these series, the legacies of the systems of oppression imbued in them remain invisible. Slotkin characterizes the essence of Turner's frontier mythology. He explicitly comments on the role of race therein but does not note the normalization of patriarchy in conjunction with white supremacy. However, he does touch upon some of the parallel dichotomies that shape the frontier ethos: "The moral landscape of the Frontier Myth is divided by significant borders, of which the wilderness/civilization, Indian/White border is the most basic. The American must cross the border into 'Indian Country' and experience a 'regression' to a more primitive and natural condition of life so that the false values of the 'metropolis' can be purged and a new, purified social contract enacted."[36]

In the blue-collar frontier series, the wilderness functions as the primary antagonist, and Native Americans are absent, or more accurately, remain outside of the observable frame of these series. Despite this, the frontier myth, no matter its iteration, is always already predicated upon the erasure of indigenous peoples. The blue-collar frontier shows present the ritualized journey of frontiersmen, which Slotkin describes above as travelling "to a more primitive and natural condition of life so that the false values of the 'metropolis' can be purged and a new, purified social contract enacted."[37]

The vary basis of the conceptualization of the frontier, as articulated by Turner, is that it exists as an empty wilderness awaiting the frontiersman, who somehow transforms the nation-state via his personal transformation. As discussed extensively in chapter one, the popular appeal of the blue-collar frontier shows resides in their depiction of "real men." As per Turner and Slotkin's description above, the idea that men must leave the city for the wilderness to appropriately perform hegemonic masculinity speaks to the critical role of place therein. In short, the frontier corresponds with dominant conceptualizations of both "real men" and "real America," and the blue-collar frontier shows reify the hegemony of the two during a time of widespread economic and cultural anxiety in the United States, particularly for white, working and middle-class men.

Turner asserts that "moving westward, the frontier became more and more American."[38] He implies that the farther the frontiersman moves away from the Eastern metropolises and into "primitive" territory, the more truly American he becomes. I explore this notion more specifically in relation to the series that film in Alaska. This echoes my contention that the frontier functions as a white male spatial imaginary, which brands itself as the seemingly race and gender-neutral landscape of "real America." Turner develops this further and emphasizes the separation between the Eastern and the Western United States: "From the time the mountains rose between the pioneer and the seaboard, a new order of Americanism arose. The West and the East began to get out of touch with each other . . . But the over-mountain men grew more and more independent. The East took a narrow view of American advance, and nearly lost these men."[39]

It is critical to stress that Turner conceives of U.S. exceptionalism as being preserved not only through white men taming the wilderness, but through their doing so as part of the wider settler-colonizing march westward. Thus,

94   *Chapter Three*

he expresses alarm regarding the "closure" of the frontier. His claim that U.S. exceptionalism can only be reified through never-ending imperialism, which is the reality of westward expansion, suggests that the settler-colonization of indigenous peoples is natural, inevitable, and desirable.

Theodore Roosevelt, whose embodied performance of white, rural, working-class masculinity as an aristocratic politician from the East Coast is discussed in the fourth chapter, rhetorically built upon Turner's thesis. On April 10, 1899, Roosevelt gave a speech before the Hamilton Club in Chicago entitled "The Strenuous Life." In this landmark address, Roosevelt espouses his belief that (white) American men must not remain docile, inactive, and cautious: " . . . I wish to preach, not the doctrine of ignoble ease, but the doctrine of the strenuous life, the life of toil and effort, of labor and strife . . . to the man who does not shrink from danger, from hardship, or from bitter toil . . . "[40] He addresses the audience as the "men of the great city of the West."[41] His emphasis on the West cannot be overlooked within the context of Turner. Roosevelt, who was born into a wealthy family in New York City, also echoed Turner's sentiment that the West was where American exceptionalism thrived. It is through Roosevelt that one can directly observe the effects of the frontier thesis on mainstream U.S. political discourse and public policy.

As Gail Bederman explains in *Manliness & Civilization: A Cultural History of Gender and Race in the United States, 1880–1917*, Roosevelt performed as a frontiersman to attain political legitimacy: " . . . he constructed a powerful male identity for himself in the terms of the Western adventure story . . . Now, shooting buffalo and bullying obstreperous cowboys, he could style himself the real thing."[42] As contemporary iterations of Western, frontier myths, the blue-collar frontier shows operate within the same codes as Roosevelt's political performance. As was the case for Roosevelt, "the Western adventure story" continues to be a reliable cultural force for ideologically reasserting white supremacist capitalist heteropatriarchy and colonial logics in U.S. culture, in which these systems of oppression remain simultaneously concealed and bolstered.

Like Turner, Roosevelt does not delineate between one's personal behavior and the wider national objectives of the United States: "As it is with the individual, so it is with the nation."[43] It is critical to reiterate that Roosevelt's conceptualization of "the individual" mirrors Turner's: the individual is assumed white and male. Bederman pinpoints how Roosevelt ideologically championed both white male supremacy and U.S. imperialism: "As he saw it, the United States was engaged in a millennial drama of manly racial advancement, in which American men enacted their superior manhood by asserting imperialistic control over races of inferior manhood."[44] Bederman further contextualizes Roosevelt's "The Strenuous Life" address as demonstrative of the fact " . . . that his strenuous manhood was inextricably linked to his nationalism, imperialism, and racism."[45]

One can envision the fishermen, loggers, gold miners, and ice road truckers of the blue-collar frontier programs as signifying Roosevelt's ideal of the "strenuous life" when he proclaims that ". . . . it is only through strife, through hard and dangerous endeavor, that we shall ultimately win the goal of true national greatness."[46] Again, Roosevelt and Turner conceive of rugged individualism on the frontier as the exclusive, rightful terrain of heteronormative, white men. Therefore, the mythical frontiersman is underpinned by logics of white male supremacy, capitalism, and settler-colonialism, which remain hidden via the related myths of rugged individualism and U.S. exceptionalism. As I have mentioned, the mythical frontier landscape itself is grounded in the historical and ongoing colonization of indigenous peoples in its dominant construction, as articulated most notably by Turner and Roosevelt, as an empty, uninhabited wilderness. To fully account for the implications of frontier mythology in relation to the symbolic and material violence it imposes upon indigenous nations, I must foreground indigenous critical theory in this analysis.

In *The Transit of Empire: Indigenous Critiques of Colonialism*, Jodi Byrd outlines indigenous critical theory, which makes the oppressive structures that constitute the frontier ethos visible. Byrd illuminates the inherent tension between indigenous critical theory and postcolonialism, in which the former calls attention to the false perception that currently colonized spaces and peoples, including the indigenous peoples of North America, exist in a 'post"-colonial state. For the indigenous nations residing within its borders, the United States remains an active colonizing agent. She challenges how settler-colonial logics have problematically constructed the social category of "the Indian" or what she refers to as "paradigmatic Indianness" to begin with: " . . . it suggests a cultural and racial homogeneity that does not exist. There are over five hundred and sixty indigenous nations and/or communities and hundreds of language stocks within the lands that constitute the United States alone that would fall under the category 'Indian.'"[47] This collapse of indigenous nations into a seemingly unidimensional, racial category within a framework of liberal multiculturalism obfuscates the enduring legacy of settler-colonialism. She further elucidates how the frontier ethos deepens settler-colonial logics and currently configures "the Indian": "Although critical theory has focused much attention on the role of frontiers and Manifest Destiny in the creation and rise of U.S. empire, American Indians and other indigenous peoples have often been evoked in such theorizations as past tense presences. Indians are typically spectral, implied and felt, but remain as lamentable casualties of national progress who haunt the United States on the cusp of empire and are destined to disappear with the frontier itself."[48]

96   *Chapter Three*

Byrd's provocation guides this analysis in terms of its engagement with frontier mythology: it is imperative not to reinforce the notion that Native Americans have somehow been relegated to the past tense, or as is the case with the blue-collar frontier shows, that they have somehow been always already gone. The filming locations of these programs are framed as perpetual empty wildernesses, awaiting the arrival of the rightful frontiersmen to stake their claims. Without Byrd's intervention of indigenous critical theory, one fails to recognize the full extent of the consequences of the replication of frontier mythology. Simply put: Frontier mythology is inseparable from the violent settler-colonization of America's indigenous peoples.

Byrd contends that "the United States needs 'cowboys and Indians' to inhabit the 'frontiers' of its borders . . . "[49] The blue-collar frontier shows can be understood as an attempt to fulfill one of the "needs" of hegemonic U.S. culture: to document and preserve the actions of contemporary cowboys on the frontier, in which their primary conflict is with nature. Despite indigenous peoples not being within the observable purview of the blue-collar frontier shows, indigenous critical theory provides the lens through which to detect how they are always already interpellated within frontier mythology and discourses. It is important to clarify here that I am not suggesting that indigenous peoples should somehow be represented within the narratives of the blue-collar frontier shows—representation alone would not rectify the pernicious cumulative effects of frontier mythology. My goal here is to aid in disrupting the normalization and veneration of frontier mythology in U.S culture, so that its role in ideologically justifying white male supremacy and settler-colonialism can be unmasked and subsequently destabilized.

Byrd argues that "U.S. frontier discourses" suggest that " . . . the only way to become 'true' American citizens is to first go native and then carve democracy out of the wilderness."[50] This encapsulates Turner's thesis, and it is important to emphasize that the notion of "going native" is at the expense of Native Americans. Within frontier mythology, it is white, heteronormative men who are the rugged individuals that foment U.S. democracy out of their dangerous encounters in the wilderness. I argue that during this time of widespread socioeconomic and cultural anxiety and anger among white males in the United States, the mythology of the frontier is being rearticulated within the logics of commercial television to assuage those fears. In *Land of Savagery, Land of Promise: The European Image of the American Frontier in the Nineteenth Century*, Ray Allen Billington provides insight into a key reason why frontier mythology continues to flourish in U.S. culture: " . . . That those frontiers never did exist is not important; they are nonetheless real to their creators and wondrously suited to the psychological needs of today."[51] Although Billington fails to recognize the place of white male supremacy and settler-colonialism within frontier mythology, he does touch upon the power of an imagined frontier in meeting "the psychological needs of today." However, he does not address whose needs precisely are fulfilled via frontier mythology and at whose expense.

With the revelation that frontier mythology serves to ideologically justify and conceal the intertwined systems of white male supremacy, capitalism, and settler-colonialism under the seemingly benevolent guise of celebrating rugged individualism and U.S. exceptionalism, I will now detail how the blue-collar frontier shows specifically exemplify the frontier ethos.

THE FRONTIER: "REAL MEN" IN "REAL AMERICA" ON "REAL TV"

Several media studies scholars have engaged with the role of the frontier within U.S. cable's blue-collar reality terrain. In Augie Fleras and Shane Michael Dixon's "Cutting, Digging, and Harvesting: Re-masculinizing the Working-Class Heroic," the authors provide a thorough and theoretically nuanced content analysis of the blue-collar frontier shows, specifically attending to *Deadliest Catch*, *Ice Road Truckers*, *Sandhogs*, and *Ax Men*. Fleras and Dixon assert that these series are " . . . redramatizing the mythic (frontier) struggle between men and untamed wilderness."[52] The anthology, *Reality Television: Oddities of Culture*, contains two highly pertinent chapters for critically examining frontier mythology within the blue-collar reality shows: Burton P. Buchanan's "Portrayals of Masculinity in the Discovery Channel's *Deadliest Catch*" and William C. Trapani and Laura L. Winn's "Manifest Masculinity: Frontier, Fraternity, and Family in Discovery Channel's *Gold Rush*." Buchanan recognizes the ways in which *Deadliest Catch* depicts hegemonic masculinity and appropriately situates hegemonic masculinity as inextricably linked with whiteness. He elucidates what this representation of hegemonic masculinity means at this juncture and pinpoints the role of place therein: " . . . white male power has endured encroachment as women, gays and minorities have gained social power in recent decades. *Deadliest Catch* serves as a fine example of a reality television program that demonstrates an environment where traditional masculinity is exercised, a place where white males can perform masculine rituals, compete with one another *in an adverse environment* [emphasis added] and reassert their position in the social cultural hierarchies."[53]

Buchanan critically posits that "frontiersmanship" is one of the primary characteristics of hegemonic masculinity in U.S. culture. He reiterates the cultural importance of Turner's frontier thesis: "As Frederick Jackson Turner put forth, the frontiersmen were those *rugged individuals* [emphasis added], daring and romantic who helped build up the American continent and left a lasting image that remains symbolic of America."[54] As his description implies, this positions rugged individualism, one of the prized tenets of U.S. culture, as the exclusive domain of white males embodying working-class aesthetics and/or engaging in manual labor on the frontier. Despite this observation, he neglects to note the ways in which Turner's frontier thesis naturalizes settler-colonialism and erases indigenous peoples. I maintain that the concept of the mythic frontiersman is predicated upon the complex intertwinement of white supremacy, heteropatriarchy, capitalism, and settler-colonialism. Through Buchanan's description of frontiersmen, one can trace the legitimacy and symbolic power this fundamentally exclusionary and oppressive performance confers in the United States.

In Trapani and Winn's "Manifest Masculinity," the authors situate *Gold Rush* and the other blue-collar reality series as demonstrative of a "new masculinity crisis."[55] Like Kimmel, they trace the development of this crisis, in which the economic downturn beginning in the late 2000s serves as a flashpoint: "Indeed, the recent economic meltdown that began in 2007 set off the newest and perhaps deepest yet anxiety over the role of men in the social order."[56] I attend specifically to the connections between the rise of blue-collar frontier series, the masculinity crisis, and the Great Recession in the first chapter. Trapani and Winn omit the centrality of whiteness to these hegemonic masculine narratives but do recognize the reinvigoration of frontier mythology within this subgenre of reality television. However, without explicit attentiveness to white supremacy, their analysis pertaining to the frontier needs further development. As they explain in relation to the symbolic objective of *Gold Rush*, " . . . we read the 19th Century advance to the 'frontier' against the proliferation of hypermasculine reality programs today . . . discovering gold is ancillary to the cause itself . . . to effect a reconnection to the symbolic order in which men are once again in charge even if it is because all *others* [emphasis added] have been evacuated from the scene."[57] This speaks to the absence of women of all races and people of color of all genders throughout these series with a few notable exceptions.

The authors do rightly connect the blue-collar frontier shows to frontier mythology. Specifically attending to *Gold Rush*, they note that " . . . the West is often characterized as the place where one can experience the last vestiges of real America."[58] With the recognition that place matters within hegemonic masculinity, it is predictable then that *Gold Rush, Ax Men, Ice Road Truckers,* and *Deadliest Catch* feature panoramic, overhead shots of wilderness landscapes in nearly every episode, typically accompanied by narration at points of introduction or transition. The prominence of scenic landscape shots within these series speaks to the visuality of frontier mythology. These shots suggest that these forests, mountains, seascapes, and frozen tundra signify "real America"—even if they are filmed in Canada, as is the case with *Ice*

Road Truckers and occasionally *Gold Rush*. As Wallmann notes, "Because the frontier serves as the symbolic 'cutting edge' of American civilization and progress, there is no specific region or time period, and consequently there are westerns set on the Canadian frontier, the Alaskan frontier . . . "[59] Thus, geopolitical borders are not as important as the mythical notion that this seemingly vast and sparsely populated terrain awaits the frontiersman to demonstrate his masculine prowess and rugged individualism to symbolically "make America great again"—to echo Trump's campaign slogan. I maintain that this is the subtext of the blue-collar reality shows: a reinvigoration of frontier mythology reclaiming "real America" for "real men."

I will begin with the most recent series in the sample, *Gold Rush*, since it is the most overtly aligned with frontier mythology in its overarching narrative structure, as per the discussion of Todd Hoffman's comments at the beginning of the chapter. The first season was entitled *Gold Rush: Alaska* before the series began to follow mining crews in the Yukon. The show situates itself within the lineage of the historic Klondike Gold Rush in the Yukon and Alaska from 1896 to 1899; occasionally showing black-and-white photos of miners and stating facts about the mining expeditions of the period. As narrator Paul Christie notes in the pilot episode, "Back in the Klondike Gold Rush in the 1890s, less than one percent of those who set out struck it rich."[60] The goal for miners is not to achieve a comfortable standard of living, but to strike it rich. The show commends attempting to join the ranks of the one percent during the Great Recession.

This all-or-nothing, every-man-for-himself mentality mirrors Turner's conceptualization of rugged individualism. Despite the acknowledgment of the grim economic and environmental realities Klondike miners endured in the late nineteenth century, the show still romanticizes the pursuit for gold and accumulated wealth. It promotes the idea that there is honor in the journey itself, since this is what real men do in the face of economic hardship. As per Todd Hoffman's comments, regardless of the risks, he is honoring his imagined ancestral legacy by following his supposed forefathers' path since " . . . they balls-ed up, and they went out into the frontier."[61] Within this romanticized pursuit of riches, the Hoffmans themselves hardly break even the first few seasons. Throughout the series, they never reach the upper echelons of wealth and status through mining.

The episode description on *Amazon* for the pilot episode, "No Guts, No Glory," provides insight into how the series is framed and promoted: "When the going gets tough, *the tough seek new frontiers* [emphasis added]. Six recession-hit patriots from Oregon become greenhorn old miners and head north to Alaska to dig for gold and save themselves from financial ruin."[62] Framing these miners as "patriots" speaks to the relationship between frontier mythology and U.S exceptionalism. The message is that patriots are real men (white, rural, working-class men) who seek new frontiers. In the opening sequence, Todd Hoffman is seen asking the camera rhetorically: "Can't a guy risk it all in America anymore?"[63] Todd is setting out to prove that he can. This rhetorical question is in conversation with Trump's campaign slogan of "Make America Great Again." Hoffman's inclusion of the word "anymore" gestures toward the idea that at one time it was possible for "a guy" to "risk it all in America." Rather than address economic inequality as a systemic, long-term problem that requires collective action, the series glamorizes frontier mythology, so as not to point toward a deeper examination of the complex, neoliberal economic policies that fostered the Great Recession in the first place. The show reinscribes the dominant U.S. mythology of rugged individualism and upward economic mobility, which are central to neoliberalism, at a time when it should logically come under increased scrutiny and critique.

In keeping with frontier mythology, the Hoffmans and their crew journey northwest to Alaska. As the narrator explains in the first episode, "To find a gold claim, the Hoffmans are travelling to *America's last frontier* [emphasis added]. Buried in the Alaskan wilderness is an estimated $250 billion worth of gold."[64] The claim that Alaska is America's "last frontier" is common, and the phrase is even included on one of the state's recent license plate designs.[65] One might logically gravitate toward Alaska as "the last frontier" in the United States in relation to Turner's assertion that "moving westward, the frontier became more and more American."[66] Within the logic of frontier mythology, Alaska is then the focal point of "real America" because it is the farthest western U.S. continental territory. It contains a vast and largely uninhabited wilderness seemingly awaiting brave frontiersmen, who are always configured as white, rural, working-class men, like the Hoffmans and their crew. Frontier mythology has become so naturalized and ubiquitous in U.S. culture that its ideological roots in white male supremacist heteropatriarchy and settler-colonialism remain hidden.

Within the logic of frontier mythology and in *Gold Rush* by extension, "real men" are white, rural, working-class men and Alaska typifies "real America." What also constitutes Alaska as a designated frontier within frontier mythology is that its terrain, particularly the mining sites featured in the series, are highly remote and hazardous. As Jack Hoffman, Todd's father, says to the camera as they finally arrive at their site after a risky trek with their massive load of equipment: "It takes some kahunas to do this. There are dangers every time we turn around."[67] Thus, the frontier functions as a white male spatial imaginary upon which hegemonic masculinity can be ritualistically enacted.

Later in the episode, Jack Hoffman gives a rousing speech to his crew after they arrive at their gold claim and admire the surrounding mountainous landscape. Standing tall and pointing at the adjacent areas, he loudly proclaims: "Everything you see right here is ours. All this down here is ours. Up there is ours."[68] Indigenous critical theory problematizes such statements. Jack reinforces the idea that these originally indigenous lands are rightfully theirs for the taking. His proclamation does more than just state the obvious: yes, this is the land upon which they will mine for gold. His declaration implies something more grandiose and sweeping—that the land *belongs* to them. This is consistent with frontier mythology, which configures the wilderness as the *exclusive* terrain of white men who must ultimately tame and subdue it. This colonial conceptualization of land and nature, in which natural resources are valued solely in relation to their ability to be extracted and monetized within the capitalism system, speaks to another pernicious aspect of frontier mythology. All the shows included in the sample document and glamorize the destruction of the natural environment to simultaneously fulfill material, capitalistic, as well as ritual, heteropatriarchal, needs and desires. Unlike indigenous nations, the dominant white supremacist, heteropatriarchal, capitalist culture does not approach the environment with a sense of reverence and appreciation. If anything, these series demonstrate how the dominant culture continues to rationalize and celebrate environmental destruction.

In season One: Episode 10: "Never Say Die," Paul Christie reminds the viewer of the narrative framework of the series at the beginning of the episode: "Last spring, six down-on-their-luck men left Oregon . . . for the Alaskan wilderness . . . They dropped everything to find gold . . . to live the American dream."[69] The voiceover is intercut with footage of the miners and cuts to an American flag flapping in the wind upon Christie mentioning the American dream. *Gold Rush* demonstrates how frontier mythology serves as a highly visceral and effective shorthand for appealing to U.S. exceptionalism. Despite the crew experiencing equipment failures, bad weather, and other misfortunes, their struggle for riches is still glamorized as a ritualistic exercise of hegemonic masculinity and suggests that this is the proper way to honor the American dream.

As the series progresses, the cameras document the trials and tribulations of other white male gold mining crews in Alaska and the Yukon. The other crews are included to keep the show engaging, and as is the case with the other blue-collar frontier shows under examination, to frame the shows as competitions for who can rake in the most money. This allows the rugged individualism endemic to frontier mythology to come even more flagrantly to the forefront. Rugged individualism tends to mask itself as a gentler form of Social Darwinism. As Wallmann notes regarding the mythology of Westerns, "Only the strong were able to survive."[70] The element of manufactured

102   *Chapter Three*

competition within these series speaks to the Western, frontier tradition, and therefore, has implications beyond functioning as a plot device.

In Season Two: Episode Two: "Virgin Ground," Todd gives his crew a pep talk during a mining season already marked by mishaps, especially in comparison to the other two crews featured in the second season. Todd addresses his skeptical crew: "If you guys got the cajones, let's team up again and really hit it hard, 100 percent . . . We represent the best country in the world. That's where we live, that's where we were born, and people have died for the freedoms that we have. So who's with me?"[71] It is striking that he makes a dramatic appeal to both hegemonic masculinity and U.S. exceptionalism in convincing his crew to continue supporting an incredibly risky business venture, in which they are all taking considerable economic and physical risks. Todd's message is clear: If you are a real man and a true American patriot, then you will continue to support his mining expedition. Therefore, if any of his crew were to back out, they would risk being emasculated and being perceived as unpatriotic. This suggests that the frontier is for real men who are simultaneously designated as real Americans—the two conceptualizations remain inextricably linked. Todd's remarks reveal the extent to which frontier mythology and its interrelated myths of rugged individualism and U.S. exceptionalism bolster white male supremacist and capitalist systems.

Moving to *Ax Men*, one can observe the imprints of frontier mythology throughout its nine seasons. The series, which is also narrated by producer Thom Beers, places various logging crews in a manufactured competition with one another for who can haul the most loads. In Season Two: Episode Seven: "One Weak Link," Beers begins the episode with a sense of urgency: "Tonight on Ax Men . . . the race for loads is on . . . It's man . . . versus the wild . . . and not everyone will make it."[72] His voiceover epitomizes frontier mythology. Even though each logging crew consists of multiple loggers working together, Beers frames the episode as though "It's man . . . versus the wild." As per Turner's thesis, it is fundamental that rugged individualism remain at the epicenter of frontier mythology. Furthermore, Beers demonstrates the Social Darwinian aspect of rugged individualism when he dramatically declares that "not everyone will make it." Of course, this dramatic exaggeration builds suspense.

It is worth reemphasizing that frontier mythology necessitates the construction of a seemingly independent frontiersman overcoming nature. For the frontiersman to be exceptional, it requires the relational construction of those who fail to tame the wilderness or those who do not "make it." Of course, as is the case with *Ax Men*, none of these men are logistically unaided, and their social advantages as white males remain hidden or at least unremarkable within the dominant discourse. Because frontier mythology is constructed as a masculinized, individualistic encounter with nature, it is unsurprising that the Social Darwinian foundations of rugged individualism are frequently articulated within frontier discourses. As Dwayne Dethlefs of the Pihl logging company says in Season One: Episode 11: "Storm of the Century," "You gotta be tough to live in the West."[73] The role of place, specifically the Western wilderness, within contemporary U.S. hegemonic masculinity cannot be overstated. The frontier functions as the white male spatial imaginary through which "real men" or "rugged individuals" solidify the legacy of U.S. exceptionalism.

In Season Two: Episode 11: "Clash of the Titans," the plot centers on a heightened sense of competition between the Rygaard Logging and J.M. Browning Logging companies. Beers begins the episode: "Deep within the mountains of Oregon and Washington, an epic battle rages between two titans of logging."[74] Euphemisms for war and violence are also interwoven throughout the series—a standard practice within representations of hegemonic masculinity, as discussed at length in the first chapter. The episode first heads to the Browning site in Oregon. Beers includes an overt reference to the Western film and television genre when he describes Jesse Browning, the son of the company's eponymous owner as follows: "Jay's son Jesse has been top gun at shingle mill."[75] This is a prime example of the series trying to discursively situate itself within the legacy of the Western to achieve broad-based commercial appeal with U.S. audiences. Although there is no usage of guns or firearms within the show, the narrative framings often contain a violent subtext.

Beers concludes the episode with more melodramatic language invoking the rugged individualism of frontier mythology: "The men of the mountain battle for pride . . . for survival . . . and for the title, king of the mountain."[76] *Ax Men* awards the owner of the logging company that hauls the most loads at the end of the season with the symbolic title, "king of the mountain." Despite the labor and teamwork of an entire crew making their operations run smoothly, the owner of the logging company becomes the proverbial king. The mythology of the frontier is one of survival of the fittest and fosters a false sense of masculinized self-reliance and independence for the frontiersman. Furthermore, the suggestion that cutting down a massive number of trees enables a single man to somehow dominate or "own" nature further legitimizes environmental destruction in the name of celebrating masculine prowess.

In Season Three: Episode 13: "King of the Mountain," Gabe Rygaard, heir of Rygaard Logging, says to the camera after an exhausting nonstop, overnight shift of dangerous downhill logging: "You know, I'm tired. I feel like crap. But I'll tell you what: Me and my crew own this mountain."[77] It is noteworthy that Gabe does credit his crew, which momentarily disrupts the winner-take-all narrative. However, the capitalistic notion of private ownership defines his relationship to his line of work. He does not only own a company that cuts down trees—he somehow conceives of himself as also owning the mountain from which they spring. *Ax Men* exemplifies the idea that hegemonic masculinity must be tested and celebrated on the frontier, in which nature itself only serves as a proving ground. I maintain that hegemonic masculine status remains contingent upon the appearance of mastery over nature, in which environmental destruction is but another casualty.

Like *Gold Rush*, *Ax Men* reinforces the perception that Alaska is somehow the last frontier. In Season Four: Episode One: "Alaska," the cameras begin to document the Papac Alaska Logging company. Beers begins the episode with the bold claim: "The Ax Men strike out into uncharted territory: Alaska."[78] This echoes the idea that Alaska is a mythical and uninhabited wilderness. The panoramic overhead shots of Alaska also include wildlife, notably wolves and bears. As per Turner's thesis, the farther West and more remote the terrain, the more truly American it becomes. Alaska is situated as a more venerable proving ground for hegemonic masculinity because of the harsher weather and presence of more dangerous animals.

Beers introduces Papac Alaska Logging as follows: "700 miles north of the lower 48, a new outfit is pushing logging all the way to America's final frontier."[79] The designation of Alaska as either the final or last frontier implies that no other terrain surpasses it as an ultimate test of manhood. As Mike "Coatsy" Coats of Papac brags to the camera, "And it's just the terrain's way tougher up here. I mean, my daughter could log down there where Rygaard logs [Washington]."[80] Coatsy also speaks to the capitalist underpinnings of frontier mythology: "Bigger risk in Alaska. Bigger reward. That's why I come up here. For the big money."[81] The message is clear: Real men prove their masculine authenticity through attempting to strike it rich in hazardous terrain. Even if these frontiersmen fall short of accumulating substantial wealth—as most of them do—undertaking the ritualized frontier journey itself confers a superior masculine status.

Deadliest Catch also finds itself in Alaska—more specifically, the frigid waters of Alaska's Bering Sea. The series incorporates the frontier mythology of rugged individualism through its construction of a competition between the five to six boats prominently featured each season. The show keeps a running "crab count" for how many pounds of king or opilio crab each boat catches in the November and January fishing seasons respectively. Narrator Mike Rowe frequently reminds the audience that Alaskan crab fishing is statistically the most dangerous job in the world. Of all the programs in this sample, *Deadliest Catch* maintains the distinction of documenting fatalities, including a crew of six fishermen during its first season. Although this was not a boat the series was following closely, stark reminders of the dangers of the job appear frequently, as the U.S. Coast Guard makes multiple appearances throughout the series on search and rescue missions.

Despite remaining a highly dangerous occupation, Alaskan crab fishing has gotten much safer overall since new quota rules were implemented for each fishing vessel after the show's first season.[82] Captain Sig Hansen of the *Northwestern* is featured throughout the show's eighteen seasons and bemoans the end of "derby-style" fishing, in which boats such as his would regularly take extreme risks to haul as much as crab as possible—putting profits over safety. In Season One: Episode Nine: "The Clock's Ticking," Sig invokes U.S exceptionalism and rugged individualism in his opposition to the new regulation: "I like the way it is . . . It's the American way to me. Go for it and do it yourself and all that."[83] He seems to be placing greater value on the potential for increased profits than prioritizing crew safety. Rowe narrates in Season One: Episode 10: "The Final Run" that " . . . this is the final season for free-spirited entrepreneurs to win big on the Bering Sea."[84] The end of cutthroat and potentially deadly competition for the sake of capitalist ends is framed as a mournful development. Despite the class hierarchies that exist between the captain and his crew, they are all collapsed into the category of "free-spirited entrepreneurs" in accordance with the capitalist foundations of frontier mythology. Government regulation for the benefit of workers' health and safety is at odds with frontier mythology and neoliberal capitalism, and this is but one telling example.

In relation to overt associations with the Western genre, the show's opening theme song is Bon Jovi's "Wanted Dead or Alive," in which cowboy imagery figures prominently in the lyrics.[85] In addition to including panoramic land-scape shots of the Bering Sea and the Alaskan shoreline, the camera occasion-ally flashes to a wild American bald eagle, such as in Season Three: Episode Seven: "New Beginnings" (2007), Season Six: Episode 10: "The Darkened Seas" (2010), and Season Seven: Episode One: "New Blood (2011). The inclusion of the U.S. national bird is a nod to U.S. exceptionalism and signals an attempt at associating the commercial fishermen with patriotism. Despite the structure of the occupation itself requiring a substantial amount of team-work, the rugged individualism dimension of frontier mythology remains a staple of the series. In Season Nine: Episode Two: "Dagger in the Back," Rowe melodramatically intones, "The hunt is on . . . And it's every man for himself."[86] The ways in which systems of power structure the life chances of the captains and their crews in various ways remains invisible. These fisher-men are framed as both unencumbered and unaided by structural realities.

Frontier mythology also tends to anthropomorphize nature itself. Considering the occupations featured in the blue-collar frontier shows often cause significant environmental harm, it is important to emphasize that nature functions as a proving ground for authentic masculinity and capitalistic resource extraction within the logic of the frontier myth. There is no respect for nature beyond the challenge it poses to the individual men attempting to tame it. In "The Final Run," Rowe minimizes tragedy in preserving frontier mythology, while autotomizing nature: "Six men died before the sea finally showed mercy. These fishermen risk their lives for the opportunity to make fast cash."[87] The idea that the sea autonomously shows mercy, or independently "decides" to take some lives and not others, feeds into the fatalistic Social Darwinism that accompanies frontier mythology. The idea that people die in an attempt "to make fast cash" is glamorized, not problematized, or challenged. In "Season Three: Episode Seven: "New Beginnings," Rowe again demonstrates this tendency to anthropomorphize nature: " . . . The vicious Bering Sea will unleash surprises . . . on the 400 brave souls tempting fate for fortune . . . Now the hunt continues . . . for the deadliest catch."[88] In keeping with Turner's thesis, fetishizing the frontier is necessary for conserving U.S. exceptionalism. Thus, even when these dominant, intertwined mythologies face increased public scrutiny, such as during the Great Recession, dominant institutions such as commercial television reinvest in them. This is not only because these myths appeal to mainstream U.S. audiences, which then assures advertising revenue, but also because the corporate-owned networks have an ideological stake in the preservation of the neoliberal capitalist status quo. Romanticized narratives of rugged individualism seek to deter class consciousness and organizing.

Frontier rhetoric also figures prominently in *Ice Road Truckers*. Thom Beers too produces and narrates the series and begins Season One: Episode Four: "The Big Chill" as follows: "For half a century, truckers have hauled heavy loads over the frozen lakes of Northern Canada, bringing supplies to the remote outposts of civilization. They are the trailblazers of our time."[89] Beers overtly situates these truckers within the lineage of the mythic frontiersman. Hugh Rowland, who is featured throughout the show's eleven seasons, also wears a cowboy hat while driving in this episode. The show further cements the connection between these contemporary truckers and Western pioneers as "trailblazers" in Season Eight: Episode Seven: "Blazing the Trail" (2014) and Season Nine: Episode Three: "Trailblazers" (2015). The series frequently refers to the ice roads as being located at the edges of "civilization." As Slotkin notes, the frontiersman must journey "to a more primitive and natural condition of life so that the false values of the 'metropolis' can be purged and a new, purified social contract enacted."[90] Indigenous critical theory unmasks and destabilizes the settler-colonial and white supremacist logics that construct relational classifications of "civilized" and "primitive." According to Turner's thesis, the civilized (white male) frontiersman must encounter "primitive" territories and peoples to transform both himself and the nation.

Thom Beers invokes "civilization" again when describing driver Jay Westgard's route in "The Big Chill": "Jay is leaving the last outpost of civilization and driving into a vast expanse where help, if he needs it, can be hundreds of miles away."[91] The more remote and dangerous the frontier, the more celebrated it is within frontier mythology. In Season Three: Episode Two: "Rookie Run," Beers declares at the beginning of the episode that "At the top of the world . . . there's a job only a few would dare."[92] The perception that Alaska in particular is the most dangerous frontier is reinforced in this season as well. After focusing on truckers in far Northwestern Canada in the first two seasons, the series frames a locational shift to Alaska as a plot point of heightened danger: "This season, two old pros join four of America's bravest truckers to tackle the continent's deadliest ice passage . . . Ice Road Truckers take on Alaska."[93] This also reifies U.S. exceptionalism in relation to Canadian truckers and terrain: Only the toughest can handle Alaskan ice roads.

The show follows the truckers to Manitoba in its seventh season, and the formulaic reinstatement of frontier mythology continues unabated. In Season Seven: Episode One: "Collision Course," Beers opens the episode with his nearly standardized introduction: "In a remote corner of North America . . . join the grudge match on the world's most dangerous frontier."[94] The camera then cuts to driver Hugh Rowland declaring that "these are the roughest, toughest roads in North America."[95] Are the roads in Manitoba tougher than Alaska or the Yukon? Again, the factual basis of these statements is not important; a critical aspect of the performance of frontier mythology is the continual reassertion that any given frontier is somehow the most dangerous. This rings true in the blue-collar frontier world, in which this claim recurs throughout the sample of shows included here. The importance of stressing that the frontier is dangerous speaks to the Social Darwinian aspect of rugged individualism. The more dangerous the frontier, the more "fit" the man is who overcomes it. As driver Darrell Ward poignantly encapsulates moments later in the same episode: "It all comes down to survival of the fittest."[96]

The drivers are also placed in a manufactured competition with each other for who can haul the most loads across the ice by the end of each season. Beers frequently refers to it as "the dash for the cash." This maximizes the viewer's perception that this occupation is a masculinized test of rugged individualism on the frontier serving capitalist ends. I discuss the show's problematic and tokenizing framing of Lisa Kelly, one of only two women truckers featured in the series, at length in the second chapter. In "Rookie Run," Beers characterizes her efficient handling of the Alaskan passage as surprising and suggests that she has yet to fully prove herself in relation to her male counterparts: "Lisa is surprisingly confident on the ice, but she still has 375 miles of raw *frontier* [emphasis added] ahead."[97] His narration casts doubt on her ability to conquer the frontier—a white male spatial imaginary.

108   *Chapter Three*

Irrespective of her performance, her presence as a white woman remains incongruous within frontier mythology.

CONCLUSION

The hegemonic conceptualization of the frontier in the United States exemplifies how a mythical, imaginary place can yield tremendous power and material consequences. In the dominant U.S. discourse, the frontier is often cast as a race and gender-neutral construct—a place devoid of any deeper ideological or material struggle. Not only did U.S. historian Frederick Jackson Turner falsely conceive of the frontier as empty backwoods, but he also portrayed life on the frontier as a necessary rite of passage for white men to continually reconstitute U.S. exceptionalism and rugged individualism through their taming of the wilderness. Without stating it explicitly in his "frontier thesis," Turner provides an ideological template for justifying continued settler-colonization of indigenous peoples and their lands; perpetual environmental destruction to satiate capitalist greed; and white manhood as the normative standard for ideal citizenship. In configuring the frontier as a "white male spatial imaginary," I aim to make visible how frontier mythology naturalizes the presence of white males in remote wilderness settings at the expense of women, indigenous peoples, and people of color. The frontier is not neutral or uninhabited: It is a contested site upon which imperial white supremacist capitalist heteropatriarchy is ritualistically enacted and resisted.

The blue-collar frontier shows provide an illustrative contemporary example of how the mythic frontier continues to serve as a proving ground for hegemonic masculinity. "Real men" prove their masculinity in "real America"—as Turner infamously conceived of the frontier. These series document white men performing hazardous occupations in remote, wilderness settings to reinvigorate frontier mythology at a time in which its intertwined core tenets, including rugged individualism, white male supremacy, and unregulated capitalism, are facing considerable public scrutiny on multiple fronts. Both the Great Recession and systemic challenges to white male supremacy elicited the proliferation of this subgenre of reality television programming—a conservative reaction to a changing U.S. sociocultural landscape. Blue-collar frontier television seems to discursively suggest that it is only through going back to the frontier that—per Trump's campaign slogan—white men can "make American great again."

NOTES

1. Stuart Hall, "The Rediscovery of 'Ideology': Return of the Repressed in Media Studies," in *Culture, Society and the Media*, ed. M. Gurevitch (London: Methuen, 1982), 65.

2. John Storey, *Cultural Theory and Popular Culture: An Introduction*, 6th edition, (New York and London: Pearson, 2012), 3.

3. Paul M. Gaston, *The New South Creed: A Study in Southern Mythmaking* (New York: Knopf, 1970), 9.

4. Richard Slotkin, *Gunfighter Nation: The Myth of the Frontier in Twentieth Century America* (Norman: Oklahoma University Press, 1998), 5.

5. Richard Slotkin, *Gunfighter Nation*, 6.

6. Ibid., 9.

7. *Gold Rush: Alaska*, season 1, episode 1, "No Guts No Glory," narrated by Paul Christie, aired December 3, 2010, *Raw TV* for *Discovery Channel*.

8. Richard Drinnon, *Facing West: The Metaphysics of Indian-Hating and Empire-Building* (Norman and London: University of Oklahoma Press, 1997), 465.

9. Paul Gaston, *The New South Creed*, 9.

10. Cheryl Harris, "Whiteness as Property," in *Critical Race Theory: The Key Writings That Formed the Movement* Crenshaw, eds. N. Gotanda, G. Peller, & T. Kendall (New York: The New Press, 1995), 277.

11. Cheryl Harris, "Whiteness as Property," 281.

12. Ibid.

13. George Lipsitz, *How Racism Takes Place* (Philadelphia: Temple University Press, 2011), 6.

14. Lipsitz, *How Racism Takes Place*, 13.

15. Ibid., 29.

16. Ibid., 30.

17. Frederick Jackson Turner, *The Significance of the Frontier in American History* (London and New York: Penguin Books, 2008), 2.

18. Stuart Hall, "Encoding and Decoding in the Television Discourse" in *Channeling Blackness: Studies on Television and Race in America*, ed. D. M. Hunt, (New York and Oxford: Oxford University Press, 2005), 50.

19. Stuart Hall, "Encoding and Decoding in the Television Discourse," 50.

20. Slotkin, *Gunfighter Nation*, 25.

21. Gary A. Yoggy, *Riding the Video Range: The Rise and Fall of the Western on Television*, (Jefferson, NC and London: McFarland & Company, Inc., 1995), 2.

22. Jeffrey Wallmann, *The Western: Parables of the American Dream* (Lubbock, TX: Texas Tech University Press, 1999), 9.

23. Wallmann, *The Western*, 17.

24. J. E. O'Connor and P. C. Rollins, "Introduction: The West, Westerns, and American Character" in *Hollywood's West: The American Frontier in Film, Television, and History*, (Lexington, KY: The University Press of Kentucky, 2005), 31.

25. Wallmann, *The Western*, 22.

110   *Chapter Three*

26. R. Phillip Loy, *Westerns in a Changing America, 1955–2000*, (Jefferson, NC and London: McFarland & Company, Inc., 2004), 144.

27. Gary A. Yoggy, *Riding the Video Range*, 82.

28. Wallmann, *The Western*, 9.

29. Dana Jennings, "Grab a Brew While They Face Death," *New York Times*, March 24, 2011, http://www.nytimes.com/2011/03/27/arts/television/coal-on-spike -aims-to-attract-male-viewers.html?_r=2.

30. Richard Slotkin, *Gunfighter Nation*, 633.

31. Turner, *The Significance of the Frontier in American History*, 2.

32. Ibid., 44.

33. Ibid., 48.

34. Ibid., 30.

35. Ibid., 4–5.

36. Richard Slotkin, *Gunfighter Nation*, 14.

37. Ibid., 14.

38. Turner, *The Significance of the Frontier in American History*, 4.

39. Ibid., 17.

40. Theodore Roosevelt, *The Strenuous Life* (Stilwell, KS: Digireads.com Publishing, 2008), 7.

41. Roosevelt, *The Strenuous Life*, 7.

42. Gail Bederman, *Manliness & Civilization: A Cultural History of Gender and Race in the United States, 1880–1917* (Chicago and London: The University of Chicago Press, 1995), 174–75.

43. Roosevelt, *The Strenuous Life*, 8.

44. Bederman, *Manliness & Civilization*, 171.

45. Ibid., 193.

46. Roosevelt, *The Strenuous Life*, 13.

47. Jodi Byrd, *The Transit of Empire: Indigenous Critiques of Colonialism* (Minneapolis and London: University of Minnesota Press, 2011), 73, Kindle.

48. Byrd, *The Transit of Empire*, Kindle, Location 191–199.

49. Ibid., 209.

50. Ibid., 191.

51. Ray Allen Billington, *Land of Savagery, Land of Promise: The European Image of the American Frontier in the Nineteenth Century* (New York and London: W.W. Norton & Company, 1981), 313.

52. Augie Fleras and Shane Michael Dixon, "Cutting, Driving, Digging, and Harvesting: Re-Masculinizing the Working-Class Heroic," *Canadian Journal of Communication* 36, no. 4 (2012), 589.

53. Burton P. Buchanan, "Portrayals of Masculinity in The Discovery Channel's *Deadliest Catch*," in *Reality Television: Oddities of Culture*, eds. A.F. Slade, A.J. Narro, & B.P. Buchanan (Lanham, Maryland: Lexington Books, 2014), 2.

54. Burton P. Buchanan, "Portrayals of Masculinity in The Discovery Channel's *Deadliest Catch*," 10.

55. W. C. Trapani and L. L. Winn, "Manifest Masculinity: Frontier, Fraternity, and Family in Discovery Channel's *Gold Rush*, in *Reality Television: Oddities of Culture*,

eds. A. F. Slade, A. J. Narro, & B. P. Buchanan (Lanham, Maryland: Lexington Books, 2014), 185.

56. Trapani and Winn, "Manifest Masculinity," 186.

57. Ibid., 185.

58. Ibid., 194.

59. Wallmann, *The Western*, 9.

60. *Gold Rush: Alaska*, season 1, episode 1, "No Guts No Glory," narrated by Paul Christie, aired December 3, 2010, *Raw TV* for *Discovery Channel*.

61. *Gold Rush: Alaska*, season 1, episode 1, "No Guts No Glory."

62. *Gold Rush: Alaska*, season 1, episode 1, "No Guts No Glory," Episode Description, *Amazon.com*, https://www.amazon.com/Gold-Rush-Alaska-Season-1/dp /B004FK9CTQ.

63. *Gold Rush: Alaska*, season 1, episode 1, "No Guts No Glory."

64. Ibid.

65. Alexandra Gutierrez, "Grizzly License Plates Ready for Issue," *Alaska Public Media*, May 5, 2015, http://www.alaskapublic.org/2015/05/05/grizzly-license-plates -ready-for-issue/.

66. Turner, *The Significance of the Frontier in American History*, 4.

67. *Gold Rush: Alaska*, season 1, episode 1, "No Guts No Glory."

68. Ibid.

69. *Gold Rush: Alaska*, season 1, episode 10, "Never Say Die," narrated by Paul Christie, aired February 17, 2011, *Raw TV* for *Discovery Channel*.

70. Wallmann, *The Western*, 22.

71. *Gold Rush*, season 2, episode 2, "Virgin Ground," narrated by Paul Christie, aired November 4, 2011, *Raw TV* for *Discovery Channel*.

72. *Ax Men*, season 2, episode 7, "One Weak Link," narrated by Thom Beers, aired April 20, 2009, *Original Productions* for *History Channel*.

73. *Ax Men*, season 1, episode 11, "Storm of the Century," narrated by Thom Beers, aired May 19, 2008, *Original Productions* for *History Channel*.

74. *Ax Men*, season 2, episode 10, "Clash of the Titans," narrated by Thom Beers, aired May 11, 2009, *Original Productions* for *History Channel*.

75. *Ax Men*, season 2, episode 10, "Clash of the Titans."

76. Ibid.

77. *Ax Men*, season 3, episode 13, "King of the Mountain," narrated by Thom Beers, aired April 18, 2010, *Original Productions* for *History Channel*.

78. *Ax Men*, season 4, episode 1, "Alaska," narrated by Thom Beers, aired December 12, 2010, *Original Productions* for *History Channel*.

79. *Ax Men*, season 4, episode 1, "Alaska."

80. Ibid.

81. Ibid.

82. Les Christie, "'Deadliest Catch' Not So Deadly Anymore," *CNN Money*, July 27, 2012, http://money.cnn.com/2012/07/27/pf/jobs/crab-fishing-dangerous-jobs/.

83. *Deadliest Catch*, season 1, episode 9, "The Clock's Ticking," narrated by Mike Rowe, aired June 7, 2005, *Original Productions* for *Discovery Channel*.

84. *Deadliest Catch*, season 1, episode 10, "The Final Run," narrated by Mike Rowe, aired June 14, 2005, *Original Productions* for *Discovery Channel*.

85. J. B. Jovi and R. Sambora." Wanted Dead or Alive," on *Slippery When Wet* (United States: Mercury Records), mp3 file.

86. *Deadliest Catch*, season 9, episode 2, "Dagger in the Back," narrated by Mike Rowe, aired April 23, 2013, *Original Productions* for *Discovery Channel*.

87. *Deadliest Catch*, season 1, episode 10, "The Final Run," narrated by Mike Rowe, aired June 14, 2005, *Original Productions* for *Discovery Channel*.

88. *Deadliest Catch*, season 3, episode 7, "New Beginnings," narrated by Mike Rowe, aired May 15, 2007, *Original Productions* for *Discovery Channel*.

89. *Ice Road Truckers*, season 1, episode 4, "The Big Chill," narrated by Thom Beers, aired July 8, 2007, *Original Productions* for *History Channel*.

90. Slotkin, *Gunfighter Nation*, 14.

91. *Ice Road Truckers*, season 1, episode 4, "The Big Chill."

92. *Ice Road Truckers*, season 3, episode 2, "Rookie Run," narrated by Thom Beers, aired June 7, 2009, *Original Productions* for *History Channel*.

93. *Ice Road Truckers*, season 3, episode 2, "Rookie Run."

94. *Ice Road Truckers*, season 7, episode 1, "Collision Course," narrated by Thom Beers, aired June 9, 2013, *Original Productions* for *History Channel*.

95. *Ice Road Truckers*, season 7, episode 1, "Collision Course."

96. Ibid.

97. *Ice Road Truckers*, season 3, episode 2, "Rookie Run."

Chapter Four

When Wealthy White Men Perform "Real Manhood"

But I have a theory about how they [media experts] missed the Trump train. They don't hang out with regular folks like us who like to hunt and fish and pray and actually work for a living. Hey, I don't even know that they know how to talk to people from Middle America. I mean, when I tell'em I'm from Louisiana they really start talking real slow and real loud. Let me tell you why I've been on the Trump train from the beginning. See when you're from the South and you grow up with *rednecks* [emphasis added], there are some occasional disagreements. Sometimes those disagreements turn into fisticuffs. But any time I was ever in a bad spot, I always knew my brothers would have my back. And today in a lot of ways, America is in a bad spot, and we need a president who will have our back.

—Willie Robertson, CEO of Duck Commander, and star of *Duck Dynasty*, endorsing Donald Trump for president at the Republican National Convention in Cleveland, Ohio, on July 18, 2016.[1]

Sporting his trademark American flag-patterned bandana and long, disheveled beard and hair, Willie Robertson of *Duck Dynasty* began his speech at the 2016 Republican National Convention with a Christian prayer—openly eschewing the dictum of separation of church and state. This is particularly noteworthy at a presidential nominating convention, in which Islamophobia was also one of the unabashed rhetorical strategies.[2] Robertson self-righteously comments that "As some of you know, we end every episode of *Duck Dynasty* with a family prayer at the dinner table."[3] He then suggests that more prayer is required " . . . with the way things are going in this country."[4] Since the Republican nominee, Donald Trump, was a former reality television star himself, it may not seem incongruous to have Robertson appear as a credible endorser. However, it is highly unlikely that when *Duck Dynasty* premiered in 2012 that anyone would have predicted the Robertson

114 *Chapter Four*

family of West Monroe, Louisiana charting a course toward political relevance in 2016.

Willie claims that he and Trump have three things in common: they are successful businessmen; have hit television series; and are married to women who are more intelligent and better looking than they are. His remarks draw laughter and applause, but it is highly revelatory that he fails to mention some of their most obvious commonalities: they are both white, cisheteronormative men who have inherited considerable wealth from their fathers. Thus, they have been conferred a unique constellation of structural advantages, which belie the self-made, upward mobility mythology that rationalizes U.S. capitalism. Willie's lack of acknowledgment of these shared experiences illuminates how white supremacy, heteropatriarchy, and capitalism function covertly and present as "commonsense." Trump and Willie's shared racial and gender identities would likely never occur to either of them or most mainstream political commentators, since they are the norm to which all non-dominant gender and racial groups are measured.

As was extensively elucidated in the first chapter, white supremacy and patriarchy retain their power in large part because whiteness and maleness seem unremarkable. Additionally, if they are spotlighted as advantaged social locations in public discourse, it remains an exceptional and highly contested instance, such as with the battle over including critical race theory in public school curriculum in 2021.[5] Willie and Trump's lived experiences enable them to never self-reflexively consider their own race or gender. Furthermore, neither of them has ever publicly acknowledged that the class-based advantages bestowed upon them from birth have factored heavily in their own economic "success." In response to fellow Republican presidential candidate Marco Rubio's accusation that he inherited $200 million from his father; Trump defended himself by claiming that he only received "a small loan" to start his real-estate empire.[6] Glenn Kessler explains in *The Washington Post* that although the $200 million figure cited by Rubio is too high, that Trump received extensive financial assistance from his father, Fred Trump, who was himself once one of the wealthiest people in the United States due to his own real estate dealings. Kessler summarizes the benefits Trump received at the behest of his wealthy father: "He benefited from numerous loans and loan guarantees, as well as his father's connections, to make the move into Manhattan. His father also set up lucrative trusts to provide steady income. When Donald Trump became overextended in the casino business, his father bailed him out with a shady casino-chip loan—and Trump also borrowed $9 million against his future inheritance."[7] Because the rugged individualism myth remains embedded and celebrated in U.S. culture and political discourse, Trump's inherited wealth, in theory, should have been a liability in relation to his claims of hard work and self-made success.

In a related fashion, Willie is now the CEO of Duck Commander, a multi-million-dollar business which manufactures duck calls for hunters and was originally established by his father, Phil Robertson. Willie attained this position through nepotism in concert with an array of social advantages linked to systems of power, such as white supremacy, heteropatriarchy, and capitalism. With an awareness of his social privileges, it is almost comical when he suggests that media experts " . . . don't hang out with regular folks like us who like to hunt and fish and pray and *actually work for a living* [emphasis added]."[8] How is his occupation as the CEO of a duck call company founded by his father considered more legitimate work than that of journalists? Willie's occupation and socioeconomic status more closely align with the professional-managerial class than with workers. More insidiously, he is trying to ingratiate himself with the white working class via this rhetorical performance, wherein he deceitfully casts himself as somehow less elite than members of the mainstream media.

Willie characteristically commits to his performance of a "redneck" identity, which is showcased throughout *Duck Dynasty*. I will unpack the raced, gendered, and classed implications of this performance in greater depth momentarily, but in only a few short minutes in this speech, he taps into the symbolic capital this performance confers. Through his embodied performance, he proclaims that he is just one of the "regular folks" from "Middle America." Through a critical discourse analysis of *Duck Dynasty*, it becomes overwhelmingly clear that the Robertsons have much more materially in common with the East Coast elites they self-consciously attempt to distance themselves from than with "regular folks." As Helen Wood and Beverly Skeggs explain in *Reality Television and Class*, more overt signifiers of social class are typically replaced with an alternative discourse that subjugates class consciousness: "The term 'ordinary' is one of the many euphemisms used to stand in for 'working-class,' because in many different nations it is no longer fashionable to speak about class identifications."[9] "Regular" and "ordinary" discursively gesture toward a white, working-class social location. This speaks to the power of white supremacy, in that whiteness is considered an "ordinary" or normalized racial identity. I contend that this obfuscation of explicitly class-based discourse not only occurs on reality television, but in U.S. public discourse writ large. Therefore, Willie Robertson, despite his assertions, is unmistakably a white, college-educated multi-millionaire with no socioeconomic connection to the working class. His rhetorical strategy and embodied performance can be read as a fledgling attempt to effuse the masculine authenticity stereotypically associated with white, rural working-class men.

As Willie's speech culminates with an endorsement of Trump, he discursively deploys another salient euphemism in the 2016 presidential election cycle: "He [Trump] may not always tell you what you want to hear, and you may not always agree, and it may not always be *politically correct* [emphasis added]. But when your father is Phil Robertson, I'm used to that, okay?"[10] The Republican party, political conservatives, and most prominently, Donald Trump, use the term "politically correct" and its various iterations to delegitimize individuals or organizations calling attention to and challenging racism, sexism, homophobia, and other systems of oppression. The term also functions to deflect and justify social inequities. It is telling that Willie mentions his father Phil to much applause. Significant public controversy arose following the revelation of Phil's racist and homophobic beliefs in late 2013, which led to a significant decline in *Duck Dynasty*'s ratings.[11] Essentially, Willie's praise of political incorrectness in relation to Trump and his father Phil can be deciphered as a thinly veiled defense of racism, sexism, and homophobia.

Trump's 2016 campaign slogan, "Make America Great Again," has generated substantial controversy because it implies that the modest inroads made in recent years by women, people of color, and LGBTQ-identified groups, and those living at those intersections, must be overturned. Trump's racist, sexist, Islamophobic, and anti-immigrant rhetoric has provoked considerable condemnation in the mainstream media, as well as a robust critique of Trump's supporters. His base is often characterized in mainstream media coverage as white, working-class males, who are unapologetic, reactionary bigots.[12] During the 2020 election, Tom Nichols of *The Atlantic* claimed that working-class white men were " . . . the most reliable component of Trump's base . . . "[13] Interestingly, Trump made significant gains with both Black and Latinx voters between 2016 and 2020.[14] Additionally, a *New York Times* analysis of 2020 polling data indicated that the demographic that Trump lost the most support from in 2020 was white male voters.[15] Despite these recalibrations, approximately 58 percent of white male voters still supported Trump in 2020.[16]

Although there appears to be plenty of bigotry within the ranks of Trump's followers, the common claim that most of his devotees, who are majority white and male, also belong to the working class is subject to considerable debate. Jeffrey Bartash summarizes the misconception: "Here's an emerging theme of the 2016 election: The improbable rise of Donald Trump has been fueled by a rapid shift of working-class, economically struggling white men into the Republican ranks. Only problem is, there's not much hard evidence to support that."[17] As Nate Silver further elucidates in "The Mythology of Trump's 'Working Class' Support," his followers are comparatively affluent overall: "The median household income for non-Hispanic whites is about $62,000, still a fair bit lower than the $72,000 median for Trump voters."[18] Silver further explains that Trump's supporters are more formally educated than is often presented: "Likewise, although about 44 percent of Trump supporters have college degrees, according to exit polls . . . that's still higher than the 33 percent of non-Hispanic white adults, or the 29 percent of American adults overall, who have at least a bachelor's degree."[19] In political reporting about class, the absence of a college degree often serves as a euphemism for working-class status. As I will elucidate momentarily, Pierre Bourdieu's conceptualization of class in relation to economic, cultural, and social capital is highly useful for parsing out class distinctions, in which both education and income factor into the calculus of class rank. In relation to Silver's 2016 findings, Trump still boasted 46 percent of college-educated whites in 2020.[20] Based upon the voting data, it appears that the news media magnifies the perception that the paradigmatic Trump supporter is a white, working-class male. In short, Trump's more affluent and educated White supporters, who comprise a significant slice of his base, receive significantly less scrutiny in terms of collective culpability for Trump's rise, as well for white supremacist and heteropatriarchal hegemony more broadly.

This begets the question: How did overt racism, sexism, and homophobia become almost exclusively associated with working and lower-class whites? White supremacy and bigotry certainly exist within this demographic, but why do charges of racism and sexism not collectively stick to middle and upper-class whites in the same stigmatizing fashion? Joan C. Williams speaks to this phenomenon in *White Working Class*. She explains that of course both working-class and professional-managerial class whites can be racist and sexist—the difference resides in their typical expression of those prejudices: "Among the professional elite, where the coin of the realm is merit, people of color are constructed as lacking in merit. Among the white working class, where the coin of the realm is morality, people of color are constructed as lacking in that quality."[21] I build on this claim in noting that journalists and other opinion leaders in the news media often hail from and remain firmly ensconced in the professional-managerial class.[22] Thus, the class status of news media professionals precludes them from recognizing their own racism or implicating themselves in social problems—it is far more convenient to scapegoat their lower-class white counterparts. As Williams explains "implicit association test results show that MDs, college grads, and MBAs did not score lower for implicit racial bias than did high school grads."[23] A dominant perception persists that one can simply be educated out of racist thinking and behaviors, which also shifts the focus away from structural racism and promotes the perception that racism is simply a matter of interpersonal animus stemming from ignorance. This is a convenient narrative for highly educated whites, and it elides the reality that groups who are systemically advantaged are invested in retaining those benefits, whether they recognize it consciously or not. As Williams succinctly encapsulates " . . . professional-class racism slides conveniently out of sight in discussions about working-class whites."[24]

118   *Chapter Four*

This is somewhat confounding given that Trump, who has deliberately made racism and sexism centerpieces of his administration's platform, is himself one of the wealthiest persons in the United States. Certainly, this is a manifestation of how classism operates within whiteness, since middle and upper-class whites avoid collective stigmatization because of their economic advantages. I posit that this can also be partially attributed to the permeation of the stylized *performance* of white, rural, working-class masculinity, as taken up by highly visible and (mostly) politically conservative wealthy, white males, such as Willie Robertson at present, and Theodore Roosevelt, Ronald Reagan, and George W. Bush in the past. As I argue in the first chapter, this form of masculine performance constitutes a hegemonic form of masculinity in the current U.S. neoliberal context, since it confers legitimacy and symbolic power. Although Trump's gender performance is not explicitly rural, which I will dissect shortly, the style and content of his speech coincides with a white, working-class masculine performance.

Case in point, J. D. Vance, author of *Hillbilly Elegy: A Memoir of a Family and a Culture in Crisis*, in which he discusses his experiences growing up in an impoverished white family in rural Appalachia, touches upon the symbolic power of white, working-class, masculine performances in relation to Trump. In an interview in *The American Conservative*, Vance suggests that his political traction and appeal are rooted primarily in white, working-class identification with his rhetoric: "No one seems to understand why conventional blunders do nothing to Trump . . . it's not really a blunder as much as it is a rich, privileged Wharton grad connecting to people back home *through style and tone* [emphasis added] . . . People don't want to believe they have to speak like Obama or Clinton to participate meaningfully in politics, because most of us don't speak like Obama or Clinton."[25]

I do not refute that Trump's rhetorical strategy has effectively garnered a sizeable contingent of white, working-class support. Notably, in the same interview, Vance comments that some elites are "entertained" by his discursive performance. It is telling though that he stops short of suggesting that elites may also enthusiastically agree with Trump's rhetoric and policy proposals; he implies that they are too sophisticated to experience anything more than detached amusement. Vance also discusses Trump's eschewment of political correctness—implying that Trump's white, working-class backers long for a president and a dominant culture that will condone the bigoted speech to which they (and evidently only they) are accustomed. He fails to acknowledge the demographic reality that Trump's base is comprised of comparatively more affluent white males overall and reifies the notion that bigoted rhetoric chiefly appeals to lower and working-class whites. In short, racism, sexism, and the push for subverting the supposed reign of "political correctness" is not the exclusive domain of lower and working-class whites, but middle and upper-middle class whites as well. The fact that lower and working-class whites are often collectively branded as bigoted and intolerant in U.S. media, and subsequently, in the public consciousness, whereas middle and upper-class whites avoid that collective characterization, speaks to how classism manifests itself within whiteness.

I have previously argued that through the lens of *Duck Dynasty*, one can discern the symbolic power embedded within the performance of white, rural, working-class masculinity *when coopted by affluent white males*.[26] I explicate the connection between the Robertsons' self-proclaimed "redneck" performance and other white, rural, working-class, masculine rhetorical performances in U.S. electoral politics, specifically in relation to the U.S. presidency both past and present. I attend to the particularities of Trump's performance, in which it lacks a more typical rural character, but as Vance notes above, echoes stereotypical notions of white, male, working-class speech. Trump's performance can be situated within this lineage, and I maintain that based on the demographics of his supporters, his performance also appeals to middle and upper-class white males because of the association between working-class, white masculinity and dominant conceptions of "real men." Like Trump's supporters, viewers of *Duck Dynasty* are also mostly comparatively affluent white males.[27] It is even more telling that according to National Media, a Republican ad-buying firm, the typical *Duck Dynasty* viewer resides in Southern and/or rural areas that characteristically lean Republican.[28] It is unsurprising then that Trump's campaign asked Willie Robertson to speak at the convention—Trump's supporters are demographically more likely to have watched *Duck Dynasty*.

Therefore, through situating *Duck Dynasty* in relation to the embodied performances of prominent wealthy, white male political figures in contemporary and historical contexts, one can trace the symbolic power of this performance because of the confluence of white supremacy, heteropatriarchy, and capitalism within U.S. culture. It exemplifies the tension endemic to class as a social category, in which it simultaneously operates as a socioeconomic location in the capitalist system and as an individual, stylized performance, in which the latter conceptualization is granted primacy in U.S. popular culture and politics.

I approach *Duck Dynasty* as a case study that exemplifies the power relations that underpin "redneck," "country boy," or "frontiersman" performances when taken up by wealthy white males, in which class hierarchies are suppressed and white male supremacy is bolstered. In short, a critical discourse analysis of *Ducky Dynasty* makes the systems of power that encompass the dominant conceptualization of "real men" in the United States visible and pinpoints the motivation for this working-class performance at the behest of comparatively wealthy, white men. It is critical to stress that a

120   *Chapter Four*

working-class structural location itself is cast as undesirable, but the credibility of white, working-class masculinity is actively sought, as demonstrated by the Robertson men, Trump, and George W. Bush.

DUCK DYNASTY: A CASE STUDY IN
HEGEMONIC MASCULINE PERFORMANCE

A&E's reality television program, *Duck Dynasty* (2012–2017), was the most-watched nonfiction series in cable television history, peaking with a record audience of 11.8 million viewers for its season four premiere in August 2013.[29] Despite the show's comparative decline in the Nielsen ratings in later seasons—a drop that has been largely attributed to the publication of Phil's racist and homophobic comments in *GQ* magazine in late 2013[30]—it remained relatively popular for cable television with its season 10 premiere bringing in 1.3 million viewers that evening.[31] The series centers on the wealthy Robertson family of West Monroe, Louisiana. Despite their economic largesse, the male members of the clan proudly tout their "redneck" credentials through hunting, fishing, perpetually wearing camouflage, and sporting long, unkempt beards with lengthy, unruly hair to match. Headed by their patriarch Phil, who originally made his millions through establishing Duck Commander—his family-run business, which manufactures duck calls for hunters—the program documents their lifestyle.

Each episode replicates a highly formulaic trajectory across the show's 11 seasons. The Robertson men are often depicted outdoors either hunting or fishing, and the Robertson women typically appear in the home performing domestic duties, particularly cooking. At times, traditional gender roles are almost hyperbolically enforced. Phil frequently makes remarks regarding who in the family is "appropriately" behaving in accordance with "redneck" standards and who is deviating from the preferred mode in a "yuppie" fashion. Each episode ends with Phil leading a Christian prayer as the whole family enjoys dinner together, while Willie, Phil's son and CEO of Duck Commander, recaps the "lesson" of the episode in a voiceover narration.

One of the core themes of the show is that not only do the family members habitually invoke their "redneck" bona fides, especially Phil, they also frequently assert their superiority in relation to so-called "yuppies." Although the term "yuppies" commonly refers to young (white) urban professionals, Phil applies the term generously to anyone who does not embrace his lifestyle of hunting and fishing. The show discursively configures "rednecks" as authentically masculine and yuppies as feminine, which therefore implies the superiority of the former over the latter in a heteropatriarchal context.

David McKillop, general manager and executive vice president of A&E, sums up the appeal of the Robertson family on *Duck Dynasty*: "The Robertsons represent a lot of things we as Americans cherish: self-made wealth, independence, three generations living together."[32] It is evident that A&E has tapped into salient aspects of U.S. culture given the show's record ratings. The Robertson family has also generated $400 million in sales from *Duck Dynasty* merchandise—establishing the Louisiana clan as a highly marketable brand.[33] Narratives of rugged individualism and upward social mobility remain hegemonic in U.S. culture, especially in the current neoliberal discourse and in reality television by extension.

In this chapter, I explicate and historicize the political significance of upper-class white male public figures and politicians embracing a white, rural, working-class performance through the lens of *Duck Dynasty*. I separate *Duck Dynasty* from my analysis of the other blue-collar frontier reality series for several reasons. First, the Robertson family is far more affluent than the crab fishermen of *Deadliest Catch*, the loggers of *Ax Men*, the drivers of *Ice Road Truckers*, and the miners of *Gold Rush*. This is even the case for the comparatively economically advantaged captains, managers, and company owners featured as the principal stars of said programs. Although *Duck Dynasty* frequently follows members of the Robertson family to the Duck Commander warehouse where they are filmed "on the job," the program does not center on their occupation in the same way as the other blue-collar frontier series. The recreational and leisure activities of the Robertson men are more heavily emphasized in relation to their masculinity; a distinction that I will attend to in significant detail.

In short, the Robertsons are far removed from the trials of the U.S. working class, but they strategically perform as though they are firmly ensconced within its ranks. I will detail through Judith Butler's groundbreaking framework of gender performance how the embodied performances of the Robertson men differ in relation to the embodied performances depicted on the other blue-collar frontier series examined herein. Through the lens of this program, the fraught dynamic between the dual conceptions of social class as both a socioeconomic category and as stylized performance in the United States can be richly observed.

Second, *Duck Dynasty* specifically invokes and valorizes the Robertson men's self-proclaimed "redneck" identity, unlike the other shows, which do not mention the term explicitly. I explore the contested boundaries of the redneck identity and its shifting meanings throughout U.S. history. Third, all the series are structured by the genre conventions of reality television, but there is a noteworthy division between the format of *Duck Dynasty* and the other programs: It mostly focuses on the Robertsons as a family unit in their home environment and remains more in line with the twenty-two-minute sitcom structure, whereas the other series center on the workplace and are more emblematic of forty-four-minute dramas. Lastly, there are more women characters on *Duck Dynasty*, and as I will discuss, policing of traditional, binary gender roles encompasses many of the plot lines.

Throughout my analysis of *Duck Dynasty*, I will draw parallels between the embodied white, rural, working-class masculine performances of the Robertson men and prominent wealthy, white male political figures who have done the same. Although Donald Trump's white, working-class, masculine performance does not strictly adhere to the explicitly rural character of George W. Bush, Ronald Reagan, and Theodore Roosevelt's performances, I elucidate the crossover within entrepreneurial masculinity or "transnational business masculinity" as Connell coins it, and Hooper's conceptualization of "frontier masculinities" within the contemporary globalized economy.[34] I also emphasize how language maintains a performative function, which Trump most aptly exemplifies with his highly masculinized, white, working-class *stereotypical* manner of speaking.

My core objective here is to illuminate the motivation behind these performances. Why would some of the most structurally advantaged subjects— wealthy, white, heteronormative men—self-consciously perform white, working-class masculinity? It is critical to reiterate that this performance remains rooted in white male supremacy, as it inherently excludes women and people of color of all genders. I maintain that Pierre Bourdieu's theorization of capital illuminates why this performance has become a rhetorical strategy for certain affluent, white male politicians. Bourdieu conceives of social life and the struggle for power through the lens of three fundamental and interrelated concepts: habitus—an individual's predispositions toward certain actions or behaviors, capital—sources of power in its economic, cultural, social, and symbolic forms, and field—a spatial metaphor for the relative distribution of power in a specific context.[35] He characterizes the various forms of capital an individual can acquire as the following: "economic capital (money and property), cultural capital (cultural goods and services including educational credentials), social capital (acquaintances and networks), and symbolic capital (legitimation)."[36]

In the case of Phil Robertson, the primary patriarchal figure on *Duck Dynasty*, he not only has a comparatively large amount of economic capital, but he also possesses the cultural capital of a master's degree in education.[37] Furthermore, because of Phil's prominence as a successful business owner and reality television star, this accords him a significant degree of social capital. As I have previously maintained, Phil and the male Robertsons adopted their televised appearances to attain the symbolic capital that the "redneck" image confers in the U.S. context.[38] In *Country Boys: Masculinity and Rural Life*, Hugh Campbell, Michael Mayerfield Bell, and Margaret Finney contend that white, rural, working-class masculinity implies authenticity, and therefore, legitimacy, since it signifies the most preferred form of masculinity in the U.S. gender hierarchy. Again, working-class status as determined by a lack of economic and cultural capital remains undesirable unto itself in the dominant domain. However, the appearances, consumption practices, and recreational activities associated with white, rural, working-class men hold tremendous symbolic power as markers of masculine authenticity.

Based on Bourdieu's understanding of social class, the Robertson family possesses far too many forms of capital in abundance to truly be considered "rednecks"—at least in the socioeconomic sense—a point I will return to. Within this line of reasoning, select white male political figures, who tend toward ideological conservatism, embrace this performance because they seek to gain the symbolic capital and legitimacy of masculine authenticity. This is unsurprising given that political conservatism in the United States remains more *overtly* associated with heteropatriarchal and sexist rhetoric and policies. I argue that white, male, rural, working-class masculinity or "redneck" masculinity constitutes a form of hegemonic masculinity in the current U.S. neoliberal moment—thus making this performance appealing to men across the ideological spectrum. In accordance with this standard of masculinity, white male political conservatives are highly invested in appealing to their base as "real men."

It is important to briefly revisit the parameters of hegemonic masculinity. Raewyn Connell originally coined the concept of hegemonic masculinity in *Gender and Power: Society, the Person, and Sexual Politics* in 1987. In a more recent article, *Hegemonic Masculinity: Rethinking the Concept* (2005), Connell and James W. Messerschmidt claim that " . . . the concept of hegemonic masculinity is in need of reformulation in four main areas: the nature of gender hierarchy, the geography of masculine configurations, *the process of social embodiment* [emphasis added], and the dynamics of masculinities."[39] In essence, hegemonic masculinity should not be collapsed into a monolithic, fixed set of traits. In *Staging Masculinities: History, Gender, Performance*, Michael Mangan succinctly encapsulates the challenges inherent to neatly conceptualizing hegemonic masculinity: "Hegemonic masculinity is that form or model of masculinity which a culture privileges above others . . . Hegemonic masculinity is by nature paradoxical, since it seems to stand still but in fact is always on the move."[40] This necessitates intersectional, socially contextualized approaches to understanding hegemonic masculinity and gender performances more broadly.

The Robertson men are not specifically or overtly coded in *Duck Dynasty* as white, rural, working-class men—their embodied performances imply a visual shorthand for "real men" in U.S. culture. It is only armed with a critical race feminist lens that a viewer could consciously discern that the

Robertsons' race (white), gender (cismen), sexual orientation (heterosexuality), place (rural Louisiana), and class-based aesthetics (working-class) are each mutually constitutive of their perceived legitimacy as real men. I concur with Campbell, Bell, and Finney's assessment that white, rural, working-class masculinity implies authenticity, and therefore, legitimacy, since it signifies the most preferred form of masculinity in the U.S. gender hierarchy. In keeping with the contingent nature of hegemonic masculinity, this does not imply that rural masculinities are ahistorical and static. However, I think one can safely assert that this constellation of traits reflects a dominant conceptualization of hegemonic masculinity in the current U.S. neoliberal context.

Prominent political figures, such as former President George W. Bush, publicly performing a white, rural, working-class masculinity with a cowboy hat, boots, t-shirt, and jeans on his Crawford, Texas ranch, reveals the extent of its symbolic capital: " . . . rural occupational and general 'country boy' representations are often appropriated by individuals for self-serving political and commercial purposes. Like the banners of God and flag, rural 'salt-of-the-earth' occupations confer widespread legitimacy."[41] Historicizing this style of political performance even further, one can trace its origins back to Theodore Roosevelt in the late nineteenth century. As Gail Bederman notes in *Manliness & Civilization*, Roosevelt self-consciously embraced a highly masculine identity that echoes the Robertsons' contemporary performance of hegemonic masculinity to attain political legitimacy: " . . . he constructed a powerful male identity for himself in the terms of the Western adventure story . . . Now, shooting buffalo and bullying obstreperous cowboys, he could style himself the real thing."[42]

Before further analyzing the white, working-class performances of affluent white, male presidents who hail from the Northeastern and Midwestern United States, including Theodore Roosevelt, Ronald Reagan, George W. Bush, and Donald Trump, it is critical to note that this performance has recognizable limits in conferring symbolic capital. This white, working-class performance only seems to be embraced in the political arena when these figures possess either bourgeois or upper-crust pedigrees. In contrast, white male politicians who truly sprung from working-class, white, Southern roots, such as presidents Lyndon Johnson and Bill Clinton, had to overcome and distance themselves from their backgrounds since they were cast as potentially shameful political liabilities.

As Nancy Isenberg notes in *White Trash: The 400-Year Untold History of Class in America*, when Johnson became president after Kennedy's assassination, he had to self-consciously distance himself from his origins: "Yet what made LBJ different from his democratic predecessor was the necessity that he reinvent himself by shedding the predictable trappings of a southern backwater identity—which he did without unlearning his famous Texas drawl."[43]

Isenberg explains that Bill Clinton had to similarly overcome his rural, working-class Arkansas upbringing: "By calling on a Jefferson or a Kennedy in his speeches, Clinton was attempting to distance himself from his home state and class background."[44] This speaks to the reality of class hierarchies in the United States: It is fashionable and advantageous to present as though you are a working-class, "ordinary" or "real" man, if and only if you are a white, heteronormative man with inherited economic privilege. Otherwise, your impoverished or working-class, rural upbringing is something to be ashamed of and overcome if you properly assimilate into the professional-managerial class (PMC). Thus, if the Robertsons of *Duck Dynasty* were truly "rednecks" in the socioeconomic sense, then the production logic of reality television would more likely frame them as objects of ridicule instead of as subjects of masculine admiration. In this sense, *Duck Dynasty* does not fall in line with the so-called "rednexploitation" series, such as *Here Comes Honey Boo Boo*, which focus on poor and working-class, rural whites, wherein they are comically mocked for eschewing middle-class sensibilities and social mores.[45]

DUCK DYNASTY: A REDNECK DRAG SHOW

After public controversy ignited following the revelation of Phil's homophobic and racist comments in late 2013, the family's starkly contrasting appearances before the reality show also surfaced in the popular media. Through a series of widely publicized photographs, it became clear that the Robertsons had fully embraced so-called "yuppie" appearances before their careers on A&E.[46] The discursive deployment of "redneck" as an authentically masculine, superior identity and "yuppie" as a feminized, subordinate label remains one of the organizing rhetorical principles of the series. The irony of the Robertsons having previously performed as "yuppies" themselves elicited significant media commentary.

In these "before" photos, the Robertson men are on the beach and golf course looking clean-shaven with short haircuts, as they pose wearing khakis and button-down shirts.[47] In a family portrait of Willie Robertson, his wife, and children on the beach, Willie presents a drastically different look than during his speech at the Republican National Convention. With his short, frosted-tipped hair, he and his family look like the prototypical, suburban family from the 2000s.[48] These images sharply contrast with their trademark long beards, hair, and camouflage. These photos prompted several mainstream media commentators to decry the Robertsons as "fake."[49] Critics drawing parallels with the drag show as a site of gender performance in relation to the Robertsons' redneck performance is evidenced in the headline

126   *Chapter Four*

from the Daily Kos: "Duck Dynasty is a Fake Yuppies-in-Red-Neck-Drag Con Job."[50]

As Drew Magary notes in his now infamous *GQ* profile on Phil, *Duck Dynasty*'s $400-million merchandising empire includes an iPhone game, which according to the press release, describes the goal of the game as follows: "'As players successfully complete the challenges, their beards grow to epic proportions and they start to transform from a yuppie into a full-blown redneck!'"[51] The irony of the game's description in relation to the Robertson men's real-life transformation from yuppies to rednecks is comical. As Daniel Luzer effectively summarizes regarding the emergence of the photographs in *Washington Monthly*, "Indeed, Jep and Phil (who has a master's degree in education from Louisiana Tech University) might think of themselves as rednecks . . . But if ol' frosted tipped, barefoot on the beach Willie is a redneck, I don't know what a real southern gentleman even is. A&E appears to have taken a large clan of affluent, college-educated, mildly conservative, country club Republicans, common across the nicer suburbs of the old south, and repackaged them as the Beverly Hillbillies."[52]

This examination is highly informed by Judith Butler's groundbreaking work on gender performance, in which Butler treats gender as an embodied social construction that one "does" or "performs" either in accordance with or in subversion of hegemonic gender expectations. In the preface to the 1999 edition of *Gender Trouble*, Butler critically elucidates the interconnectedness of gender and sexuality: " . . . under conditions of normative heterosexuality, policing gender is sometimes used as a way of securing heterosexuality."[53] Policing binary gender roles is a prominent current that runs throughout *Duck Dynasty*'s 11 seasons. The Robertson men are often depicted outdoors either hunting in the woods or fishing in the swamp and are rarely shown wearing anything other than their camouflage attire. The Robertson women typically appear in the home, usually dressed in middle-class, business casual or leisure attire, as they perform domestic duties, particularly cooking. Overall, the Robertson women are rarely portrayed as active in either indoor or outdoor environments. As John Berger once noted regarding patriarchal gender depictions in the dominant visual order in *Ways of Seeing*: " . . . *men act* and *women appear*."[54] *Duck Dynasty* exemplifies this adage.

Phil at times hyperbolically enforces traditional gender roles, as he makes frequent remarks regarding who in the family is "appropriately" behaving in accordance with masculine "redneck" standards and who is deviating from the preferred mode in a feminized "yuppie" fashion. One can infer from Phil's homophobic comments in *GQ* that his preoccupation with performing an authentic masculinity is connected to his belief in compulsory heterosexuality. It is essential to contextualize that Phil's beliefs are consistent with hegemonic and inherently oppressive ideologies regarding the relationship between normative performances of gender and sexuality.

Within Butler's formulation of gender performance, it is crucial to understand that the male Robertsons are always already performing masculine identities in accordance with their male sex assignment at birth. As Butler explains in *Gender Trouble*, " . . . the action of gender requires a performance that is *repeated*. This repetition is at once a reenactment and re-experiencing of a set of meanings already socially established . . . "[55] Even when they were performing "yuppie" masculine identities prior to their careers on *A&E*, they were not deviating from the limited spectrum of characteristics and behaviors ascribed to normative standards of gender and sexuality. However, the "yuppie" masculine identity is not configured as the most preferred or legitimate within masculine hierarchies. It is then useful to draw an analytical distinction between *performativity* and *performance*. Building off Butler's framework, Helen Wood and Beverly Skeggs explain in *Reality Television and Class* that " . . . perform*atives* are unconscious repeated gendered and classed enactments, while performances are full-blown conscious actions. What we often see on reality television is the perfomative made explicit."[56] The male Robertsons' on-camera performances of redneck masculinity appear more self-conscious and calculated based upon their prior appearances. To echo Pierre Bourdieu's theorizing, I surmise that despite possessing significant amounts of economic and cultural capital (college degrees), the Robertsons were still missing the symbolic capital of masculine legitimacy. Thus, their embrace of redneck *performances*.

To further illustrate the relevance of class performativity to the analysis of reality television more broadly, Vicki Mayer explains in *Reality Television and Class* how her experience in the industry spotlights the importance of understanding social categories in relation to how they are performed: "My experience with the reality casting process revealed its emphasis on embodied performances. Casters search not only for people within certain demographics, but also for those who act appropriately to the demographic."[57] Therefore, one must often perform *stereotypically* in relation to social categories within the commercial logic of reality television. Through the lens of reality television programs typically seeking out those who embody certain class-based characteristics that reflect their actual socioeconomic location, the Robertsons presenting as rednecks despite their economic largesse becomes even more incongruous. It is highly instructive then to situate their self-proclaimed redneck presentation as a performance and not as an unconscious performative expression. The masculine performances of the male subjects of *Deadliest Catch*, *Ax Men*, *Gold Rush*, and *Ice Road Truckers* would fall more in line with unconscious performative expression because they are not wealthy, white men who have self-consciously decided to perform as though they rightfully belong among working-class men—they are workers, as well as some middle-class managers, performing manual labor, as discussed in the first chapter.

Butler is widely recognized for pinpointing the drag show as a site of gender performance that destabilizes the naturalized rigidity of the gender binary: " . . . *drag implicitly reveals the imitative structure of gender itself—as well as its contingency* . . . In the place of the law of heterosexual coherence, we see sex and gender denaturalized by means of a performance which avows their distinctness and dramatizes the cultural mechanism of their fabricated unity."[58] It is critical to distinguish that Butler does not suggest that drag is necessarily subversive unto itself. As exemplified by the Daily Kos headline, "Duck Dynasty is a Fake Yuppies-in-Red-Neck-Drag Con Job,"[59] there is nothing transgressive about the Robertsons' performances. These wealthy white men self-consciously perform a redneck identity to gain legitimacy, broad-based appeal, and commercial success. If anything, *Duck Dynasty* covertly performs the ideological work of reifying the gender binary, white supremacy, and the neoliberal dictums of rugged individualism and upward mobility.

As Butler explicates in her chapter "Imitation and Gender Insubordination" in *The Lesbian and Gay Studies Reader*, "Identity categories" discipline bodies within regulatory regimes, whether for hegemonic or counterhegemonic ends.[60] It is integral to understand that performances constitute subject formation. In other words, subjects become intelligible through performances. It is noteworthy then that marginalized groups are often discursively, socially, and legally deprived of subjectivity. This accounts for the anxiety produced when individuals do not conform or neatly fit within socially constructed categories, such as transgender individuals. Gender nonconforming individuals are only intelligible as "others" within hegemonic framings. This process of relationally marking certain bodies as either naturalized or "other" through the lens of social categories and interrelated structures of domination only has a fictional, socially constructed ideological basis. As Butler asserts, "If a regime of sexuality mandates a compulsory performance of sex, then it may be only through that performance that the binary system of gender and the binary system of sex come to have intelligibility at all."[61]

Building off Butler's formulation, the Robertson men went on television to perform as "real men" for a national audience. Compulsory heterosexuality and the gender binary produce conceptions and discourses of "real men" and "real women"; these are the fictionalized "original" standards to which all bodies are measured. As Butler cautiously elucidates, they are socially constructed notions, but have *real* effects and embodied consequences via the naturalization and repetition of gender performances. This does not imply that the characteristics associated with "real men" and "real women" do not shift or evolve according to context, but standardized barometers of authentic masculinity and femininity unto themselves, in some form or another, always remain.

In *Sex, Drag, and Male Roles: Investigating Gender as Performance*, Diane Torr and Stephen Bottoms crucially recognize that masculine drag performances are not confined to the stage, in which male roles are performed by bodies socially marked as female, such as with drag kings. Torr and Bottoms provide a lens through which everyday masculine gender performances can be made legible as form of drag: "It is almost commonplace nowadays to suggest that men, too, are male impersonators . . . imitating the available models of masculinity and anxiously trying to live up to some idealized notion of what a 'real man' looks like."[62] When one approaches the male cast of *Duck Dynasty* as male impersonators, their quest to be seen as real men becomes visible.

A&E promotes the Robertsons as real men because they know such a narrative will attract viewers and advertising dollars. The program's overarching narrative trajectory, in which "real men" hunt and "real women" cook, appeals to a more conservative, mainstream audience's familiarity and comfort with the gender binary. Moreover, perhaps the series speaks to viewers' own personal attempts to approximate masculine and feminine ideals respectively. Looking back at Willie Robertson's comments at the Republican National Convention, one can infer that the "media experts" he is referring to must be men, when he states that "they don't hang out with regular folks like us who like to hunt and fish and pray and actually work for a living."[63] Willie is attempting to feminize, and therefore, delegitimize them, because they do not engage in the appropriate hegemonically masculine activities.

The policing of gender roles on *Duck Dynasty* is not restricted to the male Robertsons. In Season One: Episode Three: "High Teck Redneck," Phil takes his teenage grandson, John Luke, hunting. He proclaims in a cutaway interview (a common narrative device utilized in reality television) that through hunting animals: "We teach them valuable knowledge about life, manhood."[64] The integral connection between manhood and hunting is reinforced throughout the series. Miss Kay, Phil's wife, is shown wearing her apron in the kitchen, which is how she is typically presented. As she finishes up cooking squirrels, she tells John Luke as he is leaving to go hunting with Phil: "You bring home the game or you're not a man. That's what I say."[65] This illuminates how patriarchy is not only maintained by men, but by women who have internalized patriarchal values as "common sense." Later in that same episode, Phil informs John Luke while they are hunting: "If you catch squirrels for your woman, your woman will never cut you off in bed." The link between hunting and masculine sexual prowess within compulsory heterosexuality is comedically cemented.

130 *Chapter Four*

TRUMP'S PERFORMANCE: NOT
FAR FROM THE FRONTIER

Although Trump is not known for hunting himself, he is a gun owner who made virtually unrestricted access to firearms a centerpiece of his campaigns—garnering him an endorsement from the National Rifle Association. His sons, Donald Trump, Jr. and Eric Trump, generated significant controversy when photos of them posing with a dead leopard, elephant, and buffalo that they had hunted in Zimbabwe circulated on social media in 2012 and again in 2015.[66] Trump has defended his sons and speaks of their hunting activities with pride.[67] Theodore Roosevelt is famously associated with hunting big game,[68] and George W. Bush was an avid hunter during his presidency.[69] Although Reagan was not known for hunting specifically, he was publicly photographed holding rifles,[70] and his "cowboy" public persona was solidified through being frequently photographed while riding horseback and sporting a cowboy hat.[71]

As is emphasized throughout *Duck Dynasty*, real men wield guns, hunt, and have a general proclivity toward violence. Willie Robertson underscores the place of violence within his performance of white, working-class masculinity when he draws a parallel between Trump and his own brothers in his speech at the RNC: "See when you're from the South and you grow up with *rednecks* [emphasis added], there are some occasional disagreements. Sometimes those disagreements turn into fisticuffs. But any time I was ever in a bad spot, I always knew my brothers would have my back. And today in a lot of ways, America is in a bad spot, and we need a president who will have our back."[72] The rhetorical inference is that Trump, like his "redneck" brothers, will use violence as president. This begat a prescient question before Trump's election: *Who* exactly would Trump use violence against and in defense of *whom* in the United States? Who are the subjects of the "our back" Willie refers to in conjunction with his own? Clearly, Trump's racist, sexist, and anti-immigrant policies demonstrated that "defending" primarily white men was an organizing principle of his administration. The events of January 6, 2021, evidenced that Trump was willing to agitate for violence in service of himself, wherein white men could expect protection and women and people of color could expect threats to their rights and safety.

In a frightening turn of events, Trump implied in August 2016 that his Democratic opponent, Hillary Clinton and/or her potential Supreme Court nominees, should be shot. At a rally in Wilmington, North Carolina, Trump casually commented regarding Hillary's potential choices for Supreme Court: "If she gets to pick her judges — nothing you can do, folks. Although, the Second Amendment people. Maybe there is. I don't know."[73] Trump has also directly incited violence with his rhetoric numerous times against protestors at his rallies,[74] which then culminated with him spurring the insurrection at the Capitol. Highly masculinized threats of violence; aggressive posturing; racist, sexist, and xenophobic speech; and the glamorization of gun ownership have become hallmarks of Trump's performance on the campaign trail and in the White House.

I situate Trump's stereotypical white, working-class rhetorical performance within Kenway, Kraack, and Hickey-Moody's synthesis of Hooper and Connell's conceptualizations of "frontier masculinities" and "transnational business masculinity" respectively.[75] Trump consistently appears in public wearing conventional male business attire—a suit and tie. Trump has been a well-known real-estate mogul for decades and dresses the part accordingly. Unlike the Robertsons and the other white, affluent male political figures included in this examination, Trump rarely deviates from his professional attire in public, and he does not embrace an explicitly "rural" or "blue-collar" wardrobe of jeans, t-shirts, camouflage, and so on. The only notable exception to this was when Trump adorned his now iconic red, baseball cap with his campaign slogan, "Make America Great Again," scrawled across the front during the campaign. The hat signifies a concerted attempt to connect with white, working-class voters, and as I contend, gestures toward Trump's strategic effort to present as authentically masculine.

Furthermore, Trump taps into salient aspects of white, working-class or hegemonic masculinity within the transnational corporate realm as well. Kenway, Kraack, and Hickey-Moody interpret Hooper's conceptualization of "frontier masculinities," which speaks to the nature of Trump's performance: " . . . 'frontier masculinities,' have been reinscribed or recontextualized in relation to globalization . . . the kind of masculine behavior that was integral to the process of English imperialism and American frontiers has been updated and become fundamental to global corporate zones of influence . . . "[76] Essentially, Trump's performance in the boardroom and on the campaign trail is commensurate with the white supremacist, patriarchal imperialism endemic to the mythic frontier, as is discussed at length in chapter two. As Isenberg notes in *White Trash*, Donald Trump's performance on his reality television series, *The Apprentice*, was " . . . billed as a 'seductive weave of aspiration and Darwinism,' [which] celebrated ruthlessness."[77] Trump's merciless catchphrase from the series, "you're fired!," became iconic in U.S. popular culture. Even though rural, working-class dress and other frontiersman characteristics are absent from Trump's performance, the attitude, sensibility, and rhetoric remain.

Historicizing Trump's performance of hegemonic masculinity in relation to Theodore Roosevelt is instructive regarding the relationship between mainstream conceptions of "real manhood" and white supremacist, patriarchal,

132   *Chapter Four*

imperialist discourses. Roosevelt said himself in his famous 1899 address "The Strenuous Life": "As it is with the individual, so it is with the nation."[78] Gail Bederman provides a critical lens in *Manliness & Civilization* for interpreting Roosevelt's speech, in which he aggressively advocated for the U.S. to colonize Cuba, Puerto Rico, and the Philippines: " . . . Ostensibly, the speech never mentions gender at all. Yet the phrase 'the strenuous life' soon began to connote a virile, hard-driving manhood . . . "[79] She notes that is vital to understand " . . . that his [Roosevelt's] strenuous manhood was inextricably linked to his nationalism, imperialism, and racism."[80] I argue that is vital to read Trump's performance of manhood in a similar fashion—it cannot be delinked from his racist, sexist, and nationalistic aims.

A critical caveat to Butler's theorization of gender performance is the notion that most subjects will always already fail to reproduce gender ideals. As Jonathan Culler summarizes, "To be a subject at all is to be given this assignment of repetition, but—and this is important for Butler—an assignment which we never quite carry out according to expectation, so that we never quite inhabit the gender norms or ideals we are compelled to approximate."[81] Few bodies naturally approximate the fictionalized standards of "real men" and "real women," especially when configured within a global context wherein these categories are continually underpinned by compulsory heteronormativity and white supremacy. Bodies of color and gender nonconforming bodies are precluded from "the real" standards of gender at the outset. I conclude that it is this overarching anxiety of not measuring up to masculine ideals that, in part, compelled the Robertson men to shed their so-called "yuppie" appearances in favor of a more authentically masculine, redneck performance in the first place.

Trump's performance can be situated similarly. In the chapter, *Sexually Suspect: Masculine Anxiety in the Films of Neil LaBute,* in the anthology, *Performing American Masculinities: The 21st-Century Man in Popular Culture*, Brenda Boudreau discusses what Michael Kimmel refers to as "Marketplace Man": a well-groomed, nicely dressed, white-collar professional man who asserts his masculinity through overt displays of money and status.[82] "Marketplace Man" would directly coincide with the characterization of "yuppies" on *Duck Dynasty* and is also applicable to Donald Trump. Boudreau notes the tenuous position of marketplace masculinity, since its essence resides in white male professionals appearing to deliberately invest time and money into their personal presentation. For example, Trump is often criticized for appearing to wear a hairpiece and sporting a fake tan.[83] It is important to contextualize that part of what makes redneck-type masculinities appear authentic is that they imply a lack of time and energy expenditure on one's own appearance. The inference is that real men do not care about how they look—they effortlessly effuse masculine authenticity. Ironically, the Robertsons' calculated switch to a redneck presentation indicates quite the opposite.

Boudreau succinctly captures the inherent anxiety and tension within performances of so-called marketplace masculinity: "Thus, while their class position gives these men the time and freedom to worry obsessively about appearances, it has paradoxically emasculated them, revealing the performativity of masculinity (and, hence, its vulnerability)."[84] One can then insinuate that the Robertson men felt the same degree of emasculation when they were performing as yuppies, and thus sought out redneck drag as a refuge to ensure their masculine bona fides. In the same vein, Trump's hyper-masculine and violent rhetoric seeks to combat any perceived feminization that comes with a "Market-Place Man"-style performance. However, as per Hooper's conceptualization of "frontier masculinities" within the globalized economy, Trump's performance can also be understood as overlapping with white, rural, working-class masculinity's intertwined settler-colonial and rugged individualist sensibilities.

A highly representative instance in *Duck Dynasty* of the anxiety that drives gender policing is with Jase Robertson, Phil's son and Willie's brother, who also perpetually wears camo with a long beard and unkempt hair, in Season Three: Episode Nine: "Ring Around the Redneck." The narrative arch of the episode centers on Jase's reluctance to wear a replacement wedding ring because he previously lost it frog hunting twenty years ago. Jase is only doing so at the behest of his wife, Missy Robertson. As Jase says to the salesclerk at the jewelry store: "I'm not a ring type of guy."[85] When they are looking at the display case in the store, Missy suggests a ring that has diamonds in it. Jase puts it on, and then immediately takes it off saying with disgust, "No. That's way too feminine."[86]

Later in the episode, when Jase is at the Duck Commander warehouse spinning his new ring on the table, Jase's Uncle Si, Phil's brother and a U.S. Army veteran, comments: "He's been stripped of his manhood, boys. She finally won." Willie jumps in and adds: "Today a wedding ring, tomorrow a fanny pack!"[87] Jase maintains a tenuous grasp on real manhood in the eyes of his family, as simply wearing a wedding ring can somehow threaten to destabilize his masculine authenticity. Although the tone of the series is comedic, it does not transcend the anxiety around this seemingly light-hearted gender policing. For example, Jase appears sincere after his wife, Missy, and Willie's wife, Korie, challenge Jase and the other men to a game of ping-pong, and he says: "We can't lose to the women. That's embarrassing."[88]

134   *Chapter Four*

TOUGH TALK: HOW "REAL MEN" SPEAK

In *Literary Theory: A Very Short Introduction,* Jonathan Culler reveals how language itself has performative and regulatory functions linked to subject formations. Culler cites how everything from gendered pronouns to derogatory gender and sexuality-based pejoratives function to interpellate subjects. For example, if I am referred to as "she" by my relatives from birth, this repetitive language subjects me to a social expectation of feminine performativity. The "yuppies versus rednecks" dichotomous discourse on *Duck Dynasty* has a similar "performative force."[89] Via the show's narrative framing, Phil Robertson repeatedly utters the term "redneck" in contexts that discursively reassert his claims to hegemonic masculinity, while simultaneously defining inferior, feminized others as "yuppies" in relation to himself. As per Culler's theorizing, this discursive repetition carries as much performative power as the Robertson's embodied performances.

The performative function of language is overwhelmingly apparent with Donald Trump. It is not only his aggressive finger-pointing (literally and figuratively) as he speaks, but his name-calling and bullying rhetoric. As Willie implies, real men hunt, fish, pray, and are "politically incorrect" like his father Phil and Trump. Although I do not want to reproduce Trump's numerous sexist, racist, and homophobic statements, I want to highlight that his domineering, mocking, and violent rhetoric is commensurate with white, male supremacist ideology. Again, "real men" are always already implied to be white men in U.S. culture. Trump is not genteel in his speech—his rhetorical performance is coded as evincing a working-class ethos. As Vance notes, Trump's performative speech mirrors the discourse of Vance's own white, rural, working-class upbringing in Appalachia. It is not only the content of his words, but his body language and aggressive posturing. It is worth underscoring that Trump approximates a *stereotypical* white, working-class masculine manner of speech—in which he delinks this rhetorical performance from its structural location. This reifies a neoliberal tendency of framing social categories as primarily performative enactments delinked from power relations—thus enabling their stylistic co-optation in certain instances, such as with Trump taking up a white, rural, working-class rhetorical style.

Trump's performance provides a glimpse into the central place of violence within hegemonic masculinity, especially given that his rhetoric has incited violence at his rallies and most notably, during the insurrection at the Capitol on January 6, 2021. In Season Two: Episode Seven: "Spring Pong Cleaning," one can observe a representative instance of violence being normalized and celebrated in relation to evincing masculine prowess. Jase Robertson states in a cutaway interview from a scene in which he and the other employees at the Duck Commander warehouse play a game of ping-pong: "Everyone likes a little violence . . . how can we make ping-pong more violent?"[90] Hunting itself is also inherently violent. In Season Three: Episode Nine: "Ring Around the Redneck," Jase reluctantly goes shopping for a wedding ring with his wife Missy to replace the one he lost. He states in the cutaway interview: "The only metal that I find precious . . . is the metal that they use to make guns."[91] (2013). Again, guns, hunting, and violence are core characteristics of stereotypical conceptions of white, rural, working-class masculinity.

Trump's rhetoric is overtly anti-intellectual, which is also a stereotypical and stigmatizing characteristic of white, rural, working-class discourse. One of the primary features of a working-class structural location is lacking higher education—typically because of expense, especially in the United States. Trump's deployment of anti-intellectual rhetoric is ironic given that he is a graduate of the elite Wharton School of the University of Pennsylvania. In *Duck Dynasty*, Phil often ridicules anyone who relies on technology—either labeling them "yuppies" or "nerds." In Season One: Episode Three: "High Tech Redneck," Phil declares in a cutaway interview about taking his grandsons hunting: "I would consider it an obligation to my grandkids to show them the great outdoors, as they say. The last thing I would want for my grandkids is to grow up to be nerds."[92] It is important to emphasize that Phil is not referring to his female grandchildren. He conceives of a "nerd" as a feminized male identity that he wants to ensure his grandsons do not gravitate toward. To reiterate, he recognizes hunting and the outdoors as linchpins to masculine authenticity. In Season Two: Episode Seven: "Spring Pong Cleaning," Phil once again chastises his grandsons for playing video games and declares: "The last thing we need is more nerds."[93]

The series humorously celebrates anti-intellectual endeavors and behaviors, despite several of the Robertson men possessing advanced degrees. When the Robertson men engage in some drills with the West Monroe Fire Department in Season Six: Episode Four: "Quackdraft," Willie asserts in a cutaway interview: "As a redneck myself, I can safely say that when it comes to fire, we're usually the ones setting the fire . . . Definitely not putting them out."[94] As always, Willie explicitly self-identifies as a redneck—discursively strengthening the association with white, working-class masculinity and anti-intellectual, dangerous behavior, such as setting fires. In Willie's closing voiceover narration of Season Eight: Episode Two: "Induckpendence Day," he notably solidifies the critical place of anti-intellectual rhetoric and behavior within white, rural, working-class masculine drag performances. As he espouses his view of the symbolic importance of the Fourth of July and its hegemonic association with personal freedoms, he announces: "That includes the freedom to say what we want, like your uncle calling you a 'maggot,' or the freedom to do what we want, like setting off a crate full of

136   *Chapter Four*

fireworks."[95] Interestingly, the sentiment here echoes Willie's RNC speech, in which he defends his father and Donald Trump's racist, sexist, and homophobic rhetoric, or in other words, their right "to say what they want." Given the systemic erosion of civil liberties post-9/11, it is telling that Willie identifies "setting off a crate full of fireworks" as an example of a cherished and protected personal freedom. However, this remains in line with his redneck drag performance—he wants to present as anti-intellectual and violent—as "real men" supposedly are.

Former President George W. Bush is still widely remembered for his anti-intellectual rhetoric. His mispronunciations, grammatical errors, and oversimplified explanations provided ample fodder for late-night comedians. Bush memorably espoused anti-intellectual, Western frontier rhetoric just days after the 9/11 terrorist attacks. Regarding the search for Osama bin Laden, Bush remarked on September 17, 2001: "I want justice. And there's an old poster out West, I recall, that says, 'Wanted: Dead or Alive.'"[96] Obviously, Bush is referring to the posters he had seen in fictional Western films. Bush's cowboy rhetoric matched the cowboy persona he cultivated on his Crawford, Texas ranch, also known as the Western White House during his tenure.[97]

In the 2004 presidential election, Bush was characterized in the mainstream media as the more authentically masculine candidate as compared to his Democratic opponent, John Kerry. Meredith Conroy analyzes the media coverage of the 2004 election at length in *Masculinity, Media, and the American Presidency.* Conroy argues that the mainstream media branding Bush as authentically masculine and Kerry as effete and feminine was a contributing factor in Kerry's electoral defeat.[98] In a 2004 Pew Research poll, 56 percent of respondents answered that Bush came off to them as more of a "real person" than Kerry.[99] I suggest that the designation of "real person" could logically be extended to the more gendered designation, "real man."

The notion that high intelligence is an undesirable, feminizing trait for men has emerged at other prominent moments within U.S. presidential politics. As Isenberg notes in *White Trash*, 1956 Democratic presidential nominee Adlai Stevenson was pejoratively described as an "egghead."[100] President Obama's performance in one of the 2012 presidential debates against Republican candidate Mitt Romney was negatively characterized as "professorial" by numerous political pundits.[101] Although overtly gendered terms were not utilized in describing Obama's performance, the notion that speaking in a professorial or intellectual manner indicates weakness was apparent in the critical commentary following the debate. In a patriarchal context, weakness and femininity are linked, as is masculinity and strength. Fox News contributor Mark Sanford portrayed the debate as follows: "As Romney leaned in, Obama seemed to retreat rather than engage. Keep it up for a few more debates and the president might be putting that *professorial* style to good use—in academia."[102] Romney is portrayed as aggressive and decisive, which aligns with hegemonic masculinity. Therefore, in the case of Trump and the Robertsons, their anti-intellectual, brutish speech signals that they are, in fact, real men, and not feminine nerds or wimps.

Moving forward, it is critical to chart the contingent meaning of the term "redneck," which the Robertson men discursively unleash so frequently. Although Trump does not use this term in reference to himself, it is clear in Willie's RNC speech that he identifies Trump as behaving similarly to him and his fellow self-proclaimed rednecks. What does the redneck identity signify, and how has its meaning changed throughout the years?

WHAT DOES IT MEAN TO PLAY REDNECK?

The wealthy and highly educated Robertsons embracing a so-called "redneck" lifestyle raises critical questions about what the term signifies in the contemporary, neoliberal context. The family's redneck self-identification is seemingly incongruous given their comparative wealth. Is redneck still a *classed* term in contemporary discourse? Is it now only used to signify white, rural Southerners who are drawn to a lifestyle that appreciates the outdoors regardless of their socioeconomic status? With Bourdieu's configuration of social class in mind, one can analytically juxtapose the notions that the term redneck signifies both a working-class structural location and a stylized performance marked by white, rural, working-class masculinity. The latter conceptualization of redneck is particularly relevant in the current hegemonic, neoliberal discourse, which deemphasizes class consciousness and social location in favor of individualism and stylistic performance. Trent Watts quotes Charles Reagan Wilson's description of the contemporary, neoliberal characterization of a redneck in mainstream discourse in *White Masculinity in the Recent South*: "The Southern working-class version of redneck is becoming the national version, and it's good-natured, it has humor, and in some ways, it's a *performance* [emphasis added]."[103]

The word redneck is most widely documented as having its roots as a derogatory term used by aristocratic whites in reference to white rural laborers in the American South, particularly Mississippi, in the late nineteenth century.[104] Despite its negative connotation, the term seems to have gained mainstream acceptance in recent years. Edward W. Morris succinctly encapsulates the parameters of the term in his ethnographic study of a rural school in "Rednecks, Rutters, and 'Rithmetic": "The term 'redneck' is a well-known popular culture identity that implies being blue-collar, rebellious, and southern. On a more tacit level, 'redneck' also strongly represents masculinity and

138   Chapter Four

whiteness . . . This identity is unabashedly white, but opposed to middle- and upper-class whiteness."[105]

Morris explicates the interconnection of race and gender within social class in terms of white masculinity's indispensability to the redneck identity, as is exemplified on *Duck Dynasty*. He further explains the resurgence of the term in the rural location of his study because of the white male subjects there investing more in their whiteness and masculinity, evidently, because of their economic marginalization: "Uses of the term 'redneck' captured a sense of pride embedded in living in this 'rough,' white working-class, rural location. Through the implication of toughness and opposition to elitist sophistication, this regional category offered a classed and raced template consistent with local hegemonic masculinity."[106]

Isenberg discusses how the redneck identity became more prominent in popular culture as part of a collective embrace of multiculturalism in the 1970s: "The same impulses would soon be used to refashion the redneck and embrace white trash as an authentic heritage . . . Vernon Oxford [the country music singer] defined 'redneck' as 'someone who enjoys country music and likes to drink beer.'"[107] Isenberg attends to the ongoing class conflicts that persisted, even as the redneck identity appeared superficially to have attained mainstream acceptance: "Many southern suburbanites had no sympathy for the white trash underclass in their section. They drew a sharp class line between the lower-class rednecks and the 'upscale rednecks.'"[108]

Isenberg pinpoints the structural limitations of a redneck performance: A person who occupies a white, male, rural, working-class structural location is still maligned for not achieving the American dream of self-made, upward economic mobility. Thus, the Robertsons can be admired and emulated as real men because their redneck performance coincides with a higher socioeconomic status, whereas the truly working-class, largely female, self-proclaimed redneck Shannon-Thompson family of TLC's *Here Comes Honey Boo Boo*, were subjected to ridicule and criticism for their on-camera performances.[109] The dominant culture will only truly accept and celebrate comparatively affluent white men "playing redneck."

Isenberg speaks to the rigid gendered aspect of the redneck performance. She observes that in the 1990s, "Redneck was no longer the exclusive province of country singers. It had become part of the cultural lingua franca, a means of sizing up *public men* [emphasis added], and a strangely mutated gender and class identity."[110] This suggests that there was a steady process by which the redneck identity became continually dislodged from the structural realities of social class. It was morphing into an identity that would fall in line with neoliberal, multiculturalism, in which the power differentials that exist between identities are suppressed in the public discourse and consciousness. She identifies two women authors from white, rural, working-class backgrounds, Dorothy Allison and Carolyn Chute, whose contributions to popular understandings of white, rural, working-class life did not receive the same type of mainstream adulation. She pinpoints that "what they showed instead was that women cannot wear 'white trash' or 'redneck' as a badge of honor."[111] Simply put, only class-privileged, white, heteronormative men can.

Interestingly, Isenberg does not recognize the tension of the Robertsons occupying a higher socioeconomic status than their truly working-class, reality television counterparts: "After 2008, a new crop of TV shows came about that played off the white trash trope . . . The modern impulse for slumming also found expression in reviving the old stock vaudeville characters. One commentator remarked of the highly successful *Duck Dynasty*, set in Louisiana, 'All the men look like they stepped out of the Hatfield-McCoy conflict to smoke a corncob pipe.'"[112]

Indeed, *Duck Dynasty* emerged as part of this wider trend in reality television. However, the fact that the Robertson men are treated as subjects worthy of admiration because of their wealth and masculine prowess, and not derided as lower-class degenerates, needs to be acknowledged.

Phil Robertson's continual usage of the word redneck is almost always in relation to his criticism of yuppies (young urban professionals or young upwardly mobile professionals). Phil employs the terms redneck and yuppie in a context that does not overtly signify class status; he uses them as expressions that represent two divergent, gendered, and asymmetrical lifestyles. It seems the redneck versus yuppie dichotomy in many ways mirrors the gender binary. The redneck lifestyle is constructed as authentically masculine, while the yuppie lifestyle is situated as feminine and inauthentic, and therefore, subordinate. According to Phil throughout the series, yuppies are not "real men" because they live in urban areas, have professional occupations, wear formal attire, and do not hunt or fish.

This central theme in *Duck Dynasty* is encapsulated in the compilation clip titled "yuppies." The clip summarizes Phil's characterizations of who he identifies as a yuppie. It not only includes Phil's comments, but his son Jep and Jep's wife Jessica's opinions about what being a yuppie means:

> *Phil [to his grandson]:* Don't marry some yuppie girl . . . find you a kind-spirited country girl . . . if she knows how to cook . . . now there's a woman.

> *Jep:* A dude that's clean-shaved, that's wearing like a shirt and tie, oh he's a yuppie . . . pretty much anybody that doesn't spend time in the woods, that's a yuppie.

> *Jessica*: City people that, you know, don't generally know anything about hunting or live that lifestyle.[113]

140 *Chapter Four*

Unsurprisingly, Phil's conception of the ideal woman is heavily tied to traditional domestic duties, such as cooking. This suggests by logical extension that so-called yuppie women do not fulfill these roles adequately. Again, the understanding of the term yuppie as a category of social class is subsumed by rhetoric that delineates it solely as a stylized performance and lifestyle orientation tied to geographic location. Although Phil and the others do not state it explicitly here, it is implied that men are typically the ones who fish and hunt, while women remain in the kitchen. Throughout the series, the men and women of *Duck Dynasty* strictly adhere to these ascribed gender roles, including Phil's wife Miss Kay. These roles are only occasionally "transgressed," such as when Phil takes his granddaughters fishing in Season Four: Episode Two: "So You Think You Can Date?"[114]

A particularly demonstrative moment regarding the policing of gender roles occurs in Season Five: Episode Four: "From Duck 'til Dawn." Miss Kay is painting her nails with her two young granddaughters in the kitchen when Phil enters. The girls ask if they can sleep over, and Phil is reluctant. Leaning back in his recliner, the two girls hop on Phil's lap, and ask him repeatedly and excitedly if they can sleep over. He then asks them a series of questions before he agrees:

Phil: "Who's the best hunter in the world?

Girls: "You!"

Phil: "Who's a great fisherman?"

Girls: "You!"

Phil: "Who's a great cook?"

Girls: "Grandma Kay!"[115]

Phil's granddaughters respond to each question without hesitation. Although Phil does not refer to yuppies or rednecks in this scene, the discursive policing of gender roles is ever-present throughout the series. It suggests that the masculine authenticity of the redneck identity does not merely speak for itself but needs to be continually reinscribed and uttered aloud.

Instances in which gender roles are policed in relation to the grandchildren are particularly troubling. It suggests the considerable anxiety underpinning the drive for "proper" gender performances, in which adults voice concerns that young members of their family will not live up to gendered expectations. In Season Two: Episode Seven: "Spring Pong Cleaning," Phil returns to his home after taking his two older grandsons fishing. Miss Kay is cooking jelly with her apron on, as Phil and his grandsons arrive in the kitchen. Phil asks his grandsons: "Ya'll gonna grow you some whiskers when you get big?"[116] The boys say that they are required to shave for school. In the cutaway interview, Phil proclaims: "Let that hair come out their face. That shows that they're a man. They're not doing that. That's happening on its own."[117] However, as Phil continues in a humorous tone, he objects to women allowing their hair to grow naturally without intervention: " . . . I was roaming around in South Arkansas one time and some old gals up there—woo! Women with whiskers. It's a bummer."[118]

The compilation clip, "Phil's Way of Life," encapsulates the importance of gender policing for Phil. He reiterates the importance of women being able to cook and refers to men who cook as "girlie men."[119] This clip also captures his condemnation of technology as something "real men" do not rely on. Although the terms redneck and yuppie are not specifically mentioned in this clip, the signifiers of these terms remain present. The yuppies versus rednecks—us versus them—binary is one of the show's most salient discursive features. Gender policing encompasses so much of the narrative of the series that it would be hard to imagine the show without it.

A highly illustrative episode that contains several of the core themes endemic to the series is Season One, Episode Five: "Redneck Logic." It entails the Robertson men trudging through the Louisiana swamp with their rifles, blowing up old duck blinds, and then rebuilding them for their future hunting expeditions. Although Phil is disinclined to rid of an old duck blind, his son Willie offers the following observation: "Let me tell you a little bit about redneck logic: If you wanna take something away from him just blow it up because then he's gonna be so enamored by the fire that he'll forget all about what he's losing."[120] The connection between the redneck identity and hegemonic masculinity is overt. As per Willie's commentary, rednecks are assumed male, anti-intellectual, and easily transfixed by activities and displays that are coded in the popular discourse as authentically masculine.

After one of the old duck blinds is spectacularly lit aflame, Phil returns to his home where his wife, Miss Kay, can be seen cooking dinner. Phil informs Miss Kay about having used explosives to demolish the duck blind: "Willie—he's the one that concocted that scheme. A redneck stunt if I ever seen one." Interestingly, this scene segues to Miss Kay commenting in a cutaway interview about how the family upholds traditional gender roles: "It's never dull being married to a Robertson. Never. It's just like you know, 'I'm the man, you're the woman' . . . we're like in the cave, but not really, we're in modern times."[121] Although Miss Kay does not largely appear to contest the Robertson men's preference for traditional gender roles, it remains noteworthy that she considers their dynamic to be antiquated.

142   *Chapter Four*

Later in the episode, the Robertson men decide to assemble a new duck blind out of an old Recreational Vehicle. Phil hurls a possum from the RV at Willie causing him to comically run and fall to the ground. Phil remarks about Willie's reaction: "What would happen if you threw a possum on a man? Married a yuppie girl, living in a subdivision, that's what happens to you—a possum will scare you."[122] Phil emasculates Willie by claiming that he married a "yuppie girl," wherein yuppies are presumed feminine and associated with cowardice. The terms redneck and yuppie are employed in a highly gendered discursive context that naturalizes (white) masculine dominance. The class dimensions of these expressions remain muted.

Another highly illuminating moment is when the Robertson men hire a whole crew to build the new duck blind. Willie then comments about their economic largesse: "Being a wealthy redneck does have its advantages, 'cause no matter how dumb an idea is, we can always hire an entire redneck army to make sure the job gets done."[123] The celebration of anti-intellectualism is again reinscribed here. Notably, Willie is not subjected to scorn and ridicule for such a statement because he, as he himself acknowledges, is a "wealthy redneck"—a term that seems like it should be an oxymoron. *Duck Dynasty* cements the neoliberal understanding of the redneck identity—the embodied performance and lifestyle associated with hegemonic masculinity. The structural, classed implications of the redneck identity are becoming steadily subsumed by its association with hegemonic masculinity.

CONCLUSION

Duck Dynasty provides an illustrative case study for understanding the performative power of white, rural, working-class or "redneck" masculinity in the contemporary U.S. context. The power of this gender performance resides in its conferral of "real manhood" to those white males who can most closely approximate it. This is especially true for comparatively wealthy white males, such as the Robertsons, who skirt the stigma of occupying a poor or working-class socioeconomic location. Again, women of all races and people of color of all genders remain barred from taking up this performance at the outset in a manner that would be deemed authentic or celebrated in the dominant discourse. If anyone other than white men attempt to perform or claim a redneck identity, then it is perceived as inauthentic since white male supremacy is integral to dominant understandings of hegemonic masculinity or "real manhood."

The conceptualization of a redneck signifying a white, rural, Southern, working-class structural location has become subsumed by its association with hegemonic masculinity in a neoliberal context that deemphasizes class hierarchies and structural inequities writ large. This explains how the Robertons' wealth somehow does not belie the dominant perception that they are rednecks. A critical discourse analysis of *Duck Dynasty* reveals how white supremacy, heteropatriarchy, and capitalism invisibly shape seemingly benign entertainment programming. The Robertsons' support of billionaire President Donald Trump, who also derives symbolic power from his own stereotypical white, working-class rhetorical strategy, clearly discloses the Robertsons' enthusiastic support for racist, sexist, classist, and xenophobic public policies. These friendly "rednecks" on cable television demonstrate that systems of power are often reinscribed via seemingly harmless and benevolent media figures. Additionally, their wealth also indicates that contrary to dominant media discourses, racism and bigotry are not the exclusive terrains of poor and working-class whites. Donald Trump, who inherited his wealth, demonstrates how white supremacist and heteropatriarchal beliefs have always had significant traction in elite white spheres as well.

In summation, *Duck Dynasty* exemplifies the power of gender performances coded as hegemonically masculine, as well as their tenuous nature. As per Kimmel's observations regarding hegemonic masculinity throughout U.S. history, real men must continually "prove" their masculine authenticity. The Robertson men's habitual discursive reassertions that they are rednecks, when read in contrast to their former "yuppie"-style presentations, unmasks the deeper anxiety they likely carry about approximating masculine gender ideals. The social importance placed upon being a "real man" or a "real woman" demonstrates how all persons become interpellated within the heteropatriarchal logic of the gender binary. The question remains: For how long can one expect the stereotypical redneck performance to carry the valence of hegemonic masculinity in the United States? I predict that with the ascension of Donald Trump to the presidency, as well as his devoted followers calling for him to run again in 2024, white, rural, working-class masculinity will endure as a preferred way "to be a man" in the United States, even if Trump himself fails to meet those standards.

NOTES

1. Annie Nickoloff, "See 'Duck Dynasty' Star Willie Robertson's Speech at Republican National Convention," *Cleveland.com*, July 19, 2016, video, http://www .cleveland.com/rnc-2016/index.ssf/2016/07/see_duck_dynasty_star_willie_r.html.

2. Chris Fuchs, "Muslim Group Spotlights Islamophobia, Distributes 'Blind Intolerance' at RNC," *NBC News*, July 18, 2016, http://www.nbcnews .com/news/asian-america/muslim-group-spotlights-islamophobia-distributes-blind -intolerance-medicine-rnc-n611716.

Chapter Four

3. Nickoloff, "See 'Duck Dynasty' Star Willie Robertson's Speech at Republican National Convention," http://www.cleveland.com/rnc2016/index.ssf/2016/07/see_duck_dynasty_star_willie_r.html.

4. Ibid.

5. Stephen Sawchuk, "What is Critical Race Theory, and Why Is It Under Attack?," *EducationWeek*, May 18, 2021, https://www.edweek.org/leadership/what-is-critical-race-theory-and-why-is-it-under-attack/2021/05.

6. Glenn Kessler, "Trump's False Claim He Built His Empire with a 'Small Loan' from His Father," *The Washington Post*, March 3, 2016, https://www.washingtonpost.com/news/fact-checker/wp/2016/03/03/trumps-false-claim-he-built-his-empire-with-a-small-loan-from-his-father/?utm_term=.a68cc7076519.

7. Kessler, "Trump's False Claim He Built His Empire with a 'Small Loan' from His Father," https://www.washingtonpost.com/news/fact-checker/wp/2016/03/03/trumps-false-claim-he-built-his-empire-with-a-small-loan-from-his-father/?utm_term=.a68cc7076519.

8. Nickoloff, "See 'Duck Dynasty' Star Willie Robertson's Speech at Republican National Convention," http://www.cleveland.com/rnc2016/index.ssf/2016/07/see_duck_dynasty_star_willie_r.html.

9. Beverly Skeggs and Helen Wood, "Introduction: Real Class" in *Reality Television and Class*, eds. Beverly Skeggs and Helen Wood (London: Palgrave Macmillan, 2011), 2.

10. Nickoloff, "See 'Duck Dynasty' Star Willie Robertson's Speech at Republican National Convention," http://www.cleveland.com/rnc2016/index.ssf/2016/07/see_duck_dynasty_star_willie_r.html.

11. Rick Kissell, "Ratings: A&E's 'Duck Dynasty' Opens Season 6 with More Declines," June 12, 2014, https://variety.com/2014/tv/ratings/aes-duck-dynasty-opens-season-6-with-more-declines-1201219469/.

12. Lynn Vavreck, "Measuring Donald Trump's Supporters for Intolerance," *New York Times*, February 23, 2016, https://www.nytimes.com/2016/02/25/upshot/measuring-donald-trumps-supporters-for-intolerance.html?_r=1; William Galston, "New Data Why White Working Class Voters Back Trump," *Newsweek*, June 29, 2016, https://www.newsweek.com/new-data-why-white-working-class-voters-back-trump-475447.

13. Tom Nichols, "Donald Trump, the Most Unmanly President, *The Atlantic,* May 25, 2020, https://www.theatlantic.com/ideas/archive/2020/05/donald-trump-the-most-unmanly-president/612031/

14. Ashitha Nagesh, US Election 2020: Why Trump Gained Support Among Minorities," *BBC News*, November 22, 2020, https://www.bbc.com/news/world-us-canada-54972389.

15. Maggie Haberman, "Trump Had His Greatest Loss of Support in 2020 with White Voters, Particularly White Men," *New York Times*, February 2, 2021. https://www.nytimes.com/2021/02/02/us/politics/white-men-trump.html.

16. Fabiola Cineas and Anna North, "We Need to Talk about the White People Who Voted for Donald Trump," *Vox*, November 7, 2020, https://www.vox.com/2020/11/7/21551364/white-trump-voters-2020.

17. Jeffry Bartash, "Donald Trump Is Heir to Ronald Reagan in This Way," *MarketWatch*, August 4, 2016, http://www.marketwatch.com/story/shhh-dont-tell-donald-trump-is-not-the-first-republican-to-champion-white-working-class-2016-08-03.

18. Nate Silver, "The Mythology of Trump's 'Working Class' Support," *FiveThirtyEight*, May 3, 2016, https://fivethirtyeight.com/features/the-mythology-of-trumps-working-class-support/.

19. Silver, "The Mythology of Trump's 'Working Class' Support," https://fivethirtyeight.com/features/the-mythology-of-trumps-working-class-support/.

20. Andrew Prokop, "A New Report Complicates Simplistic Narratives about Race and the 2020 Election," *Vox*, May 10, 2021, https://www.vox.com/2021/5/10/22425178/catalist-report-2020-election-biden-trump-demographics.

21. Joan C. Williams, *White Working Class: Overcoming Class Cluelessness in America*, (Boston, MA: Harvard Business Review Press. 2017), 61.

22. Alex Press, "On the Origins of the Professional-Managerial Class: An Interview with Barbara Ehrenreich," *Dissent*, October 22, 2019, https://www.dissentmagazine.org/online_articles/on-the-origins-of-the-professional-managerial-class-an-interview-with-barbara-ehrenreich.

23. Williams, *White Working Class,* 61.

24. Ibid., 61.

25. Rob Dreher, "Trump: Tribune of Poor White People," *The American Conservative*, July 22, 2016, http://www.theamericanconservative.com/dreher/trump-us-politics-poor-whites/.

26. Shannon E.M. O'Sullivan, "Playing 'Redneck': White Masculinity and Working-Class Performance on Duck Dynasty," *Journal of Popular Culture* 49, no. 2 (2016): 367–84, https://doi.org/10.1111/jpcu.12403.

27. John Consoli, "Women Viewers Continue to Rule Broadcast Primetime," Nexttv.com, April 17, 2013, https://www.nexttv.com/news/women-viewers-continue-rule-broadcast-primetime-114370; Josh Katz, 'Duck Dynasty' vs. 'Modern Family': 50 Maps of the U.S. Cultural Divide," *New York Times*, December 27, 2016, https://www.nytimes.com/interactive/2016/12/26/upshot/duck-dynasty-vs-modern-family-television-maps.html?_r=1.

28. Jim Geraghty, "The Huge, GOP-Leaning Audience for 'Duck Dynasty'" *National Review Online*, August 23, 2013, http://www.nationalreview.com/campaign-spot/356553/huge-gop-leaning-audience-duck-dynasty-jim-geraghty

29. Noam Cohen, "'Duck Dynasty' Season Opens to Record Ratings," *New York Times*, August 15, 2013, https://www.nytimes.com/2013/08/16/business/media/duck-dynasty-season-opens-to-record-ratings.html?_r=1&.

30. E. Yahr, "A Year Ago, 'Duck Dynasty' Was Inescapable. Now, No One Cares," *Washington Post*, December 23, 2014, https://www.washingtonpost.com/news/arts-and-entertainment/wp/2014/12/23/a-year-ago-duck-dynasty-was-inescapable-now-no-one-cares/.

31. Mitch Metcalf, "Updated: Showbuzzdaily's Top 150 Wednesday Cable Originals and Network Finals," *Show Buzz Daily*, July 6, 2016, http://www.showbuzzdaily.com/articles/showbuzzdailys-top-150-wednesday-cable-originals-network-finals-7-6-2016.html

32. Noam Cohen, "'Duck Dynasty' Season Opens to Record Ratings," https://www.nytimes.com/2013/08/16/business/media/duck-dynasty-season-opens-to-record-ratings.html?_r=1&.

33. Julia Boorstin, "As 'Duck Dynasty' Returns to TV, Merchandisers Cash In," *CNBC*, January 15, 2014, http://www.cnbc.com/id/101339449.

34. Jane Kenway, Anna Kraack, and Anna Hickey-Moody, *Masculinity Beyond the Metropolis* (London and New York: Palgrave Macmillan, 2006), 27–8.

35. Pierre Bourdieu, "What Makes Social Class: On the Theoretical and Practical Existence of Groups," *Berkeley Journal of Sociology*, 32 (1987): 1–17.

36. David Swartz, *Culture & Power: The Sociology of Pierre Bourdieu* (Chicago: The University of Chicago Press, 1997), 74.

37. Valerie Strauss, "'Duck Dynasty's' Phil Robertson Is a Former Teacher with a Master's Degree," *The Washington Post*, December 20, 2013, https://www.washingtonpost.com/news/answer-sheet/wp/2013/12/20/duck-dynastys-phil-robertson-a-former-teacher-with-a-masters-degree/?utm_term=.93d14dc144d8

38. O'Sullivan, "Playing 'Redneck,' *Journal of Popular Culture* 49, no. 2 (2016): 367–84.

39. Raewyn Connell and J. W Messerschmidt, "Hegemonic Masculinity: Rethinking the Concept," *Gender and Society* 19, no. 6 (2005): 847.

40. Michael Mangan, *Staging Masculinities: History, Gender, Performance* (New York: Palgrave Macmillan, 2003), 13.

41. Hugh Campbell, Michael Mayerfield Bell, and Margaret Finney, *Country Boys: Masculinity and Rural Life* (University Park, Pennsylvania: The Pennsylvania State University Press 2006), 269.

42. Gail Bederman, *Manliness & Civilization: A Cultural History of Gender and Race in the United States, 1880–1917* (Chicago and London: The University of Chicago Press, 1995), 174–75.

43. Nancy Isenberg, *White Trash: The 400-Year History of Class in America* (New York: Viking, 2016), 232.

44. Isenberg, *White Trash*, 297.

45. Tanja Aho, "Reality TV and Its Audiences Reconsidered: Class and Poverty in *Undercover Boss* (CBS) in *Class Divisions in Serial Television*, eds. Sieglinde Lemke & Wibke Schniedermann (London: Palgrave Macmillan, 2016), 91.

46. Daniel Luzer, "Duck Decoy," *Washington Monthly*, January 9, 2014, https://washingtonmonthly.com/2014/01/09/duck-decoy/.

47. Ruby Turpin, "Duck Dynasty: All Four Robertson Brothers without Beards," *Starcasm*, October 9, 2012, https://starcasm.net/duck-dynasty-all-four-robertson-brothers-without-beards/.

48. Hail Boedeker, " 'Duck Dynasty'" Son Backs Up Pa," *Orlando Sentinel*, https://www.orlandosentinel.com/entertainment/tv-guy/os-duck-dynasty-son-backs-up-pa-20140327-post.html

49. Brian Lowry, "Dear 'Duck Dynasty' Fans: You Do Know It's All Fake, Right?, *Variety*, December 20, 2013, http://variety.com/2013/tv/columns/dear-duck-dynasty-fans-you-do-know-its-all-fake-right-1200980709/.

When Wealthy White Men Perform "Real Manhood" 147

50. Frank Vyan Walton, "Duck Dynasty Is a Fake Yuppies-in-Red-Neck-Drag Con Job," *Daily Kos*, December 12, 2013, http://www.dailykos.com/story/2013/12/20/1264354/-Duck-Dynasty-is-a-Fake-Yuppies-in-Red-Neck-Drag-Con-Job#.

51. Drew Magary, "What the Duck?," *GQ*, December 17, 2013, https://www.gq.com/story/duck-dynasty-phil-robertson.

52. Daniel Luzer, "Duck Decoy," https://washingtonmonthly.com/2014/01/09/duck-decoy/.

53. Judith Butler, *Gender Trouble: Feminism and the Subversion of Identity* (New York: Routledge, 2006), Location 141, Kindle.

54. John Berger, *Ways of Seeing* (London and New York: Penguin Books, 1977), 47.

55. Judith Butler, *Gender Trouble: Feminism and the Subversion of Identity* (New York: Routledge, 2006), 191, Kindle.

56. Beverly Skeggs and Helen Wood, "Introduction: Real Class" in *Reality Television and Class*, eds. Beverly Skeggs and Helen Wood (London: Palgrave Macmillan, 2011), 17.

57. Vicki Mayer, "Reality Television's 'Classrooms': Knowing, Showing and Telling about Social Class in Reality Casting and the College Classroom" in *Reality Television and Class*, eds. Beverly Skeggs and Helen Wood (London: Palgrave Macmillan, 2011), 189.

58. Judith Butler, Gender Trouble, 187.

59. Frank Vyan Walton, "Duck Dynasty Is a Fake Yuppies-in-Red-Neck-Drag Con Job," *Daily Kos*.

60. Judith Butler, "Imitation and Gender Subordination," in *The Lesbian and Gay Studies Reader,* eds. H. Abelove, M.A. Barale, and D. Halperin (New York and London: Routledge, 1993), 308.

61. Judith Butler, "Imitation and Gender Subordination," 318.

62. D. Torr and S. Bottoms, *Sex, Drag, and Male Roles: Investigating Gender as Performance* (Ann Arbor: University of Michigan Press, 2010), 8.

63. Annie Nickoloff, "See 'Duck Dynasty' Star Willie Robertson's Speech at Republican National Convention," *Cleveland.com*, July 19, 2016, video, http://www.cleveland.com/rnc-2016/index.ssf/2016/07/see_duck_dynasty_star_willie_r.html.

64. *Duck Dynasty*, season 1, episode 3, "High Tech Redneck," directed by David Hobbes, aired March 28, 2012, *Gurney Productions* for *A&E*.

65. *Duck Dynasty*, season 1, episode 3, "High Tech Redneck."

66. A. Licata, "Donald Trump on Guns, Hunting, and Conservation," *Outdoor Life*, January 22, 2016. http://www.outdoorlife.com/articles/hunting/2016/01/qa-donald-trump-guns-hunting-and-conservation

67. Alana Romain, "Does Donald Trump Hunt? He Defended His Sons' Big Game Hunting," *Romper*, July 21, 2016, https://www.romper.com/p/does-donald-trump-hunt-he-defended-his-sons-big-game-hunting-14760

68. J.D. Heyes, "Former U.S. President Theodore Roosevelt Killed Over 500 Large Game Animals on a Single Safari in 1909," *Natural News*, August 30, 2015, http://www.naturalnews.com/050987_Theodore_Roosevelt_safari_Cecil_the_Lion.html.

69. Don Sapatkin, "American Presidents Often Drawn to Hunting," *Knight Ridder Newspapers*, May 7, 2004, http://www.freerepublic.com/focus/news/1131735/posts.

70. Dave Gilson, "13 Photos of Presidents Packing Heat," *Mother Jones*, January 25, 2013, https://www.motherjones.com/politics/2013/01/photos-presidents-guns/.

71. Don Sapatkin, "American Presidents Often Drawn to Hunting," http://www.freerepublic.com/focus/news/1131735/posts.

72. Annie Nickoloff, "See 'Duck Dynasty' Star Willie Robertson's Speech at Republican National Convention," *Cleveland.com*, July 19, 2016, video, http://www.cleveland.com/rnc-2016/index.ssf/2016/07/see_duck_dynasty_star_willie_r.html.

73. S. V. Date, "Donald Trump Suggests Shooting Hillary Clinton, Her Supreme Court Picks, or Both," *The Huffington Post*, August 9, 2016, http://www.huffingtonpost.com/entry/trump-clinton-shoot_us_57aa2f6de4b0ba7ed23dd652.

74. Kate Sommers-Dawes, "All the Times Trump Has Called for Violence at His Rallies," *Mashable*, March 12, 2016, http://mashable.com/2016/03/12/trump-rally-incite-violence/#bK.3R0nrKiqY.

75. Jane Kenway, Anna Kraack, and Anna Hickey-Moody, *Masculinity Beyond the Metropolis* (London and New York: Palgrave Macmillan, 2006), 27–8.

76. Kenway, Kraack, and Hickey-Moody, *Masculinity Beyond the Metropolis*, 27–8.

77. Isenberg, *White Trash*, 306.

78. Theodore Roosevelt, *The Strenuous Life* (Stilwell, KS: Digireads.com Publishing, 2008), 8.

79. Gail Bederman, *Manliness & Civilization*, 184.

80. Ibid., 193.

81. Jonathan Culler, *Literary Theory: A Very Short Introduction*," (Oxford: Oxford University Press, 2011), 104.

82. Brenda Boudreau, "Sexually Suspect: Masculine Anxiety in the Films of Neil LaBute," in *Performing American Masculinities: The 21st-Century Man in Popular Culture*, eds. E. Watson and M. Shaw (Bloomington & Indianapolis: Indiana University Press, 2011), Kindle, Location 436.

83. Jacqueline Cutler, "Experts Urge Donald Trump to Fix His 'Reverse Raccoon' Eyes As Voters Head to Super Tuesday Polls," *New York Daily News*, March 1, 2016, http://www.nydailynews.com/news/politics/experts-urge-donald-trump-fix-reverse-raccoon-eyes-article-1.2548865

84. Brenda Boudreau, "Sexually Suspect," Location 446.

85. *Duck Dynasty*, season 3, episode 9, "Ring Around the Redneck," aired March 27, 2013, *Gurney Productions* for *A&E*.

86. *Duck Dynasty*, season 3, episode 9, "Ring Around the Redneck."

87. Ibid.

88. *Duck Dynasty*, season 2, episode 7, "Spring Pong Cleaning," aired November 7, 2012, *Gurney Productions* for *A&E*.

89. Jonathan Culler, *Literary Theory*, 104.

90. *Duck Dynasty*, season 2, episode 7, "Spring Pong Cleaning."

91. *Duck Dynasty*, season 3, episode 9, "Ring Around the Redneck."

92. *Duck Dynasty*, season 1, episode 3, "High Tech Redneck."

93. *Duck Dynasty*, season 2, episode 7, "Spring Pong Cleaning."

94. *Duck Dynasty*, season 6, episode 4, "Quackdraft," aired July 2, 2014, *Gurney Productions* for *A&E*.

95. *Duck Dynasty*, season 8, episode 2, "Induckpendence Day," directed by Jonathan Haug, aired July 1, 2015, *Gurney Productions* for *A&E*.

96. ABC News, "Bush: Bin Laden Wanted Dead or Alive, *ABC News*, September 17, 2001, http://abcnews.go.com/US/story?id=92483.

97. Mitchell Owens, "Laura and George W. Bush's Serene Retreat in Texas," *Architectural Digest*, December 16, 2016, http://www.architecturaldigest.com/gallery/laura-and-george-w-bush-prairie-chapel-ranch-texas-slideshow/all.

98. Meredith Conroy, *Masculinity, Media, and the American Presidency* (New York: Palgrave Macmillan, 2015), 136.

99. Richard Benedetto, "Who's More Likeable, Bush or Kerry?, *USA Today*, September 17, 2004, http://usatoday30.usatoday.com/news/opinion/columnist/benedetto/2004-09-17-benedetto_x.htm.

100. Isenberg, *White Trash*, 260.

101. Patrick Gavin, "Press: One Word Describes Obama," *Politico*, October 4, 2012, http://www.politico.com/story/2012/10/press-one-word-describes-obama-082023.

102. Gavin, "Press," http://www.politico.com/story/2012/10/press-one-word-describes-obama-082023.

103. Trent Watts, "Telling White Men's Stories," in *White Masculinity in the Recent South*, ed. Trent Watts (Baton Rouge: Louisiana State University Press, 2008), 5.

104. P. Huber and K. Drowne,"Redneck: A New Discovery." *American Speech* 76, no. 4 (2001): 434–5.

105. Edward M. Morris, "'Rednecks," 'Rutters," and 'Rithmetic: Social Class, Masculinity, and Schooling in a Rural Context." *Gender and Society* 22, no. 6 (2008): 741.

106. Morris, "'Rednecks," 'Rutters," and 'Rithmetic, 742.

107. Isenberg, *White Trash*, 276.

108. Ibid., 277.

109. Eric Deggans, TLC's 'Honey Boo Boo' Cancellation Shows Dangers of Exploitative TV," *National Public Radio*, October 24, 2014, http://www.npr.org/2014/10/24/358567472/tlcs-honey-boo-boo-cancellation-shows-dangers-of-exploitative-tv.

110. Isenberg, *White Trash*, 292.

111. Ibid.

112. Ibid., 307.

113. "Duck Dynasty: Yuppies," A&E, video, 2012, http://www.youtube.com/watch?v=k560-bb-1mY.

114. *Duck Dynasty*, season 4, episode 2, "So You Think You Can Date," directed by Hugh Peterson, aired August 21, 2013, *Gurney Productions* for *A&E*.

115. *Duck Dynasty*, season 5, episode 4, "From Duck 'til Dawn," directed by Hugh Peterson, aired January 29, 2014, *Gurney Productions* for *A&E*.

150   *Chapter Four*

116. *Duck Dynasty*, season 2, episode 7, "Spring Pong Cleaning."

117. Ibid.

118. Ibid.

119. "Duck Dynasty: Phil's Way of Life," A&E, video, 2013, http://www.youtube.com/watch?v=sgRb60kxUZg.

120. *Duck Dynasty*, season 1, episode 5, "Redneck Logic," directed by David Hobbes, aired April 4, 2012, *Gurney Productions* for *A&E*.

121. *Duck Dynasty*, season 1, episode 5, "Redneck Logic."

122. Ibid.

123. Ibid.

Conclusion

The Continuing Relevance of the Blue-Collar Frontier

At the time of this writing, two of the series included in this examination, Discovery's *Deadliest Catch* and *Gold Rush*, remain in production. Reality television shows venerating white, rural, working-class masculinity continue to dot programming schedules on U.S. cable. The symbolic power of this iteration of masculine authenticity has not yet lost its purchase in U.S. culture and politics. President Biden also performs his self-proclaimed authenticity via a white, working-class masculine rhetorical strategy. Although his appeals to the white working class are not overtly bigoted, his investment in speaking like he hails from Scranton's white working class has served his political career well for more than fifty years. However, his base remains far less devoted and vociferous than Trump's. After the events of January 6, 2021, it seems inevitable that calls from Trump's devotees for him to run again in 2024 will crescendo in the coming years.

The mainstream media's political coverage of the white working class includes a mix of lurid fascination; mischaracterization, especially in terms of omitting the racism and sexism of the white professional-managerial class; and occasional contempt. Undoubtedly, white, working-class male Trump backers err egregiously when they assert that they are somehow *more* deserving and worthy of economic security than women, people of color, immigrants, and members of LGBTQ communities. It unquestionably remains the media's responsibility to vigorously push back against and discredit such claims and insinuations whenever they arise in public discourse. However, the mainstream media misses the mark in their analyses of white, working-class men when they assert that the root cause of their "economic anxiety" is their failure to leverage their whiteness and maleness to succeed within the capitalist system. Even though their whiteness and maleness statistically advantage them in the labor market in relation to women workers and workers of color, especially women workers of color, it does not immunize them from capitalism's shocks and precarity. These jolts are particularly pronounced in the United States, where healthcare remains tied to employment and most Americans do not have access to pensions or secure retirement plans. In illuminating, challenging, and dismantling racism and sexism, it is vital not to do so while reinforcing the myth of meritocracy, which serves as the primary justification for all social inequities, including those based on race, gender, and sexual orientation. In essence, as all the foundational intersectional thinkers, including Crenshaw, Hill Collins, and hooks have always noted, intersectionality includes class and capitalism. At the core of intersectionality is an understanding that capitalism remains inexorably linked to white supremacy, heteropatriarchy, and settler-colonialism. Thus, meritocracy functions as an organizing principle for justifying injustice—reproducing it, in any context, undercuts efforts toward social transformation and equity.

The findings of this critical discourse analysis indicate that the blue-collar frontier shows provide a rich visual archive of performances of hegemonic masculinity in the past decade and a half. Through their framing of the highly hazardous occupations of commercial fishing, logging, truck driving, and gold mining as individualized tests of manhood, the blue-collar frontier shows solidify the connection between masculine authenticity and this type of work at a time when the nature of work itself is becoming increasingly precarious. More precisely, these series cement the linkage between "real manhood" and the type of man who performs this kind of work—white, rural, and *appearing* working-class in manner and dress.

The erasure of the class hierarchies that exist within the casts also reinforces the myth of the classless society, as these series present the embodied performance of white, rural, working-class masculinity as disconnected from one's social location within capitalism. In mapping the parameters of contemporary hegemonic masculinity in the United States, this study uncovers the systems of power, including white supremacy, heteropatriarchy, settler-colonialism, and capitalism that underpin the preferred way to present as a "real man" in the contemporary context. The blue-collar frontier shows bolster the notion that "real manhood" materializes in a vacuum, and that the cameras are just neutrally documenting these men as they "naturally" appear.

I confirm that these programs valorize white, rural, working-class masculinity as "real manhood" in direct response to Kimmel's observation that the Great Recession engendered a "masculinity crisis" for white, rural, working and middle-class men in the United States. These shows document that discursive gender policing itself is commensurate with the performance logic of hegemonic masculinity, which gestures toward an underlying insecurity many U.S. men have in relation to their place in the gender hierarchy. This reinvestment in work as a marker of masculine authenticity, as opposed to challenging the wider socioeconomic order and the restrictive construction of

The Continuing Relevance of the Blue-Collar Frontier 153

ideal masculinity, is a counterproductive and deleterious tendency in relation to alleviating the precarious nature of work under neoliberalism. Corporate-owned U.S. cable networks would much rather inject celebratory displays of white masculine prowess into their programming than foster class consciousness—a notion entirely at odds with their commercial and ideological agendas. This study further confirms commercial television's congruent economic and ideological investment in the status quo, especially at a time when social movements, such as Occupy Wall Street, Black Lives Matter, and Me Too, posed considerable challenges to the white heteropatriarchal capitalist order.

A critical assertion of this study is that the emergence of these shows signaled a profound white, rural, working and middle-class male backlash against the modest social gains made by women, people of color, and LGBTQ communities in the past two decades. This explains the near universal presence of heteronormative white males across these series, in which only white women who largely satisfy the visual desires of cisheterosexual male spectators, such as Lisa Kelly of *Ice Road Truckers*, are conditionally granted entry. Regardless of their appearances, there remains an underlying hostility toward women who dare to enter male homosocial spaces, as documented throughout these series upon women occasionally arriving on the scene. This seemingly inconsequential corner of cable television contained some inklings into a deeper white male supremacist social current, which cannot be detached from Trump's rhetorical strategy and political ascendance.

This analysis also attests to the symbolic power and material consequences of a mythical, imaginary place: the frontier. In challenging the ideological basis of frontier mythology, as articulated by renowned U.S. historian Frederick Jackson Turner via his frontier thesis, this study not only historicizes these contemporary media depictions of the frontier, but also disrupts orthodox U.S. historiographical narratives. Additionally, in noting the common conventions between the blue-collar frontier shows and the Western film and television genre, this project situates these contemporary media texts within the lineage of visual mass media representations of frontier mythology. In the dominant U.S. discourse both past and present, the frontier is often cast as a race and gender-neutral construct—a place devoid of any deeper ideological or material struggle. Not only did Turner falsely conceive of the frontier as empty backwoods, he also portrayed life on the frontier as a necessary rite of passage for white men to continually reconstitute U.S. exceptionalism and rugged individualism through "taming the wilderness." Without stating it explicitly, Turner provides an ideological justification for continued settler-colonization of indigenous peoples and their lands; perpetual environmental destruction to satiate capitalist greed; and white manhood as the normative standard for ideal citizenship.

154 *Conclusion*

In configuring the frontier as a "white male spatial imaginary," I expose how frontier mythology naturalizes the presence of white men in remote wilderness settings at the expense of women, indigenous peoples, and people of color. The frontier is not neutral or uninhabited: It is a contested site upon which imperial white supremacist capitalist heteropatriarchy is ritualistically enacted and resisted. The blue-collar frontier shows provide an illustrative contemporary example of how the mythic frontier continues to serve as the preferred proving ground for hegemonic masculine status. These series document white men performing hazardous occupations in remote, wilderness settings to reinvigorate frontier mythology at a time when its intertwined core tenets, including rugged individualism, white male supremacy, and capitalism, are facing considerable public scrutiny on multiple fronts. Both the Great Recession and activist challenges to white male supremacy elicited the proliferation of this subgenre of reality television programming—an ideologically conservative reaction to a changing U.S. sociocultural landscape. Blue-collar frontier television seems to inferentially suggest that it is only through going back to the frontier that—per Trump's campaign slogan—white men can "make America great again."

This study finds that the conceptualization of the term "redneck" as signifying a white, rural, Southern, working-class structural location has become supplanted by its association with hegemonic masculinity in a neoliberal context that minimizes class hierarchies and structural inequities writ large. This explains how the Robertons' wealth somehow does not belie the dominant perception that they are rednecks. A critical discourse analysis of *Duck Dynasty* reveals how white supremacy, heteropatriarchy, and capitalism invisibly shape seemingly benign entertainment programming. The Robertsons' support of billionaire President Donald Trump, who also derives symbolic power from his own white, working-class-style rhetorical strategy, discloses the Robertsons' support for racist, sexist, classist, and xenophobic public policies. These friendly and affluent "rednecks" on cable television demonstrate how seemingly harmless and benevolent public figures propagate systems of power. In addition, their wealth indicates that contrary to dominant media narratives about prototypical Trump supporters, racism and bigotry are not the exclusive terrains of poor and working-class whites. Donald Trump, who inherited his wealth, exemplifies how white supremacist and heteropatriarchal beliefs have always maintained significant traction in elite white spheres.

I contend that *Duck Dynasty* illustrates the power of performances of hegemonic masculinity, as well as their tenuous nature. As per Kimmel's observations regarding hegemonic masculinity throughout U.S. history, real men must continually "prove" their masculine authenticity. The Robertson men's habitual discursive reassertions that they are rednecks, when read in contrast to their former yuppie-style presentations, unmasks the deeper anxiety they likely carry about approximating ideal manhood. The social importance placed upon presenting as a "real man" or a "real woman" demonstrates how all persons become interpellated within the dominant, heteropatriarchal logic of the gender binary. The Robertsons' prior appearances indicate that the considerable economic, cultural, and social capital they had already possessed was not enough—they needed the symbolic capital of masculine authenticity.

This study illuminates how affluent white males, such as the Robertsons and Trump, take up white, working-class rhetorical performances as a strategic maneuver to increase their power. In Trump's instance, this symbolic capital contributed to his attainment of the extraordinary powers of the U.S. presidency. The question remains: For how long can one expect white, rural, working-class masculine performances to signify hegemonic masculinity in the United States? With the blue-collar frontier shows leaving an enduring imprint on U.S. cable networks, white, rural, working-class masculinity will likely continue its reign as one of the most preferred ways to "be a man" for years to come.

Lastly, this project began several years before the Trump presidency. Although these series provided clues to a deeper current of white male resentment against women, people of color, and LGBTQ communities, I distinctly remember being taken aback by Trump's emergence as the Republican front-runner for president in late 2015. However, partially because of this research project, I never felt confident that Trump would swiftly revert to his role as host of *Celebrity Apprentice*. Since 2016, news media narratives exploring the political motivations and experiences of the white working class have skyrocketed—prompting Joan C. Williams to publish *White Working Class: Overcoming Class Cluelessness in America* in 2017. Williams skillfully attends to the specificity of the social location of the U.S. white working class. Despite her prominent intervention, the descriptor, "working class," still widely circulates in U.S. media in reference to white workers without qualification.[1] This conflation reinforces the notion that the white working class, especially white male workers, are somehow *the* working class, even though women and people of color occupy most of its ranks. I hope journalists, researchers, and political strategists begin to revise dominant and inaccurate conceptions of not only social class, but the hegemonic construction of social categories writ large. Because blueprints for class consciousness, solidarity,and social transformation must be responsible and intersectional.

NOTE

1. S. Baker-Jordan, "Biden Is Teaching Democrats How to Talk to the Working Class Again," *Newsweek*, April 29, 2021, https://www.newsweek.com/biden-teaching-democrats-how-talk-working-class-again-opinion-1587528.

Bibliography

ABC News. "Bush: Bin Laden Wanted Dead or Alive. *ABC News*, September 17, 2001. http://abcnews.go.com/US/story?id=92483.

Aho, Tanja. "Reality TV and Its Audiences Reconsidered: Class and Poverty in *Undercover Boss* (CBS). In *Class Divisions in Serial Television*, edited by Sieglinde Lemke & Wibke Schniedermann, 89–119. London: Palgrave Macmillan, 2016).

Alexander, Michelle. *The New Jim Crow: Mass Incarceration in the Age of Colorblindness.* New York: New Press, 2020.

Alexander, Susan M., and Katie Woods. "Reality Television and the Doing of Hyperauthentic Masculinities." *The Journal of Men's Studies* 27, no. 2 (2019): 149–168. https://doi.org/10.1177/1060826518801529.

Arnold, Kathleen. *America's New Working Class: Race, Gender, and Ethnicity in a Biopolitical Age*. University Park, PA: Pennsylvania State University Press, 2008.

Ax Men. Season 1, Episode 2, "Risk and Reward." Narrated by Thom Beers. Aired March 16, 2008. *Original Productions* for *History Channel*.

Ax Men. Season 1, Episode 11, "Storm of the Century." Narrated by Thom Beers. Aired May 19, 2008, *Original Productions* for *History Channel*.

Ax Men. Season 2, Episode 7, "One Weak Link." Narrated by Thom Beers. Aired April 20, 2009, *Original Productions* for *History Channel*.

Ax Men. Season 2, Episode 10, "Clash of the Titans." Narrated by Thom Beers. Aired May 11, 2009, *Original Productions* for *History Channel*.

Ax Men. Season 3, Episode 13, "King of the Mountain." Narrated by Thom Beers. Aired April 18, 2010, *Original Productions* for *History Channel*.

Ax Men. Season 4, Episode 1, "Alaska." Narrated by Thom Beers. Aired December 12, 2010, *Original Productions* for *History Channel*.

Baker-Jordan, S. "Biden Is Teaching Democrats How to Talk to the Working Class Again." *Newsweek*, April 29, 2021. https://www.newsweek.com/biden-teaching-democrats-how-talk-working-class-again-opinion-1587528.

Baldoni, John. "Is Donald Trump a Role Model for Authenticity?" *Forbes,* January 2, 2016. https://www.forbes.com/sites/johnbaldoni/2016/01/02/is-donald-trump-a-role-model-for-authenticity/#1f3e753433bc.

Bartash, Jeffry. "Donald Trump Is Heir to Ronald Reagan in This Way." *MarketWatch*, August 4, 2016. http://www.marketwatch.com/story/shhh-dont-tell -donald-trump-is-not-the-first-republican-to-champion-white-working-class-2016 -08-03.

Bederman, Gail. *Manliness & Civilization: A Cultural History of Gender and Race in the United States, 1880–1917*. Chicago and London: The University of Chicago Press, 1995.

Benedetto, Richard. "Who's More Likeable, Bush or Kerry? *USA Today*, September 17, 2004. http://usatoday30.usatoday.com/news/opinion/columnist/benedetto/2004 -09-17-benedetto_x.htm.

Berger, John. *Ways of Seeing*. London and New York: Penguin Books, 1977.

Billington, Ray Allen. *Land of Savagery, Land of Promise: The European Image of the American Frontier in the Nineteenth Century*. New York and London: W.W. Norton & Company, 1981.

Boedeker, Hail. "'Duck Dynasty'" Son Backs Up Pa," *Orlando Sentinel*, https:// www.orlandosentinel.com/entertainment/tv-guy/os-duck-dynasty-son-backs-up-pa -20140327-post.html

Boorstin, Julia. "As 'Duck Dynasty' Returns to TV, Merchandisers Cash In." *CNBC*, January 15, 2014. http://www.cnbc.com/id/101339449.

Boudreau, Brenda. "Sexually Suspect: Masculine Anxiety in the Films of Neil LaBute." In *Performing American Masculinities: The 21st-Century Man in Popular Culture*, edited by *E*. Watson and M. Shaw, Location 434–735. Bloomington & Indianapolis: Indiana University Press, 2011. Kindle.

Bourdieu, Pierre. "What Makes Social Class: On the Theoretical and Practical Existence of Groups," *Berkeley Journal of Sociology*, 32 (1987): 1–17.

Bresiger, Gregory. "Americans Work Harder Than Any Other Country's Citizens: Study." *New York Post*, September 3, 2017. https://nypost.com/2017/09/03/ americans-work-harder-than-any-other-countrys-citizens-study/.

Broderick, Ryan. "The Dark Side of America's Redneck Reality TV Obsession." *Buzzfeed*, October 27, 2014. https://www.buzzfeed.com/ryanhatesthis /how-hillbilly-reality-tv-got-way-too-real?utm_term=.ao7BEy63W#.efPxN0Bq4.

Buchanan, Burton P. "Portrayals of Masculinity in The Discovery Channel's *Deadliest Catch*." In *Reality Television: Oddities of Culture*, edited by A. F. Slade, A. J. Narro, and B. P. Buchanan, 183–200. Lanham, Maryland: Lexington Books, 2014.

Burns, Alexander. "Romney: Obama Waging 'War on Job Creators.'" Politico, May 23, 2012. http://www.politico.com/blogs/burns-haberman/2012/05/romney-obama -waging-war-on-job-creators-124350

Butler, Judith. "Imitation and Gender Subordination." In *The Lesbian and Gay Studies Reader*, edited by H. Abelove, M. A. Barale, and D. Halperin, 307–318. New York and London: Routledge, 1993.

Butler, Judith. *Gender Trouble: Feminism and the Subversion of Identity*. New York: Routledge, 2006. Kindle.

Byrd, Jodi. *The Transit of Empire: Indigenous Critiques of Colonialism*. Minneapolis and London: University of Minnesota Press, 2011. Kindle.

Calhoun, Ada. "The New Midlife Crisis: Why (And How) It's Hitting Gen X Women." *Oprah.com,* https://www.oprah.com/sp/new-midlife-crisis.html.

Campbell, Hugh, Michael Mayerfield Bell, and Margaret Finney. *Country Boys: Masculinity and Rural Life.* University Park, PA: Pennsylvania State University Press, 2006.

Christie, Les. "'Deadliest Catch' Not So Deadly Anymore." *CNN Money*, July 27, 2012. http://money.cnn.com/2012/07/27/pf/jobs/crab-fishing-dangerous-jobs/.

Cineas, Fabiola, and Anna North. "We Need to Talk about the White People Who Voted for Donald Trump." *Vox*, November 7, 2020, https://www.vox.com/2020/11/7/21551364/white-trump-voters-2020.

Cohen, Noam. "'Duck Dynasty' Season Opens to Record Ratings." *New York Times*, August 15, 2013. https://www.nytimes.com/2013/08/16/business/media/duck-dynasty-season-opens-to-record-ratings.html?_r=1&.

Collins, Patricia Hill. *Black Feminist Thought.* New York: Routledge Classics, 2009.

Combahee River Collective. *The Combahee River Collective Statement: Black Feminist Organizing in the Seventies and Eighties.* New York, NY: Kitchen Table: Women of Color Press, 1986.

Connell, Raewyn. *Gender and Power: Society, the Person, and Sexual Politics.* Stanford, CA: Stanford University Press, 1987.

Connell, Raewyn and J. W Messerschmidt. "Hegemonic Masculinity: Rethinking the Concept." *Gender and Society* 19, no. 6 (2005): 829–859.

Conroy, Meredith. *Masculinity, Media, and the American Presidency.* New York: Palgrave Macmillan, 2015.

Consoli, John. "Women Viewers Continue to Rule Broadcast Primetime." Nexttv.com, April 17, 2013. https://www.nexttv.com/news/women-viewers-continue-rule-broadcast-primetime-114370;

Crenshaw, Kimberlé. "Why Intersectionality Can't Wait." *Washington Post*, September 24, 2015. https://www.washingtonpost.com/news/in-theory/wp/2015/09/24/why-intersectionality-cant-wait/.

Crenshaw, Kimberlé. "Demarginalizing the Intersection of Race and Sex: A Black Feminist Critique of Antidiscrimination Doctrine, Feminist Theory, and Antiracist Politics." In *Critical Race Feminism: A Reader*, edited by A. K. Wing, 23–33. New York: New York University Press, 2003.

Culler, Jonathan. *Literary Theory: A Very Short Introduction."* Oxford: Oxford University Press, 2011.

Cutler, Jacqueline. "Experts Urge Donald Trump to Fix His 'Reverse Raccoon' Eyes as Voters Head to Super Tuesday Polls." *New York Daily News*, March 1, 2016. http://www.nydailynews.com/news/politics/experts-urge-donald-trump-fix-reverse-raccoon-eyes-article-1.2548865

Dakss, Brian. "Is 18–49 passé as Top Demographic?." *CBS News*, November 4, 2005. http://www.cbsnews.com/news/is-18-49-passe-as-top-demographic/.

Date, S. V. "Donald Trump Suggests Shooting Hillary Clinton, Her Supreme Court Picks, or Both." *Huffington Post*, August 9, 2016. http://www.huffingtonpost.com/entry/trump-clinton-shoot_us_57aa2f6de4b0ba7ed23dd652.

160   *Bibliography*

Davis, Angela. "Recognizing Racism in the Era of Neoliberalism." *Truthout*, May 6, 2013, https://truthout.org/articles/recognizing-racism-in-the-era-of -neoliberalism/.

Deadliest Catch. Season 1, Episode 9. "The Clock's Ticking." Narrated by Mike Rowe. Aired June 7, 2005, *Original Productions* for *Discovery Channel.*

Deadliest Catch. Season 1, Episode 10, "The Final Run." Written by Ethan Prochnik. Narrated by Mike Rowe. Aired June 14, 2005. *Original Productions* for *Discovery Channel.*

Deadliest Catch. Season 3, Episode 7, "New Beginnings." Narrated by Mike Rowe. Aired May 15, 2007. *Original Productions* for *Discovery Channel.*

Deadliest Catch. Season 4, Episode 4, "Unsafe and Unsound." Narrated by Mike Rowe. Aired April 29, 2008. *Original Productions* for *Discovery Channel.*

Deadliest Catch. Season 5, Episode 3, "Stay Focused or Die." Narrated by Mike Rowe. Aired April 28, 2009. *Original Productions* for *Discovery Channel.*

Deadliest Catch. Season 5, Episode 15, "Day of Reckoning." Narrated by Mike Rowe. Aired July 21, 2009. *Original Productions* for *Discovery Channel.*

Deadliest Catch. Season 6, Episode 10. "The Darkened Seas." Narrated by Mike Rowe. Aired June 15, 2010. *Original Productions* for *Discovery Channel.*

Deadliest Catch. Season 8, Episode 4, "The Hook." Narrated by Mike Rowe. Aired May 1, 2012. *Original Productions* for *Discovery Channel.*

Deadliest Catch. Season 9, Episode 2. "Dagger in the Back." Narrated by Mike Rowe. Aired April 23, 2013, *Original Productions* for *Discovery Channel.*

Deadliest Catch. Season 11, Episode 9, "Hell's Bells." Narrated by Mike Rowe. Aired June 9, 2015. *Original Productions* for *Discovery Channel.*

Deadliest Catch. Season 4 DVD Cover Image, 2008. https://pisces.bbystatic.com/ image2/BestBuy_US/images/products/9224/9224083_so.jpg.

Deadline Team, "Deadline Team 'Gold Rush' 5th Season Debut Hits Ratings Motherlode for Discovery." *Deadline*, October 20, 2014. https://deadline.com /2014/10/gold-rush-ratings-record-5th-season-debut-discovery-channel-856046/.

Deggans, Eric. "TLC's 'Honey Boo Boo' Cancellation Shows Dangers of Exploitative TV." *National Public Radio*, October 24, 2014. http://www.npr.org/2014/10/24 /358567472/tlcs-honey-boo-boo-cancellation-shows-dangers-of-exploitative-tv.

Dehnart, Andy. "The Top 201 Reality TV shows and Their Viewers' Ages." *Reality Blurred*, October 5, 2015. https://www.realityblurred.com/realitytv /2015/10/reality-tv-show-viewer-ages/.

Deleuze, Gilles, and Felix Guattari. *A Thousand Plateaus: Capitalism and Schizophrenia*. Minneapolis, MN: University of Minnesota Press, 1987.

Dill, Bonnie Thornton, and Marla H. Kohlman. "Intersectionality: A Transformative Paradigm in Feminist Theory and Social Justice." In *Handbook of Feminist Research: Theory and Praxis*, edited by Sharlene Nagy Hesse-Biber, 3–42. Thousand Oaks, CA: Sage Publications, 2012.

Dreher, Rob. "Trump: Tribune of Poor White People." *The American Conservative*, July 22, 2016. http://www.theamericanconservative.com/dreher/trump-us-politics -poor-whites/.

Bibliography

Drinnon, Richard. *Facing West: The Metaphysics of Indian-Hating and Empire-Building.* Norman and London: University of Oklahoma Press, 1997.

Duck Dynasty. Season 1, Episode 3, "High Tech Redneck." Directed by David Hobbes. Aired March 28, 2012, *Gurney Productions* for *A&E.*

Duck Dynasty. Season 1, Episode 5, "Redneck Logic." Directed by David Hobbes. Aired April 4, 2012, *Gurney Productions* for *A&E.*

Duck Dynasty. Season 2, Episode 7, "Spring Pong Cleaning." Aired November 7, 2012, *Gurney Productions* for *A&E.*

Duck Dynasty. Season 3, Episode 9, "Ring Around the Redneck." Aired March 27, 2013, *Gurney Productions* for *A&E.*

Duck Dynasty. Season 4, Episode 2, "So You Think You Can Date." Directed by Hugh Peterson. Aired August 21, 2013, *Gurney Productions* for *A&E.*

Duck Dynasty. Season 5, Episode 4, "From Duck 'til Dawn." Directed by Hugh Peterson. Aired January 29, 2014, *Gurney Productions* for *A&E.*

Duck Dynasty. Season 6, Episode 4, "Quackdraft." Aired July 2, 2014, *Gurney Productions* for *A&E.*

Duck Dynasty. Season 8, Episode 2. "Induckpendence Day." Directed by Jonathan Haug. Aired July 1, 2015, *Gurney Productions* for *A&E.*

"Duck Dynasty: Yuppies." A&E. Video. 2012, http://www.youtube.com/watch?v=k560-bb-1mY.

"Duck Dynasty: Phil's Way of Life," A&E. Video. 2013, http://www.youtube.com/watch?v=sgRb60kxUZg.

Dubrofsky, Rachel E., and Megan M. Wood. "Posting Racism and Sexism: Authenticity, Agency and Self-Reflexivity in Social Media." *Communication and Critical/Cultural Studies* 11, no. 3 (2014): 282–287.

"Economic Status of Women of Color: A Snapshot." Women's Bureau in the U.S. Department of Labor. https://www.in.gov/icw/files/WB_WomenColorFactSheet.pdf.

Filipovic, Jill. "The Revenge of the White Man." *TIME*, November 10, 2016. http://time.com/4566304/donald-trump-revenge-of-the-white-man/.

Fisher, Milia. "Women of Color and the Gender Wage Gap." *Center for American Progress*, April 14, 2015. https://www.americanprogress.org/issues/women/reports/2015/04/14/110962/women-of-color-and-the-gender-wage-gap/.

Fleras, Augie, and Shane Michael Dixon. "Cutting, Driving, Digging, and Harvesting: Re-Masculinizing the Working-Class Heroic." *Canadian Journal of Communication* 36, no. 4 (2012): https://doi.org/10.22230/cjc.2011v36n4a2419.

Foster, Gwendolyn Audrey. *Class-Passing: Social Mobility in Film and Popular Culture.* Carbondale, IL: Southern Illinois University Press, 2005.

Fox, Justin. "Where the Job Growth Is." *Bloomberg*, February 5, 2015. https://www.bloomberg.com/view/articles/2015-02-06/job-market-gains-aided-by-slowdown-in-government-layoffs.

Friedman, Vanessa. "Why Rioters Wear Costumes." *New York Times*, January 7, 2021. https://www.nytimes.com/2021/01/07/style/capitol-riot-tactics.html.

162 *Bibliography*

Fry, Richard and Rakesh Kochhar. "The Shrinking Middle Class in U.S. Metropolitan Areas: 6 Key Findings." *Pew Research Center*. May 12, 2016, http://www.pewresearch.org/fact-tank/2016/05/12/us-middle-class-metros-takeaways/.

Fuchs, Chris. "Muslim Group Spotlights Islamophobia, Distributes 'Blind Intolerance' at RNC." *NBC News*, July 18, 2016. http://www.nbcnews.com/news/asian-america/muslim-group-spotlights-islamophobia-distributes-blind-intolerance-medicine-rnc-n611716.

Galston, William. "New Data Why White Working Class Voters Back Trump." *Newsweek*, June 29, 2016. https://www.newsweek.com/new-data-why-white-working-class-voters-back-trump-475447.

Gaston, Paul M. *The New South Creed: A Study in Southern Mythmaking.* New York: Knopf, 1970.

Gavin, Patrick. "Press: One Word Describes Obama." Politico, October 4, 2012. http://www.politico.com/story/2012/10/press-one-word-describes-obama-082023.

Geraghty, Jim. "The Huge, GOP-Leaning Audience for 'Duck Dynasty.'" *National Review Online*, August 23, 2013. http://www.nationalreview.com/campaign-spot/356553/huge-gop-leaning-audience-duck-dynasty-jim-geraghty.

Gilson, Dave. "13 Photos of Presidents Packing Heat." *Mother Jones*, January 25, 2013. https://www.motherjones.com/politics/2013/01/photos-presidents-guns/.

Glenn, Evelyn Nakano. *Unequal Freedom: How Race and Gender Shaped American Citizenship and Labor*. Cambridge, MA: Harvard University Press, 2002.

Gold Rush: Alaska. Season 1, Episode 1, "No Guts No Glory." Narrated by Paul Christie. Aired December 3, 2010. *Raw TV* for *Discovery Channel*.

Gold Rush. Season 2, Episode 17, "Frozen Out." Narrated by Paul Christie. Aired February 17, 2012, *Raw TV* for *Discovery Channel*.

Gold Rush. Season 3, Episode 3, "Secret Weapons." Narrated by Paul Christie. Aired November 9, 2012, *Raw TV* for *Discovery Channel*.

Gold Rush: Alaska. Season 1, Episode 10, "Never Say Die." Narrated by Paul Christie. Aired February 17, 2011, *Raw TV* for *Discovery Channel*.

Gold Rush. Season 2, Episode 2, "Virgin Ground." Narrated by Paul Christie. Aired November 4, 2011. *Raw TV* for *Discovery Channel*.

Gold Rush. *Raw TV* for *Discovery Channel*. Image. 2011. https://www.adgully.com/img/800/54456_gold-rush-discovery-channel.jpg.

Gotanda, Neil. "A Critique of 'Our Constitution Is Color-Blind.'" In *Critical Race Theory: The Key Writings That Formed the Movement* Crenshaw, edited by N. Gotanda, G. Peller, & T. Kendall, 257-275. New York: The New Press, 1995.

Grindstaff, Laura. "From *Jerry Springer* to *Jersey Shore*: The Cultural Politics of Class in/on US Reality Programming." In *Reality Television and Class*, edited by B. Skeggs and Helen Wood, 197–209. London: Palgrave Macmillan, 2011.

Grzanka, Patrick. "Media as Sites/Sights of Justice." In *Intersectionality: A Foundations and Frontiers Reader*, edited by Patrick Grzanka, 131–137. Boulder, CO: Westview Press, 2014.

Gutierrez, Alexabdra. "Grizzly License Plates Ready for Issue." *Alaska Public Media*, May 5, 2015. http://www.alaskapublic.org/2015/05/05/grizzly-license-plates-ready-for-issue/.

Bibliography

Haberman, Maggie. "Trump Had His Greatest Loss of Support in 2020 with White Voters, Particularly White Men." *New York Times,* February 2, 2021. https://www.nytimes.com/2021/02/02/us/politics/white-men-trump.html.

Hall, Stuart. "Encoding and Decoding in the Television Discourse." In *Channeling Blackness: Studies on Television and Race in America*, edited by D. M. Hunt, 46-59. New York and Oxford: Oxford University Press, 2005.

Hall, Stuart. "Encoding/Decoding." In *Media and Cultural Studies KeyWorks*, edited by M. G. Durham and D. M. Kellner, 163–173. Malden, MA and Oxford, UK: Blackwell Publishing, 2006.

Hall, Stuart. "The Rediscovery of 'Ideology': Return of the Repressed in Media Studies." In *Culture, Society and the Media*, edited by M. Gurevitch, 52–86. London: Methuen, 1982.

Hamilton, Laura T., Elizabeth A. Armstrong, J. Lotus Seeley, and Elizabeth M Armstrong. "Hegemonic Femininities and Intersectional Domination." *Sociological Theory* 37, no. 4 (2019): 315–341.

Hanke, Robert. "Hegemonic Masculinity in Transition." In *Men, Masculinity, and the Media*, edited by S. Craig, 190. Newbury Park: Sage Publications, 1992.

Haraway, Donna. "The Persistence of Vision." In *The Visual Culture Reader*, edited by Nicholas Mirzoeff, 356–362. London and New York: Routledge, 2013.

Harris, Cheryl. "Whiteness as Property." In *Critical Race Theory: The Key Writings That Formed the Movement* Crenshaw, edited by N. Gotanda, G. Peller, & T. Kendall, 276–291. New York: The New Press, 1995.

Hearn, Alison. "Producing 'Reality': Branded Content, Branded Selves, Precarious Futures." In *A Companion to Reality Television*, edited by L. Ouellette, 437–455. Malden, MA and Oxford: John Wiley & Sons, 2014.

Heyes, J. D. "Former U.S. President Theodore Roosevelt Killed Over 500 Large Game Animals on a Single Safari in 1909." *Natural News*, August 30, 201. http://www.naturalnews.com/050987_Theodore_Roosevelt_safari_Cecil_the_Lion.html.

Holpuch, Amanda. "No One Wants to Work Anymore': The Truth Behind This Unemployment Benefits Myth." *The Guardian*, May 7, 2021. https://www.theguardian.com/business/2021/may/07/truth-behind-unemployment-benefits-myth.

Homans, Charles. "A Soap Opera on the High Seas." *New York Times*, December 13, 2012. http://www.nytimes.com/2012/12/16/magazine/how-thom-beers-built-a-reality-tv-empire.html?pagewanted=all&_r=0.

Housing Assistance Council, "Race and Ethnicity in Rural America." *Rural Research Brief*. April 2012, http://www.ruralhome.org/storage/research_notes/rrn-race-and-ethnicity-web.pdf.

Huber, P., and K. Drowne. "Redneck: A New Discovery." *American Speech* 76, no. 4 (2001): 434–5.

Ice Road Truckers. Season 1, Episode 9, "The Big Melt." Narrated by Thom Beers. Aired August 12, 2007. *Original Productions* for *History Channel*.

Ice Road Truckers. Season 1, Episode 4, "The Big Chill." Narrated by Thom Beers. Aired July 8, 2007, *Original Productions* for *History Channel*.

Ice Road Truckers. Season 3, Episode 2, "Rookie Run." Narrated by Thom Beers. Aired June 7, 2009. *Original Productions* for *History Channel*.

Ice Road Truckers. Season 3, Episode 6, "Arctic Ice." Narrated by Thom Beers. Aired July 5, 2009. *Original Productions* for *History Channel*.

Ice Road Truckers. Season 7, Episode 1, "Collision Course." Narrated by Thom Beers, aired June 9, 2013, *Original Productions* for *History Channel*.

Ice Road Truckers. Image of Lisa Kelly. *Original Productions* for *History Channel*. https://i.pinimg.com/474x/15/ac/f3/15acf320e4523cf32d1514ae0d8398bc--cool-trucks-sexy-trucks.jpg.

Isenberg, Nancy. *White Trash: The 400-Year History of Class in America*. New York: Viking, 2016.

Jennings, Dana. "Grab a Brew While They Face Death." *New York Times*, March 24, 2011.http://www.nytimes.com/2011/03/27/arts/television/coal-on-spike-aims-to-attract-male-viewers.html?_r=2.

Johnson, David. "The Most Dangerous Jobs in America." *TIME*, May 13, 2016, https://time.com/4326676/dangerous-jobs-america/.

Jovi, J. B., and R. Sambora. "Wanted Dead or Alive." On *Slippery When Wet*. United States: Mercury Records. mp3 file.

Karter, Erin. 'Nonvoters 2020: Counted Out' Examines Reasons 80 million Americans Opted Out of Presidential Election." *Northwestern Now*, December 15, 2020. https://news.northwestern.edu/stories/2020/12/nonvoters-2020-counted-out-examines-reasons-80-million-americans-opted-out-of-presidential-election/&fj=1.

Katz, Josh. 'Duck Dynasty' vs. 'Modern Family': 50 Maps of the U.S. Cultural Divide." *New York Times*, December 27, 2016. https://www.nytimes.com/interactive/2016/12/26/upshot/duck-dynasty-vs-modern-family-television-maps.html?_r=1.

Kenway, Jane, Anna Kraack, and Anna Hickey-Moody. *Masculinity Beyond the Metropolis*. London and New York: Palgrave Macmillan, 2006.

Kessler, Glenn. "Trump's False Claim He Built His Empire with a 'Small Loan' from His Father." *Washington Post*, March 3, 2016. https://www.washingtonpost.com/news/fact-checker/wp/2016/03/03/trumps-false-claim-he-built-his-empire-with-a-small-loan-from-his-father/?utm_term=.a68cc7076519.

Kimmel, Michael. *Manhood in America: A Cultural History*, 3rd ed. New York and Oxford: Oxford University Press, 2012.

Kimmel, Michael. *Angry White Men: American Masculinity at the End of an Era*. New York: Nation Books, 2013.

Kissell, Rick. "Ratings: A&E's 'Duck Dynasty' Opens Season 6 with More Declines." *Variety*, June 12, 2014. https://variety.com/2014/tv/ratings/aes-duck-dynasty-opens-season-6-with-more-declines-1201219469/.

Klein, Naomi. *No Is Not Enough: Resisting Trump's Shock Politics and Winning the World We Need*. Chicago, IL: Haymarket Books, 2017.

Licata, A. "Donald Trump on Guns, Hunting, and Conservation." *Outdoor Life*, January 22, 2016. http://www.outdoorlife.com/articles/hunting/2016/01/qa-donald-trump-guns-hunting-and-conservation.

Lipsitz, George. *How Racism Takes Place*. Philadelphia: Temple University Press, 2011.

Lloyd, Robert. "TV's Rugged, Rural Breed." *Los Angeles Times*, December 1, 2011, https://www.latimes.com/archives/la-xpm-2011-dec-01-la-et-1130-redneck-tv-20111201-story.html.

Lockett, Christopher. "Masculinity and Authenticity: Reality TV's Real Men." *Flow*, October 15, 2010. http://flowtv.org/2010/10/masculinity-and-authenticity/.

Lowry, Brian. "Dear 'Duck Dynasty' Fans: You Do Know It's All Fake, Right?" *Variety*, December 20, 2013. http://variety.com/2013/tv/columns/dear-duck-dynasty-fans-you-do-know-its-all-fake-right-1200980709/.

Loy, Phillip R. *Westerns in a Changing America, 1955–2000*. Jefferson, NC and London: McFarland & Company, 2004.

Lufkin, Bryan. "What We're Getting Wrong about the 'Great Resignation.'" *BBC*, October 28, 2021. https://www.bbc.com/worklife/article/20211028-what-were-getting-wrong-about-the-great-resignation.

Luzer, Daniel. "Duck Decoy." *Washington Monthly*, January 9, 2014. https://washingtonmonthly.com/2014/01/09/duck-decoy/.

Mangan, Michael. *Staging Masculinities: History, Gender, Performance.* New York: Palgrave Macmillan, 2003.

Magary, Drew. "What the Duck?" GQ, December 17, 2013. https://www.gq.com/story/duck-dynasty-phil-robertson.

Martin, Christopher R. *No Longer Newsworthy: How the Mainstream Media Abandoned the Working Class.* Ithaca, NY: Cornell University Press, 2019.

Mayer, Vicki. "Reality Television's 'Classrooms': Knowing, Showing and Telling about Social Class in Reality Casting and the College Classroom." In *Reality Television and Class*, edited by Beverly Skeggs and Helen Wood, 185–196. London: Palgrave Macmillan, 2011.

Meixell, Brady, and Ross Eisenbrey. "An Epidemic of Wage Theft Is Costing Workers Hundreds of Millions of Dollars a Year." *Economic Policy Institute*, September 11, 2014. https://www.epi.org/publication/epidemic-wage-theft-costing-workers-hundreds/.

Metcalf, Mitch. "Updated: Showbuzzdaily's Top 150 Wednesday Cable Originals & Network Finals." *Show Buzz Daily*, July 6, 2016. http://www.showbuzzdaily.com/articles/showbuzzdailys-top-150-wednesday-cable-originals-network-finals-7-6-2016.html.

Miller, Claire Cain. "As Women Take Over a Male-Dominated Field, the Pay Drops." *New York Times*, March 18, 2016. https://www.nytimes.com/2016/03/20/upshot/as-women-take-over-a-male-dominated-field-the-pay-drops.html?_r=0.

Mills, Charles. *The Racial Contract*. Ithaca, NY: Cornell University Press, 1997.

Mirzoeff, Nicholas. *An Introduction to Visual Culture.* New York: Routledge, 2009.

Monbiot, George. "Neoliberalism—The Ideology at the Root of All Our Problems. *The Guardian*, April 15, 2016. https://www.theguardian.com/books/2016/apr/15/neoliberalism-ideology-problem-george-monbiot.

Morris, Edward M. "'Rednecks,' 'Rutters,' and 'Rithmetic: Social Class, Masculinity, and Schooling in a Rural Context." *Gender and Society* 22, no. 6 (2008): 728–751.

Nagesh, Ashitha. US Election 2020: Why Trump Gained Support Among Minorities." *BBC News*, November 22, 2020, https://www.bbc.com/news/world-us -canada-54972389.

Nichols, Tom. "Donald Trump, the Most Unmanly President, *The Atlantic,* May 25, 2020, https://www.theatlantic.com/ideas/archive/2020/05/donald-trump-the -most-unmanly-president/612031/.

Nickoloff, Annie. "See 'Duck Dynasty' Star Willie Robertson's Speech at Republican National Convention." *Cleveland.com*, July 19, 2016. Video. http://www.cleveland.com/rnc-2016/index.ssf/2016/07/see_duck_dynasty_star_willie_r.html.

O'Connor, J. E., and P. C. Rollins. "Introduction: The West, Westerns, and American Character." In *Hollywood's West: The American Frontier in Film, Television, and History*, 1–34. Lexington, KY: The University Press of Kentucky, 2005.

O'Sullivan, Shannon E. M. "Playing 'Redneck': White Masculinity and Working-Class Performance on Duck Dynasty." *Journal of Popular Culture* 49, no. 2 (2016): 367–84. https://doi.org/10.1111/jpcu.12403.

Ouellette, Laurie. "The Trump Show." *Television & New Media* 17, no. 7 (2016): 647–50. https://doi.org/10.1177/1527476416652695.

Owens, Mitchell. "Laura and George W. Bush's Serene Retreat in Texas." *Architectural Digest*, December 16, 2016. http://www.architecturaldigest.com/gallery/laura-and -george-w-bush-prairie-chapel-ranch-texas-slideshow/all.

Palazzolo, Joe. "Racial Gap in Men's Sentencing." *Wall Street Journal*, February 14, 2013. https://www.wsj.com/articles/SB10001424127887324432004578304463789858002.

Pape, Robert A. "What an Analysis of 377 Americans Arrested or Charged in the Capitol Insurrection Tells Us." *Washington Post*, April 6, 2021. https://www.washingtonpost.com/opinions/2021/04/06/capitol-insurrection-arrests-cpost -analysis/.

Patnaik, Arun K. "Gramsci's Concept of Common Sense: Towards a Theory of Subaltern Consciousness in Hegemony Processes." *Economic and Political Weekly* 23, no. 5 (1988): 10.

Potter, Hillary. *Intersectionality and Criminology: Disrupting and Revolutionizing Studies of Crime*. London and New York: Routledge, 2015.

Press, Alex. "On the Origins of the Professional-Managerial Class: An Interview with Barbara Ehrenreich." *Dissent*, October 22, 2019. https://www.dissentmagazine .org/online_articles/on-the-origins-of-the-professional-managerial-class-an -interview-with-barbara-ehrenreich.

Prokop, Andrew. "A New Report Complicates Simplistic Narratives about Race and the 2020 Election." *Vox*, May 10, 2021. https://www.vox.com/2021/5/10 /22425178/catalist-report-2020-election-biden-trump-demographics.

Puar, Jasbir. *Terrorist Assemblages: Homonationalism in Queer Times.* Durham, NC: Duke University Press, 2007. Kindle.

Bibliography 167

Romain, Alana. "Does Donald Trump Hunt? He Defended His Sons' Big Game Hunting," *Romper*, July 21, 2016, https://www.romper.com/p/does-donald-trump-hunt-he-defended-his-sons-big-game-hunting-14760.

Roosevelt, Theodore. *The Strenuous Life*. Stilwell, KS: Digireads.com Publishing, 2008.

Rottenberg, Catherine. "How Neoliberalism Colonised Feminism—and What You Can Do about It." *The Conversation*, May 23, 2018. https://theconversation.com/how-neoliberalism-colonised-feminism-and-what-you-can-do-about-it-94856.

Rice, Lynette. "'Deadliest Catch' Captures Biggest Audience Ever." *Entertainment Weekly*, June 23, 2010. http://ew.com/article/2010/06/23/deadliest-catch-captures-biggest-audience-ever/.

Sapatkin, Don. "American Presidents often Drawn to Hunting." *Knight Ridder Newspapers*, May 7, 2004. http://www.freerepublic.com/focus/news/1131735/posts.

Sawchuk, Stephen. "What is Critical Race Theory, and Why Is It Under Attack?." *EducationWeek*, May 18, 2021. https://www.edweek.org/leadership/what-is-critical-race-theory-and-why-is-it-under-attack/2021/05.

Scarborough, "Fishing for Discovery Channel Audience Demographics?" *Nielsen Local*, October 10, 2012. http://dialog.scarborough.com/index.php/fishing-for-discovery-channel-audience-demographics/.

Schlosser, Kurt. "King of Blue-Collar Reality TV Driven by 'Living on the Edge.'" *Today*, March 13, 2013. https://www.today.com/popculture/king-blue-collar-reality-tv-driven-living-edge-1C8842451.

Shandevel, Lauren. "A Bold Experiment in Working-Class Journalism." *In These Times*, August 3, 2021. https://inthesetimes.com/article/working-people-podcast-media-labor-stories.

Shebaya, Halim. "Trump 'Tells It Like It Is.'" *HuffPost*, May 5, 2016 https://www.huffpost.com/entry/trump-tells-it-like-it-is_b_9836974.

Silver, Nate. "The Mythology of Trump's 'Working Class' Support." *FiveThirtyEight*, May 3, 2016. https://fivethirtyeight.com/features/the-mythology-of-trumps-working-class-support/.

Skeggs, Beverly, and Helen Wood. "Introduction: Real Class." In *Reality Television and Class*, edited by Beverly Skeggs and Helen Wood, 1–29. London: Palgrave Macmillan, 2011.

Slaughter, Ann-Marie. "Why Women Still Can't Have It All." *The Atlantic*, August 15, 2012. https://www.theatlantic.com/magazine/archive/2012/07/why-women-still-cant-have-it-all/309020/.

Slotkin, Richard. *Gunfighter Nation: The Myth of the Frontier in Twentieth Century America*. Norman: Oklahoma University Press, 1998.

Smith, Jacquelyn. "10 Things the Best Leaders Never Say." *Business Insider*, September 15, 2014. http://www.businessinsider.com/successful-leaders-never-say-these-things-2014-9.

Sommers-Dawes, Kate. "All the Times Trump Has Called for Violence at His Rallies." *Mashable*, March 12, 2016. http://mashable.com/2016/03/12/trump-rally-incite-violence/#bK.3R0nrKiqY.

Stanley, T. L. "'Pawn Stars' Helps History Finish in Top Five among Cable Networks." *Los Angeles Times*, December 21, 2011. http://latimesblogs.latimes .com/showtracker/2011/12/history-pawn-stars-top-five-cable-networks.html.

Stevens, Matt. "Poorer Americans Have Much Lower Voting Rates in National Elections than The Nonpoor, a Study Finds." *New York Times*, August 11, 2020. https://www .nytimes.com/2020/08/11/us/politics/poorer-americans-have-much-lower-voting -rates-in-national-elections-than-the-nonpoor-a-study-finds.html.

Storey, John. *Cultural Theory and Popular Culture: An Introduction*, 6th edition. New York and London: Pearson, 2012.

Strauss, Valerie. "'Duck Dynasty's' Phil Robertson Is a Former Teacher with a Master's Degree." *The Washington Post*, December 20, 2013. https://www.washingtonpost .com/news/answer-sheet/wp/2013/12/20/duck-dynastys-phil-robertson-a-former -teacher-with-a-masters-degree/?utm_term=.93d14dc144d8.

Swartz, David. *Culture & Power: The Sociology of Pierre Bourdieu.* Chicago: The University of Chicago Press, 1997.

Thompson, Derek. "Who Are Donald Trump's Supporters, Really?" *The Atlantic*, March 1, 2016. https://www.theatlantic.com/politics/archive/2016/03/who-are -donald-trumps-supporters-really/471714/.

Torr, D., and S. Bottoms. *Sex, Drag, and Male Roles: Investigating Gender as Performance*. Ann Arbor: University of Michigan Press, 2010.

Trapani, W. C., and L. L. Winn. "Manifest Masculinity: Frontier, Fraternity, and Family in Discovery Channel's *Gold Rush*. In *Reality Television: Oddities of Culture*, edited by A. F. Slade, A. J. Narro, and B. P. Buchanan, 183–200. Lanham, MD: Lexington Books, 2014.

Turner, Frederick Jackson. *The Significance of the Frontier in American History*. London and New York: Penguin Books, 2008.

Turpin, Ruby. "Duck Dynasty: All Four Robertson Brothers without Beards." *Starcasm*, October 9, 2012. https://starcasm.net/duck-dynasty-all-four-robertson -brothers-without-beards/.

Tyson, Alec, and Shiva Maniam. "Behind Trump's Victory: Divisions by Race, Gender, Education." *Pew Research Center*, November 9, 2016. http://www .pewresearch.org/fact-tank/2016/11/09/behind-trumps-victory-divisions-by-race -gender-education/.

Vavreck, Lynn. "Measuring Donald Trump's Supporters for Intolerance." *New York Times*, February 23, 2016. https://www.nytimes.com/2016/02/25/upshot/ measuring-donald-trumps-supporters-for-intolerance.html?_r=1.

Wallmann, Jeffrey. *The Western: Parables of the American Dream*. Lubbock, TX: Texas Tech University Press, 1999.

Walton, Frank Vyan. "Duck Dynasty Is a Fake Yuppies-in-Red-Neck-Drag Con Job." *Daily Kos*, December 12, 2013. http://www.dailykos.com/story/2013/12/20 /1264354/-Duck-Dynasty-is-a-Fake-Yuppies-in-Red-Neck-Drag-Con-Job#.

Watts, Trent. "Telling White Men's Stories." In *White Masculinity in the Recent South*, edited by Trent Watts, 1–29. Baton Rouge: Louisiana State University Press, 2008.

Williams, Joan C. *White Working Class: Overcoming Class Cluelessness in America*. Boston, MA: Harvard Business Review Press. 2017.

Winck, Ben. "Having a Job Right Now Means Longer Hours and Slow Pay Growth." *Business Insider*, June 14, 2021. https://www.businessinsider.com/labor-shortage-employed-americans-longer-hours-slow-pay-growth-jobs-2021-6.

Yahr, E. "A Year Ago, 'Duck Dynasty' Was Inescapable. Now, No One Cares." *Washington Post*, December 23, 2014. https://www.washingtonpost.com/news/arts-and-entertainment/wp/2014/12/23/a-year-ago-duck-dynasty-was-inescapable-now-no-one-cares/.

Yancy, George, and bell hooks. "bell hooks: Buddhis, the Beats and Loving Blackness." *New York Times*, December 10, 2015. https://opinionator.blogs.nytimes.com/author/bell-hooks/.

Yoggy, Gary A. *Riding the Video Range: The Rise and Fall of the Western on Television*. Jefferson, NC, and London: McFarland & Company, Inc., 1995.

Zweig, Michael. *The Working-Class Majority: America's Best Kept Secret.* Ithaca, NY: Cornell University Press, 2000.

Index

A&E. *See Duck Dynasty*

African Americans. *See* Blacks

Aho, Tanja, 25

Alexander, Michelle, 38–39

Alexander, Susan M., 38, 39, 61

Allison, Dorothy, 141

The American Conservative, 120

American Dream, 36, 91; on *Gold Rush,* 103; individualism in, 42; "real men" and, 38

Anderson, Jake, 50

Angry White Men (Kimmel), 3, 24, 25, 36, 59, 77, 81

Appling, Ryan, 65

The Apprentice, 1, 133

assemblage: intersectionality and, 13–14; power in, 37; working class as, 10

Atlantic, 118

authentic masculinity, 7, 54; on *Duck Dynasty,* 129; in frontier mythology, 107; violence of, 56

Ax Men, x, 4, 5; dangerous conditions on, 51–52, 56; demographics of viewership for, 22, 23, 25; frontier mythology in, 86, 99, 100, 104–6; gender policing on, 64; hegemonic masculinity on, 21, 35, 105–6; white, rural, working-class masculinity on,

54; white women on, 79–80; working class on, 47, 51–52

Baldoni, John, 7

Bartash, Jeffrey, 118–19

Bederman, Gail, 21, 126, 134

Beers, Thom, 5, 39, 56, 76, 84, 92, 104, 105, 106, 108–9

Bell, Michael Mayerfield, 20, 55, 125, 126

Berger, John, 55, 75, 128

Biden, Joe, ix, 155

Billington, Ray Allen, 98–99

bin Laden, Osama, 138

Black Feminist Thought (Collins), 8–9

Black Lives Matter, 157

Black Reconstruction in America (Du Bois), 16

Blacks (African Americans): in Great Recession, 3, 38; masculinity, criminality and, 43, 58; white supremacy and, 16; women, 8, 11, 59

blue-collar frontier shows, x; casting for stereotypes for, 21; class consciousness in, 16, 26; continuing relevance of, 155–59; demographics of viewership for, 22–25, 38; frontier revival from, 18–19, 89; in Great Recession, 26, 38, 58–59,

172 *Index*

89; hegemonic masculinity in, 19, 21, 53–62; homosociality on, 40; individualism on, 83–84, 94; intersectionality of, 8–9, 11–12; Native Americans and, 17; oppression in, 8; populism from, 39–40; power and, 7–8; "real men" on, 14–15, 40, 53, 83–110; "rugged individuals" on, 15; social class on, 40; Trump, D., and, 24, 39; U.S. exceptionalism on, 83–84; Westerns and, 90–93; white, rural, working-class masculinity on, 2, 5, 25–26, 39, 44, 54, 155–59; white spatial imagery on, 88; white supremacy in, 8, 14–15; white women on, 26, 73–81; working class in, 47–53. *See also specific shows*
Bottoms, Stephen, 131
Boudreau, Brenda, 134–35
Bourdieu, Pierre, 9, 20, 21–22, 125, 139
Bradley, Matt, 50, 57–58
Broderick, Ryan, 5–6
Browning, Jay, 52, 64
Browning, Jesse, 105
Buchanan, Burton P., 61–62, 99–100
Buckwild, 5
Bush, George W., 21, 24, 122, 124; hunting by, 132; language use by, 138; white, rural, working-class masculinity and, 27, 55, 126
Butler, Judith, 20, 128, 129, 130, 134
Buzzfeed, 5–6
Byrd, Jodi, 17, 97–98

Campbell, Hugh, 20, 55, 125, 126
capital, 21, 22; frontier mythology and, 100. *See also* social capital
capitalism: on *Ax Men,* 105–6; in blue-collar frontier shows, 8; class consciousness and, 46; on *Duck Dynasty,* 121, 158; in frontier mythology, 99, 107; in mass media, 11, 12; neoliberal, 8, 108; power of, 11, 88; self-made man and, 36,

43–44; in Western modernity, 15; white working-class men and, 37
Capitol riot, ix, x–xii, 4, 6, 136–37
Celebrity Apprentice, 159
Chauvin, Derek, 41
Chiu, Danny, 63
Christie, Paul, 56–57, 80, 101, 103
Chute, Carolyn, 141
class consciousness, 159; in blue-collar frontier shows, 16, 26; cable companies and, 157; capitalism and, 46
Class-Passing (Foster), 45
Clinton, Bill, 126–27
Clinton, Hillary, x, 132–33
Coal, 24–25, 92
Coats, Mike "Coatsy," 106
Colburn, Keith, 64–65
colorblindness, 15
Connell, Raewyn, 19, 53–54, 124, 133
Conroy, Meredith, 138
Country Boys (Campbell, Bell, and Finney), 20, 55, 125
Crenshaw, Kimberlé, 11, 156
criminality: Black masculinity and, 43, 58; intersectionality of, 12
critical race theory, 15
critical whiteness studies, 15
"A Critique of 'Our Constitution is Color-Blind'" (Gotanda), 15–16
Culler, Jonathan, 134, 136
"Cutting, Digging, and Harvesting" (Fleras and Dixon), 99
"The Dark Side of America's Redneck Reality TV Obsession": (Broderick), 5–6

Davis, Angela Y., 37
Deadliest Catch, x, 4, 5; captains on, 48–50; continued production of, 155; dangerous conditions on, 48–50, 55–56, 106–7; demographics of viewership for, 22, 23–24, 25; frontier mythology in, 86, 99, 100, 106–8; gender policing on, 63;

Index

173

hegemonic masculinity on, 21, 35, 50, 99; homosociality on, 64–66; masculinity on, 48–50, 61–62; "real men" on, 7, 65; wealthy men on, 26; white, rural, working-class masculinity on, 54; white supremacy on, 57–58; white women on, 73; working class on, 47, 48–50

Deadline, 23

Deleuze, Gilles, 10, 13

"Demarginalizing the Intersection of Race and Sex" (Crenshaw), 11

Denhart, Andy, 23

Dill, Bonnie Thornton, 12–13

Discovery Channel, x, 2, 4; demographics of viewership for, 23–24, 38; stereotypes of white working-class men on, 38; white male viewers of, 3. *See also Deadliest Catch; Gold Rush*

Dixon, Shane Michael, 99

dominant-hegemonic position, 53

Dred Scott v. Sanford, 15

Du Bois, W. E. B., 16

Dubrofsky, Rachel E., 75

Duck Dynasty, 5–6, 27; "before" photos of Robertsons, 127–28; capital of, 22; as drag show, 127–39; frontier mythology in, 86; gender policing on, 131–32, 135–36, 142–44; hegemonic masculinity on, 20–21, 122–27, 158–59; hunting on, 83, 122–23, 128, 131–32; language use in, 136–39; masculinity on, 44, 83; meaning of redneck in, 139–44; merchandise sales from, 123, 128; neoliberalism and, 139; Trump, D., and, 115–18, 121–22, 132–39, 158–59; violence on, 137; white, rural, working-class masculinity in, 20–21; white women on, 122, 124, 128, 135–36, 142–43; yuppies and, 122–23, 127–28, 129, 134, 137, 141

"Encoding and Decoding in the Television Discourse" (Hall), 19, 89–90

"family values," on *Duck Dynasty,* 6

femininity: hegemonic, 74, 75, 78, 79; passivity and vulnerability of, 74; white domesticity of, 18

femininity premium, 78

feminism: blue-collar frontier shows and, 25; hegemonic masculinity and, 39; neoliberal, 77–78

field, 22

Finney, Margaret, 20, 55, 125, 126

Fleras, Augie, 99

Floyd, George, 41

Forbes, 7

Foster, Gwendolyn Audrey, 45

Fox News, 138–39

Friedman, Vanessa, x

frontier: hegemonic masculinity on, 99; individualism on, 93, 94, 99–100; revival of, from blue-collar frontier shows, 18–19; Turner on, 17–18, 26, 88–89, 93–96, 99–100, 157; U.S. exceptionalism and, 88, 94, 95–96; whiteness of, 93–94; white spatial imaginary of, 19, 26–27, 88, 157–58; white supremacy on, 94–95

Frontier, 92

frontier masculinities, 124; of Trump, D., 133, 135

frontier mythology, 83–110; in *Ax Men,* 86, 99, 100, 104–6; on *Deadliest Catch,* 106–8; on *Gold Rush,* 101–4; heteropatriarchy in, 88, 100; on *Ice Road Truckers,* 108–9; Native Americans in, 95; power in, 88, 157; U.S. exceptionalism and, 101–2

Gaston, Paul M., 84–85

Gender Advertisements (Goffman), 74

Gender and Power (Connell), 19, 54

gender policing: on *Duck Dynasty,* 131–32, 135–36, 142–44; of masculinity, 62–66

174   *Index*

Gender Trouble (Butler), 20, 128, 129
Goffman, Erving, 74
Gold Rush, x, 4; American Dream on, 103; continued production of, 155; demographics of viewership for, 23; frontier mythology in, 86, 100, 101–4; Great Recession and, 52, 85–86; hegemonic masculinity on, 21, 35, 56–57, 104; individualism on, 101; masculinity on, 52–53; mythology in, 85–86; new masculinity crisis on, 100; self-made man on, 56–57; U.S. exceptionalism on, 104; white, rural, working-class masculinity on, 54; white women on, 80; working class on, 47, 52–53
Gotanda, Neil, 15–16
GQ, 122, 128
"Grab a Brew While They Face Death" (Jennings), 24–25
Great Recession: Blacks in, 3, 38; blue-collar frontier shows in, 26, 38, 58–59, 89; *Gold Rush* and, 52, 85–86; LGBTQ in, 89; neoliberalism and, 41–42, 102; people of color in, 89; unemployment in, 59–60; white working-class men in, 4; women in, 89
Greensfelder, Abby, 5
Grindstaff, Laura, 45
Grzanka, Patrick R., 14
Guattari, Felix, 10, 13
Gunfighter Nation (Slotkin), 85

habitus, 21
Half Yard Production, 5
Hall, Stuart, 19, 84, 89–90
Hamilton, Laura T., 78
Hanke, Robert, 54
Hansen, Edgar, 49, 57–58
Hansen, Mandy, 73
Hansen, Sig, 49–50, 57–58, 106–7
Haraway, Donna, 44
Harris, Cheryl, 16–17, 87
hegemonic femininity, 74, 75, 78, 79

hegemonic masculinity: on *Ax Men*, 21, 35, 105–6; in blue-collar frontier shows, 19, 21, 53–62; capital and, 22; crisis of, 53–62; on *Deadliest Catch*, 50, 99; on *Duck Dynasty*, 20–21, 122–27, 158–59; on frontier, 99; gender and, 20; on *Gold Rush*, 56–57, 104; heterosexuality in, 58; in neoliberalism, 54, 120; power in, 74–75; on reality TV, 35–66; "real men" and, 41–47; of self-made man, 36; social class and, 84; of Trump, D., 134; violence in, 56–58; of white, rural, working-class masculinity, 58; whiteness in, 57; white supremacy in, 57–58
Hegemonic Masculinity (Connell and Messerschmidt), 19
Here Comes Honey Boo Boo, 4–5, 46, 127, 140
heteropatriarchy: in blue-collar frontier shows, 8, 18; on *Duck Dynasty*, 121, 158; in frontier mythology, 88, 100; gendered expectations of, 44; in mass media, 11, 12; power of, 11, 88, 116; of self-made man, 36; white, rural, working-class masculinity and, 157
heterosexuality: on *Duck Dynasty*, 129, 132; in hegemonic masculinity, 58
Hickey-Moody, Anna, 133
Hillbilly Elegy (Vance), 120
Hill Collins, Patricia, 8–9, 78, 156
Hillstrand, Phillip, 63
History Channel, x, 2, 4; demographics of viewership for, 23, 38; stereotypes of white working-class men on, 38; white male viewers of, 3. *See also Ax Men; Ice Road Truckers*
Hoffman, Jack, 52–53, 57, 85, 102–3
Hoffman, Todd, 52–53, 85–86, 101–4
Hollywood's West (O'Connor and Rollins), 91
Homans, Charles, 5
homophobia: on *Duck Dynasty*, 118, 122, 127, 129; political correctness

and, 118; Trump, D., and, 138; of white working-class, 119
homosociality: on blue-collar frontier shows, 40; feminine premium in, 78; masculinity in, 62–66; white women in, 76
Hooper, 124, 133, 135
How Racism Takes Place (Lipsitz), 18–19, 87–88
Huffington Post, 7
hunting: by Bush, 132; on Discovery Channel, 23; on *Duck Dynasty,* 83, 122–23, 128, 131–32; by Roosevelt, 132; white, rural, working-class masculinity and, 137
Hurt, Dustin, 80
Hurt, Fred "Dakota," 80

Ice Road Truckers, x, 4, 5; dangerous conditions on, 50–51, 56, 108–9; demographics of viewership for, 23, 25; frontier mythology in, 86, 99, 100, 108–9; hegemonic masculinity on, 21, 35; masculinity on, 50–51; "real men" on, 7; white, rural, working-class masculinity on, 54; white women on, 26, 73, 74–79, 109, 157; working class on, 47, 50–51
ideology, 84–85
indigenous critical theory, 89, 97–99, 103; settler-colonialism and, 108; white supremacy and, 108
individualism/rugged individualism: in American Dream, 42; on *Ax Men,* 105; on blue-collar frontier shows, 15, 83–84, 94; on *Deadliest Catch,* 107; in frontier mythology, 93, 94, 99–100, 104, 105; on *Gold Rush,* 101; racism and, 16; of self-made man, 43–44; on Westerns, 103; of white working-class, 60; of working class, 91
intersectionality: assemblage and, 13–14; of blue-collar frontier shows,

8–9, 11–12; of crime, 12; of power, 11, 12–13, 14
Intersectionality (Grzanka), 14
"Intersectionality" (Dill and Kohlman), 12–13
Intersectionality and Criminology (Potter), 12
In These Times (Shandevel), ix
"Is Donald Trump a Role Model for Authenticity?" (Baldoni), 7
Isenberg, Nancy, 127, 133, 138, 140–41
Islamophobia: *Duck Dynasty* and, 118; Trump, D., and, 7, 118

Jennings, Dana, 24–25
Johnson, Lyndon, 126–27
Johnson, Patrick M., xii

Katz, Josh, 24
Kelly, Lisa, 26, 73, 74–77, 109, 157
Kenway, Jane, 133
Kerry, John, 138
Kessler, Glenn, 116
Kimmel, Michael, 2–4, 24, 25, 36, 38, 40, 42–44, 54, 58–59, 62–63, 77, 81, 156
Klein, Naomi, x, 3, 37, 60
Kohlman, Marla H., 12–13
Kraack, Anna, 133

Land of Savagery (Billington), 98–99
Larson, Zack, 63
The Lesbian and Gay Studies Reader (Butler), 130
LGBTQ: advancements for, 2; blue-collar frontier shows and, 25, 26; in Great Recession, 89; hegemonic masculinity and, 35, 39; heteropatriarchy and, 8; Trump, D., and, 118; white, rural, working-class masculinity and, 157; white working-class and, 155. *See also* homophobia
Lipsitz, George, 18–19, 26, 87–88
Liske, Peter, 48–49
Literary Theory (Culler), 136

176 *Index*

Lloyd, Robert, 35
Lockett, Christopher, 7, 35, 38, 54
Los Angeles Times, 23
Loy, R. Philip, 91–92
Luzer, Daniel, 128

Magary, Drew, 128
"Make America Great Again," 89, 101, 102, 118, 133
Mangan, Michael, 19, 58, 125
Manhood in America (Kimmel), 62–63
Manifest Destiny, 97
"Manifest Masculinity" (Trapani and Winn), 99, 100
Manliness & Civilization (Bederman), 21, 126, 134
marketplace masculinity, 134–35
Martin, Christopher R., 42, 46, 47–48
masculinity, x; crisis of, 2–3, 36, 53–62, 100, 156; on *Deadliest Catch,* 48–50, 61–62; on *Duck Dynasty,* 44, 83; gender policing of, 62–66; on *Gold Rush,* 52–53; in homosociality, 62–66; on *Ice Road Truckers,* 50–51; of middle-class men, 44; of Roosevelt, 126; of upper-class men, 44. *See also specific types*
Masculinity, Media, and the American Presidency (Conroy), 138
"Masculinity and Authenticity" (Lockett), 7, 54
mass media: capitalism in, 11, 12; heteropatriarchy in, 11, 12; white supremacy in, 10, 12; on white working-class, 155–56; on working class, 46
Mayer, Vicki, 21
McDougal, Karen, 78–79
McKillop, David, 123
The Meaning of Freedom and Other Difficult Dialogues (Davis), 37
"Media as Sites/Sights of Justice" (Grzanka), 14
Messerschmidt, James W., 19
Metcalf, Mitch, 23

Me Too, 157
middle-class men, 25; at Capitol riot, 6; masculinity of, 44; for Trump, D., 121; white working-class and, 60–62; wide identification with, 46
Miller, Claire Caine, 59
Mills, Charles, 8
Mirzoeff, Nicholas, 14, 53
Moilanen, Jason, 64–65
Monbiot, George, 8
Morris, Edward W., 139–40
Mulvey, Laura, 74
mythology. *See* frontier mythology
"The Mythology of Trump's 'Working Class' Support" (Silver), 118–19

nationalism: of "real men," 134; of Trump, D., 39
National Rifle Association, 132
Native Americans: blue-collar frontier shows and, 17; as elements of past, 97–99; in frontier mythology, 95
neoliberal capitalism, 8, 108
neoliberal feminism, 77–78
neoliberalism: in Democratic Party, 3–4; *Duck Dynasty* and, 139; Great Recession and, 41–42, 102; hegemonic masculinity in, 54, 120; socia class and, 45, 46–47; working class in, 49
The New Jim Crow (Alexander, M.), 38–39
new masculinity crisis, on *Gold Rush,* 100
New York Times, x, 24–25, 59, 118
New York Times Magazine, 5
Nichols, Tom, 118
No Is Not Enough (Klein), 3, 37, 60
No Longer Newsworthy (Martin), 42, 46

Obama, Barack, 38–39, 138–39
Occupy Wall Street, 157
O'Connor, John E., 91
O'Donnell, Jennifer, xii

Index

oppression: in blue-collar frontier shows, 8; on frontier, 94; intersectionality of, 8

O'Sullivan, Gerald, xi

O'Sullivan, Julia, xi

Ouellette, Laurie, 1

Oxford, Vernon, 140

Pape, Robert A., xi

people of color: advancements for, 2; blue-collar frontier shows and, 26, 40–41; frontier defense against, 87; in Great Recession, 89; hegemonic masculinity and, 35; Trump, D., and, 118; white, rural, working-class masculinity and, 157; white male resent toward, 3; white working-class and, 155; women of, 59–60, 73–74. *See also* Blacks

"Persistence of Vision" (Haraway), 44

Pihl, Mike, 79

Plessy v. Ferguson, 15

PME. *See* professional-managerial elite

political correctness, 118

populism, 39–40

"Portrayals of Masculinity in the Discovery Channel's *Deadliest Catch*" (Buchanan), 61–62, 99

"Posting Racism and Sexism" (Dubrofsky and Wood, M.), 75

Potter, Hillary, 12

power, 9; in assemblage, 37; blue-collar frontier shows and, 7–8; from capital, 21, 22; of capitalism, 11, 88; in field, 22; in frontier mythology, 88, 157; in hegemonic masculinity, 74–75; of heteropatriarchy, 11, 88, 116; intersectionality of, 11, 12–13, 14; of "real men," 84; in self-made man, 36; of settler-colonialism, 11, 88; of white supremacy, 11, 88, 116, 117

Proctor, Leah, 79–80

professional-managerial elite (PME): white, rural, working-class masculinity and, 127; women, 43

Puar, Jasbir, 13–14

The Racial Contract (Mills), 8

racism: blue-collar frontier shows and, 25; on *Duck Dynasty,* 118, 122, 127; hegemonic masculinity and, 39; individualism and, 16; Obama and, 38–39; political correctness and, 118; of "real men," 134; Trump, D., and, 1, 59, 118, 120, 133, 138, 158; in white supremacy, 61; of white working-class, 61, 119; white working-class men and, 9

Reagan, Ronald, 27, 55, 124, 126

"real America": in frontier, 95; "real men" in, 38, 83–110; white working-class men in, 39

Reality Television (anthology), 99

Reality Television and Class (Mayer), 21

Reality Television and Class (Wood, H., and Skeggs), 41, 117, 129

"Reality Television and Doing of Hyperauthentic Masculinities" (Alexander, S., and Woods), 38

"Reality TV and Its Audiences Considered" (Aho), 25

"real men": American Dream and, 38; on *Ax Men,* 64, 105; on blue-collar frontier shows, 14–15, 40, 53, 83–110; on *Deadliest Catch,* 7, 65; on *Duck Dynasty,* 6, 125, 130–31, 158; fictionalized standards of, 134; on *Ice Road Truckers,* 7; language use by, 136–39; meaning of, 44; power of, 84; in "real America," 38, 83–110; Roosevelt as, 134; social class and, 41–47; wealthy white men as, 115–45; white, rural, working-class masculinity of, 101–2; white working-class men as, 4

180

Index

"real women": on *Duck Dynasty*, 131, 158; fictionalized standards of, 134
"Rednecks, Rutters, and 'Rithmetic'" (Morris), 139–40
rednexpoitation series, 4–6; of white working-class, 46. *See also Duck Dynasty*
Riding the Video Range (Yoggy), 90
ritualization of subordination, 74
Robertson, Jase, 135–36, 137
Robertson, Miss Kay, 142, 143–44
Robertson, Missy, 135–36
Robertson, Phil, 6, 122–25, 127–29, 131–32, 136, 137, 141–43
Robertson, Willie, 115–18, 120, 122, 127, 132, 135–36, 138, 143, 144
Robeson, Stacey, 79
Rollins, Peter C., 91
Romney, Mitt, 48, 138–39
Roosevelt, Theodore, x, 21, 124; hunting by, 132; masculinity of, 126; as "real man," 134; white, rural, working-class masculinity and, 27, 96–97
Rottenberg, Catherine, 77
Rowe, Mike, 48, 55–56, 106–8
Rowland, Hugh, 50–51, 109
rugged individualism. *See* individualism
Rygaard, Gabe, 105

Sandberg, Sheryl, 43, 77
Sandhogs, 99
Sanford, Mark, 138–39
self-made man, 36; on *Axe Men*, 52; on *Gold Rush*, 56–57; individualism of, 43–44; social class and, 42–43; white spatial imaginary and, 43
settler-colonialism: in blue-collar frontier shows, 8, 84; of frontier, 17, 18; in frontier mythology, 99, 100; indigenous critical theory and, 108; power of, 11, 88; of self-made man, 36; in Western modernity, 15
Sex, Drag, and Male Roles (Torr and Bottoms), 131

sexism: political correctness and, 118; of "real men," 134; Trump, D., and, 1, 59, 118, 120, 133, 138, 158; of white working-class, 119; white working-class men and, 9
Sexually Suspect (Boudreau), 134–35
Shandevel, Lauren, ix
Shebaya, Halim, 7
Shelby v. Holder, 15
Siber, Maya, 74
"The Significance of the Frontier in American History" (Turner), 17–18, 88
Silver, Nate, 118–19
Skeggs, Beverly, 41, 45, 117, 129
Slotkin, Richard, 85, 92–93, 94–95, 108
social capital, 22; of *Duck Dynasty*, 124, 159; social class and, 119
social class: on blue-collar frontier shows, 40; hegemonic masculinity and, 84; neoliberalism and, 45, 46–47; "real men" and, 41–47; self-made man and, 42–43; social capital and, 119; whiteness and, 45. *See also* class consciousness; *specific classes*
Social Darwinism, 103, 104, 108, 109
Spike, *Coal* on, 24–25, 92
Staging Masculinities (Mangan), 19, 58, 125
stay-at-home mothers, 43
Storey, John, 84
"The Strenuous Life" (Roosevelt), 134
strong intersectionality, 12, 13

Tallis, Melody, 80
Television & News Media, 1
Terrorist Assemblages (Puar), 13–14
TLC, *Here Comes Honey Boo Boo* on, 4–5, 46, 127, 140
Torr, Diane, 131
The Transit of Empire (Byrd), 17, 97–98
transnational business masculinity, 133
Trapani, William C., 99, 100
Trump, Donald, Jr., 132

Index

179

Trump, Donald J.: on *The Apprentice,* 1, 133; as "authentic" politician, 7; blue-collar frontier shows and, 24, 39; capital of, 22; Capitol riot for, ix, xii, 4, 136–37; on *Celebrity Apprentice,* 159; *Duck Dynasty* and, 6, 115–18, 121–22, 132–39, 158–59; frontier masculinities of, 135; hegemonic masculinity of, 134; language use by, 124, 136–39; "Make America Great Again" of, 89, 101, 102, 118, 133; marketplace masculinity of, 134–35; middle-class men for, 121; nationalism of, 39; political correctness and, 118; racism and, 1, 59, 118, 120, 133, 138, 158; sexism and, 1, 59, 118, 120, 133, 138, 158; supporters portrayal of, 1; violence and, 133, 136–37; wealthy men for, 121; white, rural, working-class masculinity and, 22, 26, 27, 137, 158–59; white supremacy and, 37; white working-class and, 3, 60, 118–19, 120–21; women and, 81; xenophobia and, 59
Trump, Eric, 132
Trump, Fred, 116
Turner, Frederick Jackson, 17–18, 26, 88–89, 93=96, 99–100, 157

Undercover Boss, 25
unemployment, in Great Recession, 59–60
upper class. *See* wealthy white men
upper-class men, masculinity of, 44
U.S. exceptionalism: on blue-collar frontier shows, 83–84; on *Deadliest Catch,* 107, 108; frontier and, 88, 94, 95–96; in frontier mythology, 89, 99, 101–2, 104; on *Gold Rush,* 104; on *Ice Road Truckers,* 109

Vance, J. D., 120, 121
violence: of authentic masculinity, 56; on *Ax Men,* 105; on *Duck Dynasty,*

137; in hegemonic masculinity, 56–58; Trump, D., and, 133, 136–37; in Westerns, 92
"Visual Pleasure and Narrative Cinema" (Mulvey), 74
Voting Rights Act, 15

Wallmann, Jeffrey, 90–91, 92, 100–101, 103
Ward, Darrell, 109
Washington Monthly, 128
Washington Post, xi, 11, 116

Wayne, John, 91
Ways of Seeing (Berger), 55, 75, 128
weak intersectionality, 12, 13, 14
wealthy white men (upper class), 21; at Capitol riot, 6; on *Deadliest Catch,* 26; as *Duck Dynasty* viewers, 121; as "real men," 115–45; for Trump, D., 121. *See also Duck Dynasty;* Trump, Donald
Webb, Janet, 51
The Western (Wallmann), 90–91
Westerns, 90–93; *Deadliest Catch* and, 107; individualism on, 103
Westerns in a Changing America (Loy), 91–92
Westgard, Jay, 108–9
white, rural, working-class masculinity, 19–20; on blue-collar frontier shows, 2, 5, 25–26, 39, 44, 54, 155–59; Bush and, 27, 55, 126; on *Duck Dynasty,* 117, 125, 126; hegemonic masculinity of, 58; hunting and, 137; language use of, 136–39; PME and, 127; Reagan and, 27; of "real men," 101–2; Roosevelt and, 27, 96–97; Trump, D., and, 22, 26, 27, 137, 158–59; women and, 77
white femininity/domesticity, 18
White Masculinity in the Recent South (Wilson), 139
whiteness: in blue-collar frontier shows, 8, 11; critical studies on,

15; on *Duck Dynasty*, 6; of frontier, 93–94; in hegemonic femininity, 74; in hegemonic masculinity, 57; as normative racial standard, 41; as "ordinary," 117; personhood from, 87; as property, 16, 87; of self-made man, 43–44; social class and, 45

"Whiteness as Property" (Harris), 16–17

white privilege, 41

white spatial imaginary: of frontier, 19, 26–27, 88, 157–58; self-made man and, 43; white supremacy and, 18, 87–88

white supremacy, 3, 44; African American slaves and, 16; in blue-collar frontier shows, 8, 14–15, 18; in demographics of viewership, 23–24; on *Duck Dynasty*, 121–22, 158; on frontier, 17, 94–95; in frontier mythology, 89, 99, 100; in hegemonic masculinity, 57–58; indigenous critical theory and, 108; in mass media, 10, 12; neoliberal feminism and, 78; Obama and, 38; power of, 11, 88, 116, 117; racism in, 61; Trump, D., and, 37; in Western modernity, 15; white spatial imaginary and, 18, 87–88

White Trash (Isenberg), 127, 133, 138

white women: on *Ax Men*, 79–80; on blue-collar frontier shows, 26, 73–81; on *Deadliest Catch*, 73; on *Duck Dynasty*, 122, 124, 128, 135–36, 142–43; on *Gold Rush*, 80; in homosociality, 76; on *Ice Road Truckers*, 26, 73, 74–79, 109, 157

white working-class: individualism of, 60; mass media on, 155–56; middle-class men and, 60–62; portrayal of, 46; racism of, 61; Trump, D., and, 60, 118–21

White Working Class (Williams), 43, 44, 46, 61, 119–20, 159

white working-class men, 44; as base of working class, 9; on blue-collar

frontier shows, 2, 5; capitalism and, 37; on Discovery, 38; dominance of, 2; in Great Recession, 4; on History, 38; in "real America," 39; as "real men," 4; stereotypes of, 38; of Trump, D., 3; in unions, xi; as viewers of History and Discovery networks, 3

white working-class women, 43

Wichrowski, Bill, 63

Williams, Joan C., 43, 44, 46, 61, 119–20, 159

Wilson, Charles Reagan, 139

Winn, Laura L., 99, 100

Wolfe, Tom, 44

women: advancements for, 2; Blacks, 8, 11, 59; blue-collar frontier shows and, 26; childrearing by, 43; domestic role of, 42–43; in Great Recession, 89; hegemonic masculinity and, 35; heteropatriarchy and, 8; of people of color, 59–60, 73–74; physical attractiveness of, 74, 76; professional-managerial elite (PME), 43; sexualization of, 75; Trump, D., and, 81, 118; white, rural, working-class masculinity and, 77, 157; white male resentment toward, 3; white working-class and, 155; working class and, 8–9; yuppie, 142. *See also* femininity; feminism; white women

Wood, Helen, 41, 45, 117, 129

Wood, Megan M., 75

Woods, Katie, 38, 39, 61

working class: as assemblage, 10; on *Ax Men*, 47, 51–52; in blue-collar frontier shows, 47–53; on *Deadliest Catch*, 48–50; on *Gold Rush*, 52–53; on *Ice Road Truckers*, 50–51; individualism of, 91; mass media on, 46; in neoliberalism, 49; as "ordinary," 45, 117; white men as dominant feature of, 9; women and, 8–9. *See also* white, rural, working-class masculinity; white working-class

The Working Class Majority (Zweig), 41

xenophobia, Trump, D., and, 1, 59, 133, 158

Yemm, Rick, 51

Yoggy, Gary A., 90, 92

yuppies, *Duck Dynasty* and, 122–23, 127–28, 129, 134, 137, 141

Zweig, Michael, 41, 47–48

About the Author

Shannon O'Sullivan is an independent scholar. She earned her PhD in media studies from the University of Colorado at Boulder in 2017. Her dissertation was recognized with the 2019 Outstanding Dissertation Award from the Critical and Cultural Studies Division of the National Communication Association.

Lightning Source UK Ltd.
Milton Keynes UK
UKHW021328201022
410805UK00004B/91